THE MAKING OF LEGAL AUTHORITY

The Making of Legal Authority

Non-legislative Codifications in Historical and Comparative Perspective

NILS JANSEN

OXFORD
UNIVERSITY PRESS

OXFORD
UNIVERSITY PRESS

Great Clarendon Street, Oxford OX2 6DP

Oxford University Press is a department of the University of Oxford.
It furthers the University's objective of excellence in research, scholarship,
and education by publishing worldwide in

Oxford New York

Auckland Cape Town Dar es Salaam Hong Kong Karachi
Kuala Lumpur Madrid Melbourne Mexico City Nairobi
New Delhi Shanghai Taipei Toronto

With offices in

Argentina Austria Brazil Chile Czech Republic France Greece
Guatemala Hungary Italy Japan Poland Portugal Singapore
South Korea Switzerland Thailand Turkey Ukraine Vietnam

Oxford is a registered trade mark of Oxford University Press
in the UK and in certain other countries

Published in the United States
by Oxford University Press Inc., New York

First published 2010

British Library Cataloguing in Publication Data
Data available

Library of Congress Cataloging in Publication Data
Data available

Typeset by MPS Limited, A Macmillan Company
Printed in Great Britain
on acid-free paper by the
MPG Books Group, Bodmin and King's Lynn

ISBN 978–0–19–958876–3

3 5 7 9 10 8 6 4 2

for l.

Preface

This book is the fruit of an extended sabbatical. Large parts were written during the autumn of 2008, when I visited Duke Law School, and during Hilary term 2009 in St. John's College and the Institute of European and Comparative Law, Oxford. I am deeply indebted to these institutions and especially to Ralf Michaels, Stefan Vogenauer, and Simon Whittaker: not only for the excellent working conditions, but, first of all, for stimulating discussions, which I will not forget.

The Cluster of Excellence at the University of Münster proved to be a permanent source of valuable interdisciplinary inspiration. I would like to express my thanks especially to Barbara Stollberg-Rilinger, who critically commented on a first draft of the text. As did—I am inclined to say as always—Ralf Michaels and Reinhard Zimmermann. Indeed, much of this book was developed in the many classes which I had the privilege of teaching together with one or the other of them in the course of the last years. I learned a lot from all their inspiration and critique.

Michael Bonell, Ole Lando and Hugh Beale, and the Beck Verlag kindly gave permission to reproduce parts of the UNIDROIT-Principles, the PECL and the *Palandt*, respectively. Matt Dyson provided invaluable help in matters of English grammar and style. In Münster, I received extremely thorough and diligent assistance from Lukas Rademacher, Max Fabian Starke, Kristin Vorbeck, and Sarah Woyciechowski. I am really grateful for all this support.

Contents

List of Abbreviations

ABA	American Bar Association
AcP	*Archiv für die civilistische Praxis*
ACQP / *Acquis Principles*	*Principles of the Existing EC Contract Law*: The Research Group on the Existing EC Private Law (ed.), *Acquis Principles. Contract I*
Acquis Group	The Research Group on the Existing EC Private Law
ALI	American Law Institute
AmJCompL	*American Journal of Comparative Law*
AöR	*Archiv für öffentliches Recht*
ARSP	*Archiv für Rechts- und Sozialphilosophie*
art.	*articulus*
BAGE	*Entscheidungen des Bundesarbeitsgerichts*, decisions of the Federal Court of Labour Law
BGHZ	*Entscheidungen des Bundesgerichtshofs in Zivilsachen*, decisions of the Federal Supreme Court in matters of private law
BVerfGE	*Entscheidungen des Bundesverfassungsgerichts*, decisions of the Federal Constitutional Court
C.	*Codex Iustinianus*
cap.	*caput*
CFR	Common Frame of Reference
CISG	Vienna Convention on the International Sale of Goods
CMLR	*Common Market Law Review*
COM	European Commission / Commission document
Const.	*Constitutio*
D.	*Digesta*

DCFR	Draft Common Frame of Reference: von Bar, Clive and Schulte-Nölke (eds), *Principles, Definitions and Model Rules of European Private Law: DCFR Outline Edition*
EC	European Community / European Communities
ECJ	European Court of Justice
ELJ	*European Law Journal*
ERPL	*European Review of Private Law*
exerc.	*exercitatio*
fol.	*folium*
GG	Grundgesetz (German constitution)
gl.	*glossa*
Gl. Ord.	*Glossa ordinaria* to the Corpus Iuris Civilis (Codex *lib.* I-IX, Antwerp 1576; Institutiones, Digesta, Codex *lib.* X-XII etc., Lyon 1552 f.)
GPR	*Zeitschrift für Gemeinschaftsprivatrecht*
HKK	*Historisch-kritischer Kommentar zum BGB,* ed. by Schmoeckel, Rückert and Zimmermann
ICC	International Chamber of Commerce
INCOTERMS	International Commercial Terms of the ICC
Inst.	*Institutiones Iustiniani*
JZ	*Juristenzeitung*
LG	Landgericht (court of first instance in Germany)
lib.	*liber*
LJ	*Law Journal*
LR	*Law Review*
MG	*Monumenta Germaniae Historica: Scriptores rerum Germanicarum in usum scholarum*
MLR	*The Modern Law Review*

NJW	*Neue Juristische Wochenschrift*
obs.	*observatio*
OJ	Official Journal of the European Union
OJLSt.	*Oxford Journal of Legal Studies*
OLG	Oberlandesgericht (court of appeal in Germany)
Palandt	Palandt, *Bürgerliches Gesetzbuch*
PECL	*Principles of European Contract Law*: Lando and Beale (eds), *Principles of European Contract Law I and II*; Lando, Clive, Prüm and Zimmermann (eds), *Principles of European Contract Law III*
PICC	UNIDROIT Principles of International Commercial Contracts
PICC-Commentary	*Commentary on the UNIDROIT Principles of International Commercial Contracts,* ed. by Vogenauer and Kleinheisterkamp
PL	*Patrologiae cursus complectus*: Migne (ed.)
qu.	*quaestio*
RabelsZ	*Rabels Zeitschrift für ausländisches und internationales Privatrecht*
Rev.	*Review*
RG	*Rechtsgeschichte. Zeitschrift des Max-Planck-Instituts für Europäische Rechtsgeschichte*
RGZ	*Entscheidungen des Reichsgerichts in Zivilsachen,* decisions of the Empire's Supreme Court in matters of private law
Rtd civ.	*Revue trimestrielle de droit civile*
SDHI	*Studia et documenta historiae et iuris*
Study Group ECC	Study Group on a European Civil Code
tit.	*titulus*
TR	*Tijdschrift voor Rechtsgeschiedenis*

U.	*University*
ULR	*Uniform Law Review*
UNIDROIT	International Institute for the Unification of Private Law
US	United States
U.S.	United States Supreme Court Reports
VG	Verwaltungsgericht (administrative court of first instance in Germany)
ZEuP	*Zeitschrift für Europäisches Privatrecht*
ZIP	*Zeitschrift für Wirtschaftsrecht*
ZNR	*Zeitschrift für Neuere Rechtsgeschichte*
ZRG (germ.)	*Zeitschrift der Savigny-Stiftung für Rechtsgeschichte / Germanistische Abteilung*
ZRG (kan.)	*Zeitschrift der Savigny-Stiftung für Rechtsgeschichte / Kanonistische Abteilung*
ZRG (rom.)	*Zeitschrift der Savigny-Stiftung für Rechtsgeschichte / Romanistische Abteilung*
ZRP	*Zeitschrift für Rechtspolitik*

List of Figures

Introduction

According to a fundamental assumption of Western legal thinking, the making of law is conceptually, normatively, and institutionally distinct from its understanding and application.[1] Legislation—a means of political domination—is authoritative *ratione imperii.* Thus, according to a modern writer, a statute or codification binds its addressees, '. . . if it has been issued in the duly prescribed way by a duly authorised organ and does not violate higher-ranking law, in short, if it is authoritatively issued'.[2] In basically the same way, the Roman lawyer Ulpian had argued that the Emperor's commands were vested with the force of law: 'Quod principi placuit, legis habet vigorem'.[3] Whether such legislation is based on reasonable, well-considered argument does not matter: in principle, Parliament may—within the relevant constitutional confines—arbitrarily implement whatever legal rule it chooses.

In contrast, legal writing, especially doctrinal texts written by legal scholars, can only be authoritative *imperio rationis.* Doctrinal argument relates, in an essentially descriptive way, to legislative texts.[4] Legal writing, accordingly, can assume authority only insofar as these texts are vague[5] or contain 'gaps' that need to be filled by means of constructive, innovative legal argument. The same is basically true for judicial decisions which are expected to give expression to and apply the law actually in force.[6] According to civilian doctrine, the finding of a 'gap' in the law determines whether a judge is empowered to develop the law in a constructive,

[1] Ulpian D. 1,4,1,1; Justinian C. 1,14,12, claiming that the right to interpret the law authoritatively was a prerogative of the prince; *Gl. Ord.*, gl. *suo proprio ad* D. 1,1,9: 'solus princeps possit facere leges'. See below 29 ff.

[2] Alexy, *Begriff und Geltung*, 142 f. / *Argument from Injustice*, 87.

[3] Ulpian D. 1,4,1 pr.: '. . . utpote cum lege regia, quae de imperio eius lata est, populus ei et in eum omne suum imperium et potestatem conferat'.

[4] Ernst, 'Gelehrtes Recht', 10 f., 15 ff. and *passim.*

[5] Alexy, *Theorie der juristischen Argumentation*, 334 ff.; Zimmermann and Jansen, 'Quieta Movere', 303 f.

[6] See below 87 f.

innovative way.[7] What is more, even where the law is vague or contains gaps, legal writing and judicial decisions are usually of persuasive authority only; hence, there is normally no room for arbitrary decision making. The authority not only of scholarly writing, but also of judicial precedent normally rests on the quality of the reasoning process employed. In most legal systems, even well-established judge-made law may be reversed in light of superior countervailing arguments.

This picture of the legal system is often connected with further assumptions. One is the idea that the validity of all law ultimately derives from the state alone.[8] Indeed, during the 20th century nearly all private law disputes discussed in academic literature had been, or could have been, brought before the state's courts, which applied, as a matter of course, a nation state's law. Usually, this was neither perceived as problematic nor in any sense as peculiar: was it not obvious that *all* law's validity depended on the state?[9] In fact, when authors such as Hans Kelsen described the positive law's validity and identity as conceptually dependant on a single basic norm (*Grundnorm*) and thus presupposing a sovereign's authority,[10] they gave expression to a common understanding. The law was exclusively made by legislators, administrations, and, in a limited way, by the courts authorized to do so. Hence, it was even argued that customary law existed only to the extent it had been recognized as such in judicial precedent.[11] True, the position of other authors, especially of H.L.A. Hart, was more complex. Hart did not conceptually identify the law with the state. He meant his concept to capture also the 'early law of many societies', and he was thus prepared to relate a rule of recognition directly to authoritative legal texts.[12] Nevertheless, Hart's analysis seems to have

[7] Cf. Canaris, *Lücken im Gesetz*, 6; cf. also 17 f., 19 ff.

[8] Cf. Ehrlich, 'Internationales Privatrecht', 425: 'Jetzt ist es selbstverständlich nur der Staat, der bestimmt, welches Recht in seinen Gemarkungen gelten solle'. See also Michaels, 'The Re-State-Ment of Non-State Law', 1245 f.

[9] For a non-representative sample of authors from various traditions, see Röhl, *Allgemeine Rechtslehre*, 184 ff., 186, 282 ff.; Grimm, 'Rechtsentstehung', 41: 'Produkt staatlicher Entscheidung'; J. Braun, *Einführung in die Rechtswissenschaft*, 216 ff.; Unger, *Knowledge and Politics*, 1975, 281–284. For a succinct summary, see Bodenheimer, *Jurisprudence*, 52 ff.

[10] Kelsen, *Reine Rechtslehre*, 196 ff. / *Pure Theory*, 193 ff.

[11] Raz, 'Legal Principles and the Limits of Law', 825, 848 f. The point had been left open by Hart, *Concept of Law*, 64.

[12] Hart, *Concept of Law*, 94 ff., 100.

taken the modern states as typical examples of legal systems of primary and secondary norms.[13] Moreover, he also held that legal systems were necessarily unified by one basic rule of recognition.[14] Even if such a rule could be complex embracing different criteria for both statutory and common law, it therefore had to be well-structured in that the 'several criteria are ranked in order of relative subordination and primacy' and 'one of them is *supreme*'.[15] Seen from a historical perspective, however, such a unification of the law was only an achievement of the modern state. Earlier legal systems were essentially pluralistic in that there was no clear hierarchy between different subsystems and sources of the law;[16] and similar features, it will be shown, can be observed in present law, as well.[17] Thus, even Hart's highly influential formulation of the concept of law was closely, even if not conceptually, connected with the modern state.

A final related assumption is that the political leaders of a state—princes, governments, and parliaments—usually pronounce their political will by means of mandatory legislation, whereas academic lawyers are expected to express their views in learned textbooks or commentaries which apply and interpret such legislation. Likewise, the function of the judiciary is primarily seen as applying the (states') law. It follows that the development of legal systems is seen as largely determined by the political process. Even if legislation is vague and if judges cannot be restrained to being *les bouches de la loi*, they have, of course, to obey to the law. The legal profession, i.e. academics, judges, and practising lawyers, may only develop the law within the limits of the actual legal system and thus within the legislative constraints determined by the political government. Indeed, the idea of a codification has, since the 19th century, been connected with the two political ideals that the law should be found in a publicly accessible legislative text and that it could be seen as an expression of a people's political will. These ideals in turn presuppose a concept of law that describes legal rules as resulting from and being determined by the political process.

[13] Hart, *Concept of Law*, 79, 114 ff.

[14] Hart qualified this assumption only in the context of public international law: *Concept of Law*, 213 ff.

[15] Hart, *Concept of Law*, 95, 100 f., 105 f.

[16] Below 30 f.

[17] See for the conceptual questions below 41 ff.

1. Problems

During the 20th century, many of these ideals and assumptions have been challenged. Common-law theorists argued that the positivistic separation of legislation and law-making on the one hand and its description or application on the other does not adequately capture the nature of common law, at least if common law is not seen as a system of legal rules based on precedent, but rather as custom and reason *in foro*:[18] customary law consisting of a 'body of practices observed and ideas received by a caste of lawyers'.[19] More generally, scholars studying legal transplants and receptions fundamentally questioned the idea of the law being essentially determined by the political process.[20]

At the same time, it became apparent that none of the political ideals connected with the concept of codification has ever been achieved.[21] On the one hand, codifications never made the law accessible to laymen: even if it is true that a Frenchman used to carry his *Code civil* with him, it is unlikely he understood it. On the other hand, codifications have never been written by legislators in Parliament and often not even by governmental administrations, but by commissions of scholars and other legal experts.[22] A democratic legitimization of the codification idea may therefore be regarded as artificial. This is not to say, of course, that core areas of private law *should* be independent of democratic decision making.[23] But it is difficult to deny that private law is in fact largely autonomous against political decision making. Hence, as a matter of fact, there must be other sources legitimizing the practice of private law.[24]

[18] Postema, 'Philosophy of the Common Law', 590 ff.; cf. also id., '*A Similibus ad Similia*'.

[19] Simpson, 'Common Law and Legal Theory', 77–99, 94.

[20] Graziadei, 'Comparative Law as the Study of Transplants and Receptions', 463 ff.

[21] This is discussed in more detail in Jansen and Michaels, 'Private Law and the State', 380 ff.

[22] J. Schröder, 'Rechtsdogmatik und Gesetzgebung', 37 f.

[23] Such an argument is made by Smits, 'European Private Law and Democracy'. The classical democratic ideal is defended by Rödl, 'Law Beyond the Democratic Order?'

[24] Among those are 'democratic' procedural values of discursive participation and transparent decision making; see below 100 ff.

In addition, neither the rise of the nation state nor the codifications really changed the structure and method of legal reasoning.[25] As a result, codifications never rendered the law static. Codifying legislation has not prevented later legal change by academic argument and judicial activity.[26] Yet, changes of the law resulting from its judicial 'application' often have a retroactive effect. Therefore, the legal professions have increasingly become aware, not only in the common law but also in codified legal systems, of the necessity of protecting the citizens' reliance on the law developed, besides statutory law and codifications, by judges and legal scholars.[27] In such an argument, legislation and judge-made law are largely equated. Even if the distinction between the making of the law and its interpretation and application may be clear in theory, it is difficult to apply in legal practice.

2. Plan of the book

This book seeks to further clarify the classical understanding of the legal process in general, and of codifications in particular. The analysis will focus on specific legal texts and their form, rather than on legal rules. Here, the main argument proceeds from the historical observation that—before and besides the modern legislative codifications—there have always been non-legislative codifications and other basic reference texts:[28] law books, laying down a comprehensive body of norms, which were not issued by legislators but nevertheless were regarded as effectively binding in legal discourse. Famous examples include the *Corpus iuris civilis* during the times of the *ius commune*, the Saxon Mirror, and the *Decretum Gratiani*.

[25] Donahue, 'Private Law', 136 f.; Behrends, 'Bündnis zwischen Gesetz und Dogmatik', 13.

[26] See below 18 f.

[27] Alexander and Sherwin, 'Judges as Rule Makers', 28 ff.; for civilian systems Zimmermann and Jansen, 'Quieta Movere'.

[28] The concept of a codification is understood in this book narrowly, as a written body of norms, which regulate a large part of the law in a comprehensive and therefore systematic way. It is a concept which historically did not appear before the enlightenment and thus does not fit well with earlier eminent *codices*, such as Justinian's *Corpus iuris* that were not systematic in structure (cf. below at 16). Yet, as far as the authority of basic legal reference texts is concerned, these pre-enlightenment *codices* must be included in the present analysis.

Today, comparable basic legal texts are often the work of 'private', state-independent institutions or groups. Thus, the American Law Institute's Restatements of the Law have long become a well-established element of the American legal system. They have achieved quasi-legislative authority that may of course be criticized,[29] but cannot be seriously disputed anymore. As observers have noted, '(i)n some states, where there is no conflicting statute or earlier case law, the Restatements are the law'.[30] Similar developments are on the global level, the International Institute for the Unification of Private Law (UNIDROIT)'s *Principles of International Commercial Contracts*[31] (PICC): rules of an alleged new 'lex mercatoria'[32] for international arbitration and trade.[33] On the European level, the *Principles of European Contract Law* (PECL), prepared by the Lando Commission on European Contract Law, have had a significant unifying effect on the last decade's development of private law;[34] and the Lando Commission's work has been continued by other groups, such as the European Group on Tort Law, the Study Group on a European Civil Code, and the Research Group on EC Private Law (Acquis Group). All these groups have presented 'Principles' of European private law: comprehensive bodies of basic rules which are meant to become a textual foundation for a new European *ius commune*.[35] Indeed, all these texts, both on the global and the European level, very much look like a modern codification, but lack the political authority of a state or a state-like legislator.

Scholars have recently coined the concept of 'private codification (*codification privée, Privatkodifikation*)' for such texts of authority,

[29] For an overview of critique directed against the American Law Institute and its Restatements, see Frank, 'Law Institute', 620 ff.; Adams, 'Blaming the Mirror'; Hesselink, 'Choices Made by the Lando Commission', 77 ff., all with further references.

[30] Frank, 'Law Institute', 638 f.; Zekoll, 'Law Institute', 115 ff. For further detail, see below 50 ff.

[31] See also Bonell, *International Restatement.*

[32] See Michaels, 'The true lex mercatoria', 448, 457 ff.

[33] Cf. also *PICC-Commentary*/Vogenauer, Introduction [11]. Other attempts of restatements of international commercial custom are the INCOTERMS and model standard contract forms; examples are the ICC model contracts on subjects such as commercial agency or sales. Yet, only the PICC use the traditional legislative form of a codification.

[34] Zimmermann, 'Comparative Law and the Europeanization of Private Law', 560 ff., 563.

[35] See for all below 59 ff.

and indeed, such texts are usually written by 'private' groups of lawyers.[36] Nonetheless, it may be doubted whether it is fully adequate to describe the professional activity of legal scholars, the main actors in this process, as 'private'. Indeed, European academics are usually based at state universities; and although their academic activity may be protected by the constitutional guarantee of academic independence, they have often identified themselves with their respective state to a remarkable degree.[37] Similarly, most American lawyers who engaged themselves in the American Law Institute strongly identified with the American society and acted out of a feeling of 'public duty',[38] although they were either professors at private law schools or worked for private law firms. Such jurists do not promote their own individual interests or the interests of a particular pressure group when drafting a system of transnational principles (they may have an interest in having their name on the codification, though). It may thus be misleading to characterize them as 'private actors' in the legal system. Therefore, in this book, the concept of a 'non-legislative codification' will be used. On the one hand, this term shall indicate that such codifications are not based on a sovereign's will and are drafted outside the political sphere of states and governments. On the other hand, unlike genuinely private self-regulation, these codifications are drafted by actors without substantial interests in the legal matters regulated. Rather these actors act in pursuit of what they perceive as the common public good.

The existence of non-legislative codifications should be taken as a reason for further reconsidering the relation of political domination and the legal process, of *auctoritas* and *ratio* (or *scientia*), of law making and law application, and especially the relation of private law and the state. The focus is on legal reference texts and on the authority that is attributed to them by those working in the legal

[36] Kessedjian, 'La codification privée', 135–149; Michaels, 'Privatautonomie und Privatkodifikation', 590 f.; for further references, see *PICC-Commentary*/Michaels, Preamble I [5]; cf. also Snyder, 'Private Lawmaking'; Bachmann, *Private Ordnung*, 37 ff.

[37] Cf. Lepsius, 'Taking the Institutional Context Seriously'; Haferkamp, 'Science of Private Law', 258 ff., both with further references.

[38] ALI, 'Report of the Committee Proposing the Establishment of an American Law Institute', 29: 'fulfillment [sic] of a public duty'.

system, i.e. by the professional lawyers applying and interpreting those texts. Of course, this focus on written reference texts and on the legal profession throughout this book may be criticized as suggesting an inappropriately normative[39] and even elitist concept of the law, which is based exclusively on the views of legal elites and does not take into account the views of the public. However, the concept of law is determined from within the legal discourse, and the legal discourse is strongly professionalized in all European and indeed in all Western legal systems. Therefore, the legal profession is probably the most important group for an empirically adequate reconstruction of the legal systems' rules or processes of recognition.[40] For the same reason, written reference texts must be regarded as a foundation of the legal system, if the legal profession normally takes such texts as a 'source of the law' and thus as an ultimate justification of legal argument.

The focus on specific legal texts and on their authority in legal discourse will make apparent that private law mostly has been and still is to a large degree autonomous from political domination. Thus, it may be said that private law is beyond the state. Non-legislative codifications are no modern peculiarity. It is thus an oversimplification to base private law essentially or conceptually on the state or a Parliament's or government's political will. Rather, jurists should try to identify the factors determining the applicability and authority of basic legal texts as sources of the law. This would enable them to understand the processes by which participants to legal discourse accept a legal text as ultimate authority without requiring further justification for doing so.[41] This book is a first step towards such analysis.

It is doubtful whether such issues can be addressed appropriately by philosophical reflection and analysis alone. A broader empirical basis may be helpful for such a study. In this work, such a basis will

[39] Indeed, the use of a highly normative concept, such as 'legal profession', is dangerous from a methodological point of view; see Bourdieu and Wacquant, *Reflexive Sociology*, 235 ff., 242 ff. Yet, being aware of the dangers of an uncritical use of such a concept may help avoiding most of them.

[40] Cf. similarly Hart, *Concept of Law*, 60, 109 f.; even more narrowly Simpson, 'Common Law and Legal Theory', 95: 'most powerful members'.

[41] See, more detailed, below 41 ff.

be provided by historical and comparative observations (Part I, Chapters 1 and 2).[42] I will compare, on the one hand, texts from different times and legal cultures, and, on the other hand, legislative codifications and non-legislative reference texts. Such a broad and complex comparison will reveal common textual structures (Part II, Chapter 3) and general factors contributing to the authority of reference texts (Chapter 4). Some of these factors, such as the procedural ideals of fair representation and transparent decision making, may come as little surprise for many lawyers, as they are often discussed in present debates as criteria of a norm's legitimacy. Other criteria, though, such as the formal presentation of a text, have mostly been underestimated in legal discourse. Nevertheless, such factors will be shown to be of the utmost importance for a legal text's authority.

In accordance with the basically empirical approach of this book, the perspective chosen must be the descriptive point of view of an external observer of legal systems. Hence, the focus here is not on the constitutional principles of legislative and judicial law-making, but rather on the factors *de facto* explaining the authority of non-legislative codifications. The applicability of a text as an authoritative legal reference always depends on its recognition by the individual members of the relevant legal profession, and such recognition is usually based on certain reasons or motives. However, not all those reasons and motives are necessarily valid arguments, if seen from the internal perspective of the law. Hence, such factors will not always be openly addressed in legal discourse. What is more, it should not even be presupposed that all these factors have the status of reasons for action, on which jurists consciously base their professional behaviour. Indeed, jurists have often applied reference texts without even asking for reasons to do so. Mostly, they simply followed a common, generally acknowledged practice. In such a case, the factual recognition of a text as legal authority may become a normative reason for treating it as such.[43]

[42] See, on the methodological assumptions in this respect, Jansen, 'Comparative Law and Comparative Knowledge'.

[43] Cf. Luhmann, *Recht der Gesellschaft*, 80 f., 133 ff. / *Law as a Social System*, 108 f., 149 ff.

PART I

TEXTUAL AUTHORITIES IN LEGAL DISCOURSE

Chapter 1

Historical Observations

It is general historical knowledge that the connection between the law and the state is of rather recent origin.[1] The state is a modern concept, at least as it is understood today as an abstract legal entity or juristic person dominating a specific people in a specific geographic part of the world.[2] In this sense, the concept of a state describes neither the Roman Republic nor ancient and medieval empires, nor even the early monarchies in Sicily, England, France, and Spain. In fact, this concept, which is intellectually based on ideas developed by writers such as Thomas Hobbes and Jean Bodin, was coined only after the religious conflicts of the 16th and 17th centuries, when the traditional monarchies were transformed into European nation states.[3] It was not until then that the state was seen as an abstract entity independent of the King's or Prince's person, that it developed an extensive, complex administration monopolizing the exercise of power, and that it gained immediate control of its citizens: before, central domination had typically been mediated by independent powers.[4] True, attempts to control and administer private law publicly can be observed long before these modern states appeared, under the Roman Emperors, by the Popes of the Catholic Church after the reforms of Gregory VII, and by the administrations of the quickly growing European cities from the 11th century onwards.[5]

[1] The following paragraphs draw on Jansen and Michaels, 'Private Law and the State'; Michaels and Jansen, 'Private Law Beyond the State?'. See also the contributions to Jansen and Michaels (eds), *Beyond the State.*

[2] Cf. Jellinek, *Staatslehre,* 174 ff., 180 ff.; van Crefeld, *State,* 1; cf. also Reinhard, *Staatsgewalt,* 15 ff.

[3] Cf. Harding, *Foundations of the State,* 295 ff., 307 ff.; van Crefeld, *State,* especially 124 ff.; Möllers, *Staat als Argument,* 215 ff., with further references.

[4] Reinhard, *Staatsgewalt,* 196 ff., 212 ff.

[5] Cf. Donahue, 'Private Law', 126 ff.

Yet, it was not before the modern states appeared on the scene that the idea of some sort of a sovereign's full public control of private law was conceivable.

I. Codifications and the State

This idea of the sovereign state's control of the law was connected with the idea of a codification from early on,[6] and this intellectual connection has remained vivid until today. In the 20th century, codifications were historically explained as an expression of the states' practical political interest in unifying and dominating private law[7] on the one hand, and of the political-theory idea of the law's validity being grounded on the state on the other.[8] This view was supported by the fact that codifications were often initiated by governmental administrations and thus originated in the political sphere of the state. And indeed, they were successful only in strong states. Thus, private law was codified in 1734 in Sweden, 1756 in Bavaria, 1794 in Prussia, 1804 in France, 1811 in Austria, but only in 1896/1900 in the German *Reich*.

It is remarkable that the present project of the European Commission to formulate a 'Common Frame of Reference' (CFR) for European contract law may likewise be understood from such a perspective. It is strongly supported by the European Parliament, which in 2002 had proposed an extremely ambitious timescale for the enactment of a European Civil Code by the year 2010.[9] True, in

[6] For Hermann Conring's arguments in favour of a codification of German private law, see Luig, 'Conring', 378. On earlier, humanistic arguments for a codification of the law, cf. Caroni, 'Kodifikation', cols. 911 f.; Coing, 'Vorgeschichte der Kodifikation', 798 ff., 805 ff.; Mohnhaupt, 'Gesetzgebung des Reichs', 103 ff. For the Prussian codification in particular, see Eckert, 'Gesetzesbegriff und Normanwendung', 573 ff.

[7] As an expression of a 'strong state', codifications have been seen by Meder, 'Krise des Nationalstaates'; Caroni, *Gesetz und Gesetzbuch*, 39 ff.; Wieacker, *Privatrechtsgeschichte*, 324, 333: 'Staatskunstwerk'; id., 'Kodifikationsidee', 41; Reinhard, *Staatsgewalt*, 301 ff.; Varga, *Codification*, 71 ff., 334 ff.: 'codification is nothing but a means for the state to assert its domination by shaping and controlling the law'. More nuanced van den Berg, *Politics of European Codification*.

[8] Cf. Kroppenberg, 'Der gescheiterte Codex', 117, 120 f.

[9] Resolution of the European Parliament on the approximation of the civil and commercial law of the Member States, OJ C140E/538.

a Communication of 2003[10] the European Commission relegated the idea of a codification to a secondary position, and in a later Communication this idea was even rejected;[11] and in response, the Council 'welcomed' 'the Commission's repeated reassurance that it does not intend to propose a "European Civil Code" which would harmonise contract laws of Member States and that Member States' differing legal traditions will be fully taken into account'.[12] Nevertheless, the idea of unifying contract law was never dismissed. Rather, the intriguing term 'CFR' was established as the official label for an instrument which is not supposed to be enacted as a piece of legislation but which, nonetheless, will have to be endorsed by the European legislators in some way or other and will, therefore, become a determining factor in the development of European contract law. Thus, even if the Commission is currently focusing on the consumer *acquis*, rather than on general contract law,[13] relying for this purpose on the traditional legal instruments of European law,[14] it seems clear that the CFR is meant to become a legal device of the European Union unifying contract law in Europe. Of course, there is still a great deal of uncertainty as to the substance, the exact form, and the legal nature of such a CFR, but it can safely be said that it is meant to become the basic reference text for European private law and that it shall be backed in some way by the legislative authority of the European Union.[15] According to such a view, the European Union is plausibly conceived of as a political, quasi-state authority; and the CFR process would be seen as the European Union taking full control over large parts of private law, thereby replacing the nation states as the ultimate foundation of the validity of private law.

Despite its plausibility at first sight, however, such a state-conception of codifications being an expression of governmental

[10] Commission (EC), 'A More Coherent European Contract Law: An Action Plan', COM(2003) 68 final, 12 February 2003.

[11] Commission (EC), 'European Contract Law and the revision of the *acquis*: the way forward', COM(2004) 651 final, 11 October 2004.

[12] Press release of 28/29 November 2005–14155/05 (press 287), 28.

[13] Commission (EC), 'First Annual Progress Report on European Contract Law and the Acquis Review', COM(2005) 456 final, 23 September 2005.

[14] Commission (EC), 'Proposal for a Directive of the European Parliament and of the Council on consumer rights', COM(2008) 614 final, 8 October 2008.

[15] Jansen, 'Traditionsbegründung', 536 ff., 540 f.

domination may be misleading. Not everybody agrees with a historical explanation of the European codification movement as a process of the state taking control over private law. Indeed, such an explanation may be the result of a one-sided focus on the development of states. Codifications have also been described, from an internal legal perspective, as 'a specific historical phenomenon that originated in ... legal science'.[16] Such a legal-system view of codification is supported by the fact that common law systems have mostly proved resistant to codification movements. This was so even though the codification debate in England is as old as that on the European continent, although the discussions in common law countries were no less intense than those in civilian systems, and although the British Crown was not weaker than continental governments.[17]

Of course, there is a bundle of different factors explaining the success and failure of codifications in civil law and common law systems. One such factor was that continental civil law consisted of complex multi-layer systems of written and unwritten legal sources of different kinds of authority.[18] As a result, the law was perceived as highly insecure and arbitrary. Another important factor was that the normative status of Roman law as a source of positive law had become untenably awkward. In the increasingly rationalistic world of the 18th century, Roman law finally lost its previous status as legal *ratio scripta*. It was therefore felt that the whole legal system was in need of fundamental reform and a unified legislative foundation. In the course of these developments, codifications became a central element of enlightened natural-law thinking that proved highly influential in 18th-century continental Europe. At the same time, codifications were regarded as a necessary means of rationally

[16] Zimmermann, 'Codification', 98; see also Mohnhaupt, 'Gesetzgebung des Reichs', 104.

[17] For the United States, see Cook, *Codification Movement*; Crystal, 'Restatement Movement', 255 ff.; for England A. Braun, 'English codification debate'; cf. also Jansen and Michaels, 'Private Law and the State', 383–387, with further references. Instead of a civil code, there are different, specifically American, outcomes of the codification debate, namely the American Restatements and the UCC, both of which have created a substantial degree of national uniformity and systematization of the law.

[18] Oestmann, *Rechtsvielfalt*. For the medieval times similarly Berman, *Law and Revolution*, 10 ff., 199–519; Grossi, *L'ordine giuridico*, 223 ff.

reordering and systematizing private law, an idea that was deeply entrenched in the civilian concept of law.

Hence, the codification movement cannot be fully understood without taking these genuinely legal aspects into account. True, codifications presuppose a strong state. But the idea of a strong state or political system taking control of the legal system does not suffice for a full explanation of successful codification processes. In the same way, it is remarkable, that the CFR process today does not originate in the political sphere alone, but is strongly supported by academic lawyers. Indeed, the *Principles of European Contract Law* (PECL) were drafted independently of any participation or influence from political actors of the European Union.[19] Again, it was felt that the present plural state of the law in Europe is unsatisfactory, and, again, the idea of a uniform European system of private law constitutes a strong motive for drafting a CFR and a corresponding non-legislative, 'academic' *Draft Common Frame of Reference* (DCFR).

Another observation casting doubts on a purely state-centric conception of legislative codifications is that even the more reformatory codifications never fundamentally dominated the legal process. On the one hand, changing the rules and principles of private law was usually not a central point on the political codification agendas. The systems, on which the codifications were based, were the result of academic debate;[20] and the individual rules, too, were mostly written outside Parliament.[21] Indeed, codifications primarily aimed at a restatement of the law in a simpler and more accessible form;[22] this is true also for 20th-century codifications. Thus, the new Dutch code was primarily meant to update the old codification both in substance and system. There are of course material changes, but these are less important than the systematic

[19] At an early stage, the European Commission did financially support the Lando Commission's work; see Lando, 'Preface', xv. This support, however, was not continued.

[20] *HKK*/Michaels, vor § 241. 'Systemfragen des Schuldrechts' [14], [19], [25] and *passim*. For the German discussion during the 19th century see Schwarz, 'Entstehung des Pandektensystems'.

[21] Above 4.

[22] Zweigert and Kötz, *Rechtsvergleichung*, 78 ff., 84 ff. (for France), 137 ff., 142 ff.; Koschaker, *Europa und das römische Recht*, 205 (for Germany). On the methodological debate see Mertens, *Gesetzgebungskunst*, 18 ff., 33 ff., 51 ff.

revision. Moreover, many of these changes are legislative restatements of earlier judge-made law. Likewise, the code was discussed in Parliament, but although these discussions had an impact on the final outcome, they did not amount to more than peripheral corrections on the original academic draft.[23]

On the other hand, codifications cannot be seen as a suitable device for controlling the law's further developments. Codifications reduce the former law's complexity into abstract systems of relatively few but dense rules.[24] Accordingly, courts have mostly been able to continue earlier lines of jurisprudence,[25] and codifications have never prevented later legal change by academic argument and judicial activity.[26] This must be taken as a clear indication of the fact that legal systems may retain large parts of their autonomy against the political and social process, even when being codified. The idea of the state taking control of private law by means of codification therefore appears misleading. Indeed, the systematic character of codifications often makes it more difficult for a political legislator to 'intervene'. In England, this has always been a reason for Parliament to oppose codification. Parliamentarians feared that an outside body might endanger their 'sovereignty over detail of legislation'.[27]

Of course, the idea of the law's autonomy is a notoriously contested notion. In the present context, however, it simply indicates

[23] For all Hondius, 'Das neue Niederländische Gesetzbuch', 378 ff., 381 ff., 386 ff.

[24] See Kroppenberg, 'Der gescheiterte Codex', 117 f., describing (successful) codifications as a 'condensed substratum of previous law (*ein verdichtetes Substrat dessen ..., was vorher rechtens war*)'; cf. also J. Schröder, 'Rechtsdogmatik und Gesetzgebung', 38 f.

[25] Zimmermann, *Civilian Tradition Today*, 55 ff., 98 ff.; *HKK*/Zimmermann, vor § 1. 'Das Bürgerliche Gesetzbuch ...' [17]; see also the contributions to Falk and Mohnhaupt (eds), *Das Bürgerliche Gesetzbuch und seine Richter*; Zweigert and Kötz, *Rechtsvergleichung*, 88 ff., 93 ff.; Gordley, 'Myths of the French Civil Code'; cf. also Kelly, 'Ancient Verses on New Ideas'.

[26] See, for France, Bürge, *Privatrecht*, 174 ff., 254 ff. and *passim*; cf. also Morin, *Révolte du droit*, describing fundamental changes of the law as a result of the joint efforts of the legislator, however outside the *Code civil*, of *la doctrine*, and of judicial law making. For Austria, see Brauneder, 'Privatrechtsfortbildung durch Juristenrecht'. For Germany, such developments can be clearly seen in most contributions to the *HKK*; see *HKK*/Zimmermann, vor § 1. 'Das Bürgerliche Gesetzbuch ...' [17], and, as an example, Haferkamp's commentary on § 242 (*Treu und Glauben*); a summary is given in [88]. See also, for the law of torts, von Caemmerer, 'Wandlungen des Deliktsrechts'; Jansen, 'Codifications, Commentators, and Courts', both with further references.

[27] See A. Braun, 'English codification debate', at 4.

the fact that private law is—at least in part—conceptually and normatively independent from the political and social discourse.[28] True, the law is normally influenced by and responsive to political and social developments and thus to general political and moral arguments. Nonetheless, the law's historical development is to a large extent determined by an inter-systemic order of its own: by peculiar institutional, normative, and conceptual constraints. Indeed, general moral or practical arguments can only become effective in legal discourse if they can be translated into legal language; only such 'translation' connects extra-legal arguments with the authoritative sources of the law. Yet the meaning of basic legal concepts cannot normally be arbitrarily interpreted as such concepts relate to other concepts and rules within the legal system; hence their meaning is determined by such concepts and rules.[29] Thus, the proposition that somebody is 'entitled' to something presupposes the existence of a legal system and a judiciary; and the concept of 'property' implies complex rules on the *rei vindicatio*, the *actio negatoria*, and the delictual protection of individually assigned legal positions. As a consequence of such conceptual and intellectual constraints, the law has its own conceptual and discursive rationality;[30] this is especially true for private law. This alone suffices for making private law—at least to a substantial degree—independent and autonomous from the general political, social, and moral discourse. It may be regretted,[31] but private law cannot be a 'mirror' of society or an immediate function of the political process.

[28] Cf. Finnis, *Natural Law*, 268 ff., 316 ff.; Berman, *Law and Revolution*, 7 ff., 37 ff.; for a critical analysis Postema, 'Law's Autonomy', 80 ff. Of course, a strong theory of strict autonomy is implausible, but this is no argument against a weakly autonomous conception of private law maintaining that arguments based on positive sources of the law normally have a *pro-tanto* priority over non-legal arguments.

[29] Hart, *Definition and Theory*, 4 ff., 9 ff., 26: 'the meaning of these words is to be found only by examining the legal rules which prescribe in what conditions such a statement is correct'. Cf. also Alexy, *Grundrechte*, 44.

[30] Cf., for Roman law, Fögen, *Römische Rechtsgeschichten*, 209 ff.; for the discussion in the 19th century and its political sub-text, see also Rückert, *Autonomie des Rechts*, 57 ff.

[31] Indeed, many authors have forcefully argued that the law should be more responsive to political and societal developments; cf. Cohen, 'Transcendental Nonsense', 821: 'Jurisprudence, then, as an autonomous system of legal concepts, rules, and arguments, must be independent both of ethics and of such positive sciences as economics or psychology. In effect, it is a special branch of the science of transcendental [sic] nonsense'; Encinas de Munagorri, 'Qu'est-ce que la technique juridique?'

II. The Textual Foundations of the *Ius Commune*

The autonomy of legal systems, and especially of private law, not only consists of the fact that judges and other professional lawyers ultimately determine the content of a codification and other legislative sources of the law, however. The legal elites also determine which texts may be applied as sources of law. From the perspective of systems theory, this is an evident truism: if social systems define their boundaries from within, the law's boundaries and thus its textual bases can only be determined from the internal perspective of the law,[32] i.e. by the professional lawyers participating in legal discourse. True, lawyers must convince their contemporaries of accepting their legal systems and conceptions of law as appropriate mechanisms of and instruments for conflict resolution; here, their motives often relate to reputation and wealth.[33] But such social struggles concern the relation of the legal system to the economic or political sector; they must be distinguished from the internal legal processes which lead to the recognition of legal authority.

Historical evidence confirms this rather theoretical assumption: the applicability and thus the validity and authority of legal texts have always been determined from within a legal system, by the participants to legal discourses. This can be seen in more detail with three fundamental reference texts of the European *ius commune*: first the *Decretum Gratiani*, the basic text of Canon Law; second the Saxon Mirror, the basic reference text for Saxon and, more generally, for large parts of German law; and third the *Corpus iuris civilis*, which from the 12th century onwards became the fundamental reference text of European private law.

[32] Luhmann, *Recht der Gesellschaft*, 15: 'Das Recht bestimmt, was die Grenzen des Rechts sind, bestimmt also, was zum Recht gehört und was nicht' / *Law as a Social System*, 58: '... the law itself defines what the boundaries of law are and what belongs to law and what does not'. See also *loc. cit.*, 98 ff. / 122 ff.; Teubner, *Recht als autopoietisches System*, 1 ff.

[33] For such processes with respect to the medieval *ius commune*, see Kantorowicz, 'Kingship under the Impact of Scientific Jurisprudence', 90 ff.; Görich, 'Kontext der roncalischen Gesetze', 318 ff. For the modern 'lex mercatoria', see the classical study by Dezalay and Garth, *Dealing in Virtue*.

1. The *Decretum Gratiani*

From the second half of the 12th century onwards, the *Decretum Gratiani*, a legal text, which was published in its final version around 1140, was long regarded as the central textual authority of Canon law. Its title expresses the later attribution of this text to Gratian: a jurist and monk, or perhaps a couple of jurists and monks, of whose life near to nothing is known.[34]

The original title of the *Decretum* had been *Concordantia discordantium canonum*, 'concordance of dissonant canons', and this title formulated a clear programme: the text integrated large parts of the earlier laws and authoritative texts of the Roman Church into a coherent body of legal norms. The *Decretum* brought together canons of church councils, letters and decretals of Popes, excerpts from Roman law, and passages from the scripture and from the church fathers' writings. Gratian re-organized all these texts, irrespective of their origin, into a single legal whole. Yet, this was a vast mass of quite distinct authorities, many of which were in apparent contradiction or 'dissonance'. Gratian confronted this problem by relating all these texts to specific questions of actual Canon law practice; this made it possible for him to uncover and harmonize apparent conflicts by distinguishing and re-interpreting these texts in the light of related authorities. For this purpose, Gratian included in between the collected individual texts of independent authority his own explanatory *dicta*: short texts that analysed, interpreted, and harmonized the Church's authorities.[35]

The *Concordantia discordantium canonum* had not been the first of such reconstructive collections of Canon law[36] which complemented

[34] 'Unfortunately, virtually everything about it, save its authority and importance, seems to be either disputed or unknown': Helmholz, *Classical Canon Law*, 7; see also Christensen, 'Introduction', xiv; Winroth, *The Making of Gratian's Decretum*, 122 ff. and *passim*. Apparently, there were at least two versions of the *Decretum*. The original version was probably written around 1139. During the immediately following years, it was substantially enriched and restructured; only at that stage Roman law found its place within the text.

[35] See for all Helmholz, *Classical Canon Law*, 7 ff.; Christensen, 'Introduction', xii ff. with further references.

[36] See especially the collection of Ivo of Chartres; for the earlier state of research, see Kuttner, 'Father of the Science of Canon Law'; Landau, 'Quellen und Bedeutung'.

the primary norms of the Church with a secondary layer of more consistent derivative norms.[37] However, it was the only successful attempt; and it standardized Canon law.[38] Within a few years, it was acknowledged by jurists and theologians as one of the most important books of medieval law and it was seen as an independent textual authority in itself.[39] During the following centuries, it was the main reference text for academic teaching and the starting point of every learned analysis of Canon law. Indeed, it was only this text that made Canon law the object of systematic academic study.[40] From then on, scholarly discussion which further developed Canon law was focused on the *Decretum*. A few decades later, the outcome of this discussion was itself canonized in the form of a Standard Gloss (*Glossa ordinaria*) by Johannes Teutonicus and Bartholomaeus of Brescia.[41] This was a quasi-official standard commentary, which usually accompanied copies or prints of the *Decretum*. Written as a marginal gloss around the text of the *Decretum*,[42] it collected the increasingly sophisticated learning of the generations of canon lawyers after Gratian. In later times, it was often regarded as a distinctive legal authority in itself.

Even if it may have been difficult in those times to draw a clear distinction between a private work and an official collection, there are no doubts that the *Decretum* was written in private in that it was independent of any official commission.[43] Only centuries later, in 1582, Pope Gregory XIII officially ratified the 'customary status' of Gratian's *Decretum*. With regard to the *Decretum's* factual authority, however, this ratification made no real difference anymore. It merely confirmed a role that the *Decretum* had long acquired: it had become the main textual basis of positive Canon law. Indeed, the

[37] Thier, 'Dynamische Schriftlichkeit', 7, 15 ff., 27 ff.

[38] Christensen, 'Introduction', xvi; see also Landau, 'Quellen und Bedeutung', 218, 227 ff.

[39] For this point, see Kuttner, 'Observations sur l'autorité des collections canoniques', 306 ff.

[40] Landau, 'Quellen und Bedeutung', 229 f.

[41] On the developments leading to the canonization of the Standard Gloss, see Weigand, 'Glossen, kanonische'.

[42] See Christensen, 'Introduction', xvi. For a picture of such a standard gloss (to the *Digest*) see below at 116. The Standard Gloss to the first 20 Distinctions of Gratian's *Decretum* is easily accessible in the English translation by James Gordley.

[43] Kuttner, 'Observations sur l'autorité des collections canoniques', 306 f.

Decretum had been included as the first part within the Roman Church's *Corpus iuris canonici*;[44] thus, it had become one of the most important reference texts of the *ius commune*. Its recognition as a legally authoritative text by the legal profession pre-dated its coming into force as mandatory legislation. In fact, the 'legislative act' was not more than an official acknowledgement by the Roman Church of the *Decretum's* status as binding law.

2. The Saxon Mirror

Comparable developments can also be seen in secular law. At the beginning of the 13th century the oral practice of the law in Germany had increasingly become confronted with the written and thus superior *ius commune* taught at Italian universities and exported throughout Europe. As a result, it was widely felt that the law should be laid down in written texts.[45] Indeed, to keep—or make—the law predictable, the form of legal sources must normally be in writing.[46]

One such text, written to lay down and update the traditional legal custom in an orderly form, was the Saxon Mirror.[47] This book was probably written on the basis of an earlier Latin version,[48] which its author, Eike von Repgow, may actually have produced himself. In substance, the text presents itself as a restatement of the customary law of the area around Magdeburg: as a mirror of the law, like a mirror for women's use.[49] Yet, Eike substantially enriched it with biblical elements;[50] and he significantly modernized

[44] See Christensen, 'Introduction', xviii f.

[45] Bertelsmeier-Kirst, *Kommunikation und Herrschaft*, 12 ff. On the function of writing in the medieval legal and institutional practice and on the related historical processes, see also the contributions to Keller *et al.* (eds), *Pragmatische Schriftlichkeit im Mittelalter*; see especially Dilcher, 'Oralität, Verschriftlichung und Wandlungen der Normstruktur'; id., 'Verrechtlichung der Lebensbeziehungen', 95 ff., 105 ff. For a view qualifying the functional necessity of written legislation, see also Mihm, 'Vom Dingprotokoll zum Zwölftafelgesetz', 56 ff.

[46] Summers, *Form and Function*, 171 f.

[47] See generally Wieacker, *Privatrechtsgeschichte*, 106 f.; Bertelsmeier-Kirst, *Kommunikation und Herrschaft*, 61 ff.; Lück, *Sachsenspiegel*, 13 ff., with further references. See also Dawson, *Oracles of the Law*, 153 f., 208 f.; Glenn, *Common Laws*, 37 ff.

[48] This is what Eike von Repgow himself claimed: Saxon Mirror, Reimvorrede 274.

[49] Saxon Mirror, Reimvorrede 178–182.

[50] Kisch, *Sachsenspiegel and Bible*, 58 ff. and *passim*.

the traditional law on the basis of the more innovative learned Canon law.[51] Altogether, the text was much more than a mere description of actual custom; and it was designed to be binding not only on the Saxons, but on all people.[52] Indeed, Eike did not write the Saxon Mirror as a scholar's description of legal custom; rather he meant it to be an authoritative statement of the law.[53]

Eike von Repgow, a man of the lesser nobility, was probably not part of a governmental administration.[54] It is possible that he was charged with the project by a local Prince, as has been suggested[55] (if so, the Saxon Mirror would bear some similarity with the DCFR).[56] Yet, even if this was not the case, Eike clearly did not regard his endeavour as a private matter: he acted out of a feeling of a 'public' duty towards God and Christianity. There is no doubt, nevertheless, that the Saxon Mirror was originally neither drafted nor enacted as formal legislation; it was, in this sense, unofficial law. Yet, within a century, it became the textual basis of the law in Saxony—and later also in other parts of Germany and especially Eastern Europe. During the first decades, it was already being used in quite distant towns such as Augsburg, Cologne, or Bremen;[57] and it became the model for other comparable texts such as the Swabian Mirror, which largely copied its provisions.[58] A politically influential learned lawyer, Johann von Buch,[59] further developed and

[51] On the sources used by Eike von Repgow, see Landau, 'Entstehungsort des Sachsenspiegels', 82 ff.; Bertelsmeier-Kirst, *Kommunikation und Herrschaft*, 86 ff.

[52] Saxon Mirror, Reimvorrede 157 ff., 183 ff.

[53] Saxon Mirror, Reimvorrede 1 ff., 36 ff., 133 ff., 183 ff., 221 ff.; cf. also Trusen, 'Die Rechtsspiegel', 17 f.; Kroeschell, 'Von der Gewohnheit zum Recht', 75 ff.

[54] On Eike von Repgow, see Pahlmann and Schröder, 'Eike von Repgow', 123 ff.; Eckhardt, *Eike von Repchow und Hoyer von Falkenstein*, 9 ff., 18 ff.; Bertelsmeier-Kirst, *Kommunikation und Herrschaft*, 66 ff.

[55] Eike von Repgow himself tells of having been charged by Earl Hoyer von Falkenstein with the translation of a prior Latin text; see Saxon Mirror, Reimvorrede 263 ff. It is disputed, though, whether he was really a public servant of Falkenstein; see Eckhardt, *Eike von Repchow und Hoyer von Falkenstein*, 21 ff.; Kroeschell, 'Rechtsaufzeichnung und Rechtswirklichkeit', 353 f.

[56] For this parallel, Hähnchen, 'Die Rechtsform des CFR', 150, 170.

[57] Kroeschell, 'Rechtsaufzeichnung und Rechtswirklichkeit', 370 f.; id., 'Von der Gewohnheit zum Recht', 82 ff. On the further influence, especially in Eastern Europe, see Lück, *Sachsenspiegel*, 55 ff.; Glenn, *Common Laws*, 38 f., both with further references.

[58] Trusen, 'Rechtsspiegel', 38 ff.

[59] See Lück, 'Johann von Buch'.

endorsed it with a standard gloss (*Buch's Gloss*),[60] which was modelled after Accursius' *Glossa ordinaria* to the *Corpus iuris civilis*; the Saxon Mirror was accepted as good law by powerful towns such as Magdeburg and Halle; and in at least one case, it was even formally ratified as the law by a local government.[61] From the 14th century onwards, it was generally recognized as the textual basis of positive Saxon law; and it was treated as such until the 20th century.[62] In fact, it was now regarded as a source of positive law in the same way as the sources of Canon law or the *Corpus iuris civilis*. As soon as it had been glossed, courts acknowledged it as the Saxon *ius commune*; hence it was applied without further proof.[63]

Leading actors in this process of recognition were, on the one hand, professional jurists, such as Johann von Buch and especially clerical lawyers, who apparently took a leading role in the use of the text in arbitration proceedings.[64] On the other hand, the text was supported by the *Schöffen* of Magdeburg and Halle,[65] lay assessors, who had some knowledge of the law. Clearly, all these men treated the Saxon Mirror as a valid expression of the law, when they made it the object of a scholarly discourse and the basis of legal argument. This becomes apparent from the fact that it was produced in comparatively high numbers, often together with *Buch's Gloss*. Even today 78 complete texts exist.[66] There can be no doubt that professional lawyers regarded these texts as highly important for their

[60] See Kannowski, *Buch'sche Glosse*, 2 ff., 6 ff., 73 ff. and *passim*; cf. also id., 'Sachsenspiegel'; id., 'Europäisches Rechtsdenken bei Johann von Buch', 80. There were also other glosses, but *Buch's Gloss* became the leading authority.

[61] Kannowski, *Buch'sche Glosse*, 87: apparently, the only place where this happened was the little town of Jerichow, which, however, had been given to Johann von Buch (see Lück, 'Johann von Buch', 135), and where Johann had actively promoted this official act of recognition; see Kannowski, *loc. cit.* More generally on the process of the Saxon Mirror's gaining legislative authority, see Kroeschell, 'Rechtsaufzeichnung und Rechtswirklichkeit', 367 ff.; cf. also Trusen, 'Rechtsspiegel', 35 f.

[62] RGZ 137, 324, 343 f. (9 July 1932); see also BGHZ 108, 110, 122 (22 June 1989).

[63] Kroeschell, 'Rechtsaufzeichnung und Rechtswirklichkeit', 379 f.; id., 'Von der Gewohnheit zum Recht', 86 ff.

[64] Kroeschell, 'Rechtsaufzeichnung und Rechtswirklichkeit', 371: 'es ist die Luft von geistlichen Gerichten und Gelehrtenstuben, die einen hier anweht, von Ratskanzleien und Bettelordenklöstern'.

[65] Trusen, 'Rechtsspiegel', 35 ff.; Kroeschell, 'Rechtsaufzeichnung und Rechtswirklichkeit', 369 f., 373 f.

[66] Kannowski, *Buch'sche Glosse*, 12 ff., 34 ff.

practice. Not for all of those men, however, was it evident that the Saxon Mirror was to be applied as good law, and they therefore looked for good reasons to do so. Some authors explained it as imperial legislation—this was an idea which could already be found in the Saxon Mirror itself;[67] and from the second half of the 13th century, it was said that the Saxon Mirror was a privilege that had been granted to the Saxon people by the Emperor Charlemagne.[68] This theory became highly influential, as it was used as a central argument in *Buch's Gloss*.

As a matter of historical fact, this legend was plainly wrong. It was a fairy tale, invented after the fact—and even confirmed through forgery of documents[69]—to legitimize the use of the text. Yet, this was probably no 'political' *coup d'État*; rather, it must be understood as an expression of the feeling of the text's dignity and of the conviction that it should be applied in legal practice. Indeed, Johann von Buch strongly paralleled the Saxon Mirror with the *Corpus iuris* and believed that some parts of it were the legislation of later Emperors, like the *Corpus iuris' Novellae*.[70] Thus, even if the Saxon Mirror's authority was probably strengthened as a result of the people believing that it was supported by imperial authority, its recognition as a valid expression of the law must have pre-dated that legend.

It follows that the status of the Saxon Mirror as the textual basis of Saxon law cannot be explained with an external political source of legal validity. Ultimately, it rested on the fact that it was recognized and treated as valid law by the participants to the legal discourse.[71] It is worth emphasizing in this context that Johann von Buch, who also embraced the legend of Charlemagne's privilege, did not usually rely on this legend as an argument for explaining the 'validity' of the text. Rather, he used the legend for more specific purposes of legal, doctrinal argument: for an occasional correction

[67] Trusen, 'Rechtsspiegel', 19.

[68] Siegel, *Die deutschen Rechtsbücher*, 2–20; Trusen, 'Rechtsspiegel', 28 f.; see also Homeyer, 'Johannes Kledonk wider den Sachsenspiegel', 385; Kannowski, *Buch'sche Glosse*, 86 f., 134 f., 498 f., 543 ff.; Kroeschell, 'Von der Gewohnheit zum Recht', 89 ff.

[69] Trusen, 'Rechtsspiegel', 29, 36 f.

[70] Kannowski, *Buch'sche Glosse*, 526 f. On the Saxon Mirror's complex description as imperial legislation *and* imperial privilege, see id., 'Europäisches Rechtsdenken bei Johann von Buch', 84 ff.

[71] See also Kannowski, 'Sachsenspiegel', 516 ff.

of the Saxon Mirror's text or for justifying the Saxon Mirror's points of departure from Roman law. Thus, the legend helped to integrate Saxon law into the learned *ius commune*.[72] Perhaps, Johann von Buch also felt a practical need to support the text's authority politically. But such an argument was probably not directed at his professional peers.[73] For Johann the authority of the Saxon Mirror was beyond doubt. For him and for later jurists it was the Saxons' *Corpus iuris, tout court*.[74]

The legend of Charlemagne's privilege was in its core clearly of a mythological nature. The legal profession telling this story was not really concerned about questions of historical fact. Indeed, the precise facts, on which the story was based, were often not very clear: Johann von Buch never clearly distinguished Charlemagne and Eike von Repgow; he described a colourful, though not very consistent, mix of imperial authority behind the text,[75] and he accepted the *Corpus iuris civilis* as another imperial authority, which could even abrogate the Saxon Mirror's provisions.[76] The modern reader should therefore not be irritated by the rather detailed and specific story and by the forgery of documents: the truth of the legend of Charlemagne's privilege did not relate to matters of historical facts in the modern understanding. Indeed, in the 14th century, the idea of imperial authority was not a matter of political domination, but rather an aspect of the political metaphysics. Imperial authority was seen as the moral foundation of the political, social, and thus also the legal order,[77] and the concept of imperial law was used as a means of expressing that a body of norms was part of the system of secular law.[78] Jurists telling such stories believed that the text was based on imperial authority because they felt obliged to apply it, rather than the other way around.

[72] Siegel, *Die deutschen Rechtsbücher*, 6 ff.; Kannowski, *Buch'sche Glosse*, 134 f., 498 f., 555 f., 593 f., with further references.

[73] On the addressees of *Buch's Gloss*, see Kannowski, *Buch'sche Glosse*, 528 f., 592.

[74] Kannowski, *Buch'sche Glosse*, 525 f., 594; Kroeschell, 'Von der Gewohnheit zum Recht', 86 ff.

[75] Siegel, *Die deutschen Rechtsbücher*, 12 f.; Kannowski, *Buch'sche Glosse*, 525 ff., 545 ff., 551 ff., 558 f.

[76] References above n. 72.

[77] Stollberg-Rilinger, 'Würde des Gerichts', 194 f. with further references.

[78] Cf. Krause, 'Kaiserrecht und Rezeption', 87 ff., 126 ff.

3. The *Corpus iuris civilis*

Modern lawyers might be inclined to explain the authority of the Saxon Mirror as being based on custom and the authority of the *Decretum Gratiani* as deriving indirectly from the primary canons of the sovereign Roman Church. Thus, both texts would be understood as secondary sources of the law, their authority being of derivative nature only. However, no such explanation exists for the authority of the *Corpus iuris civilis*, which was seen for centuries as the basic reference text of the secular *ius commune*. Its authority may therefore appear 'mysterious'.[79] Indeed, the *Corpus iuris* did not become the legal basis for the *ius commune* because an Emperor or Prince had declared it binding, but for the only reason that learned lawyers used it as the standard textual reference within their legal discourse, first in Italy and later in most other European countries (it is another question, why *ius-commune* lawyers became highly influential as experts for the resolution of social conflicts).[80] The so-called Lothar legend, according to which the use of the *Digest* had been prescribed in 1137 by the Emperor Lothar III of Supplinburg, did not come up before the 16th century; and it was of purely mythological character, similar to the legend of Charlemagne's Saxon privilege.[81]

(a) Law per excellentiam

Hence, the secular *ius commune* may *prima facie* be seen as a paradigm of private law being independent of the state. Indeed, the 11th and 12th centuries, when Roman law was 'reborn', were times without any kind of state structures.[82] What is more, the *ius commune* was quite distant from the political process. Even if the Emperors, especially Frederick I Barbarossa, supported and used legal learning and Roman law,[83] it was evident that an Emperor could not comprehensively legislate in matters of private law.

[79] Donahue, 'Private Law', 129: 'Why this became such a popular teaching book is something of a mystery'.

[80] Cf. above n. 33.

[81] See below at 35 f.

[82] See above at 13 f.

[83] Fried, *Entstehung des Juristenstandes*, 17 ff.; Struve, 'Rolle des römischen Rechts'; see also the other contributions to Dilcher and Quaglioni (eds), *Inizi/Anfänge*.

Nonetheless, the idea that the law's validity was based on the sovereign's will could already be found in the *Corpus iuris*,[84] and it was apparently accepted as a matter of course by the early medieval jurists: the authority to make the law was seen as a prerogative of the sovereign Emperor or Prince: 'solus princeps possit facere leges'.[85] Indeed, this assumption was a central element within the basic distinction of *auctoritas* or *potestas* and *ratio* or *scientia*, a distinction on which the scholars founded their academic authority.[86] For a modern observer, the overall picture is thus remarkably perplexing. These jurists emphasized, in theory, that all law was based on domination, i.e. on the Prince's command, and such a conception was indeed plausible in the context of Canon law.[87] Yet, the jurists must have been aware of the fact that the idea of Roman law being authoritatively established by an Emperor was actually absurd under their political living conditions in 11th, 12th, and 13th century Bologna.[88] It is therefore instructive to question how these jurists and their successors explained the applicability of the Roman *Corpus iuris*.

Looking to the sources, though, it proves difficult to find an explicit answer to this question within the *Gloss* to the *Corpus iuris*, the most important and influential text of medieval secular law. In any case, no such answer was given in the context of the texts concerning the concept of law[89] and the sources of the law.[90] Indeed, there was apparently not even a doctrinal concept of a *ius commune*.[91] The Roman *Corpus iuris* had the status of a positive, universal law,[92] but such an idea was

[84] Ulpian D. 1,4,1 pr.; see above at 1. [85] *Gl. Ord.*, gl. *suo proprio ad* D. 1,1,9.

[86] For further argument on this point, see Jansen, 'Das gelehrte Recht', 166 ff.

[87] Landau, 'Quellen und Bedeutung', 229 f. Yet in Canon law, the authority to make the law was connected with the *potestas* to decide cases. There could be no distinction between the power of the legislator and the judge. Nevertheless, there was, as a matter of fact, a clear distinction between the political power of the legislator and the academic profession establishing the *Decretum Gratiani* and the authoritative learning which was related to this text.

[88] Calasso, 'diritto comune', 39.

[89] Inst. 1,1: *De iustitia et iure*; D. 1,1: *De iustitia et iure*.

[90] See Inst. 1,2: *De iure naturali et gentium et civili*, D. 1,3: *De legibus senatusque consultis et longa consuetudine*, D. 1,4: *De constitutionibus principum*, C. 1,14: *De legibus et constitutionibus principum et edictis*.

[91] Calasso, 'diritto comune', 62.

[92] *Gl. Ord.*, gl. *ius civile ad* Inst. 1,2,1: *ius civile* 'dicitur quoties adiicitur aliquid iuri naturali ... vel detrahitur iuri naturali. vel additur iuri gentium ... vel detrahitur'; similarly gl. *ius civile ad* D. 1,1,6. See also J. Schröder, *Recht als Wissenschaft*, 9 ff.; Berman, *Law and Revolution*, 145 ff.

difficult to explain on the basis of the Roman distinction of local *ius proprium* and universal unwritten *ius naturale* or *ius gentium*.[93] Similarly, it was difficult to decide whether the *Corpus iuris* was based on consensus, necessity, or custom.[94] Clearly, the Roman legal categories proved inadequate with regard to the highly complex, plural state of medieval law.[95] Medieval law was characterized by a concurrence of different, partly independent legal systems:[96] while the Church claimed universal jurisdiction for all *causae spirituales*, like family law (marriage being a sacrament), law of succession, and even contract law (because contracts were often confirmed by oaths), citizens were of course subject to local law as well. Besides, the legal position of noblemen was determined by feudal law, craftsmen were subject to the statutes of their guilds and cities, and merchants did business according to the rules of the *lex mercatoria*.[97]

At the same time, however, all those legal systems were closely interconnected and integrated by the idea of a *ius commune*.[98] The Lombard *libri feudorum*, the main source of feudal law, had early been integrated into the *Corpus iuris civilis*;[99] and while Canon law maxims became part of the Roman *ius commune*, Canon law included substantial elements of Roman law: *ecclesia vivit lege Romana*.[100] Similarly, the *lex mercatoria* was not an independent body of transnational commercial law, but rather consisted of many, mostly local, norms that modified Roman law in matters of commercial practice. Normally the decisions of the merchants' courts

[93] See Gaius D. 1,1,9, and *Gl. Ord.*, gl. *suo proprio ad* D. 1,1,9: 'hic loquitur de eo iure generale quod quasi ipsa natura inter omes tenet: & proprio quod non sit generale'.

[94] See Modestinus, D. 1,3,40: 'omne ius aut consensus fecit aut necessitas constituit aut firmavit consuetude', and *Gl. Ord.*, gl. *necessitas ad* D. 1,3,39 (40), arguing that Modestinus did not speak about Natural law, *necessitas* referring to the Emperors' legal acts, 'quas necessario scire debemus' (which we all have to know).

[95] Cf. Calasso, 'diritto comune', 50 f., 60 ff., 70 f.; Jansen, 'Das gelehrte Recht', 169 ff.

[96] See Berman, *Law and Revolution*, 10 f., 199–519; Grossi, *L'ordine giuridico*, 223 ff.; Jansen and Michaels, 'Private Law and the State', 359 ff., 366 ff.

[97] The concept and existence of a *lex mercatoria* is disputed. Cf. for a discussion Basile *et al.*, 'Introduction', 13, 20 ff., 123 ff.; further references in Jansen, 'Das gelehrte Recht', 107 f.

[98] Cf. Glenn, *Common Laws*, 19 ff.: 'relational common law'; Bellomo, *L'Europa de diritto comune / Common Legal Past*.

[99] Lange and Kriechbaum, *Römisches Recht im Mittelalter II*, 188 ff.

[100] Helmholz, *Classical Canon Law*, 17 ff.

were based on the *ius commune*, which was indeed regarded as the 'mater legis mercatoriae'.[101] These Roman rules were only modified in accordance with the needs of commerce on the basis, e.g., of the idea of an *aequitas mercatoria*.[102] Altogether, this was a complex system of rules, which were at the same time concurring and complementing each other. For instance, the relationship between Canon law and the secular *ius civile* was never without tensions.[103] It is evident that such a 'system' of laws is difficult to reconstruct into clear concepts. Ideas of founding the law's 'validity'—in Roman terms—in the Emperor's or Prince's or,—in modern terms—in a sovereign state's domination,[104] would not have been helpful for those jurists.

What is more, in contrast to what is generally assumed today,[105] the concept of law was not restricted to legal norms, but also included doctrinal knowledge.[106] Accordingly, the concept of law was highly complex and could assume different meaning in different context.[107] Thus, when medieval jurists explained the *lex* as 'the wise men's doctrine',[108] they clearly did not refer to a city's or a guild's statutes, but rather to the authoritative Roman texts. Whereas statutes were meant to protect the citizen's specific interests,[109] the *Corpus iuris*

[101] This is the wording of the first known treatise on the *lex mercatoria*: 'Lex mercatoria', *cap*. 9.

[102] Donahue, 'Equity'; id., 'Benvenuto Stracca's De Mercatura', 84 ff., 109 ff. This understanding continued until the 16th century, when the commercial courts were under the control of political rulers; cf. von Gail, *Practicae Observationes, lib*. II, *obs*. XXVII [27].

[103] Glenn, *Common Laws*, 109 ff., with further references.

[104] See above at 2 f.

[105] Cf. Kelsen, *Reine Rechtslehre*, 72 ff., 196 ff. / *Pure Theory*, 70 ff., 193 ff.; Hart, *Concept of Law*, 91 ff.; Alexy, *Begriff und Geltung*, *passim*; id., *Grundrechte*, 24; for a critical discussion Jansen, 'Dogmatik', 754 f.

[106] Azo, *Summa in ius civile*, Prooemium ad summam institutionum (before Inst. 1.1) for the *dogmata* in Justinian's *Institutes*; later Zasius, *Paratitla, ad* D. 1,3,7 (*legis virtus*): 'omnes iuris regulae ... dogmaticae ... sunt, docent, erudiunt, dant regulas'; later Falck, *Juristische Encyclopädie*, 4 (§ 1). In the 18th century, legislators were therefore expected to lay down a doctrinal frame for the law: Schlosser, *Gesetzgebung*, 161, 338 ff.; for general discussion J. Schröder, 'Rechtsdogmatik und Gesetzgebung', 41 ff.; for the medieval jurists Herberger, *Dogmatik*, 177 ff.

[107] Cf. Brynteson, 'Roman Law and Legislation'.

[108] *Gl. Ord*., gl. *Nam & ad* D. 1,3,2: 'lex est sapientium dogma, & doctrina per os sapientium promulgata'; cf. also *loc. cit*. gl. *regulam*: 'id est, compendiosa doctrina'.

[109] Zimmermann, 'Statuta sunt stricte interpretanda?', 317; for examples see Koch, *Statutengesetzgebung*, 68 ff., 76 f., 99 f.; Lütke Westhues, *Kommunalstatuten*, 265 ff.

could be seen as the foundation and expression of general legal knowledge. In this sense, it was the foundation of the overall system; its 'validity' was of a different nature to the validity of statutory legislation.

All this must be kept in mind when reading the Gloss's more implicit remarks on the status of the *Corpus iuris civilis* in legal argument. In general terms, *ius*, the law, derived from *iustitia*: justice;[110] more specifically, medieval jurists regarded the *Corpus iuris* as law 'per excellentiam'.[111] Only this text could be assumed to contain answers of divine justice[112] to every legal question.[113] Justinian—so the jurists thought—had chosen and preserved legal propositions of utmost justice.[114] The *Corpus iuris* provided for legal texts of outstanding quality and thus for an objective standard of law. The medieval jurists depended on such texts of authority for deciding social conflicts more rationally and peacefully; at the same time, those texts were the basis of their professional reputation and thus for their wealth and high social prestige.[115] It is not surprising to find that those lawyers regarded the *Corpus iuris* as an immeasurably valuable gift.[116] Knowledge of private law could be seen as true philosophy;[117] and the *Corpus iuris* was even regarded as a

[110] *Gl. Ord.*, gl. *iustitia ad* D. 1,1,1 pr.: 'est autem ius à iustitia, sicut à matre sua'; for a neo-platonic interpretation of this idea Brynteson, 'Roman Law and Legislation', 435 f.

[111] *Gl. Ord.*, gl. *nostrum ad* Inst. 1,2,2 de iure natur. etc.

[112] *Gl. Ord.*, gl. *vigorem ad* C. 10,1,5: 'Id est principem, qui est vigor iustitiae: unde dicitur lex animata . . .'; see also gl. *Nam & ad* D. 1,3,2: 'nutu divino faciunt principes leges'.

[113] *Gl. Ord.*, gl. *notitia ad* D. 1,1,10: 'nam omnia in corpore iuris inveniuntur'; similarly *ad* Inst. 1,1,1; see also gl. *prima elementa ad* Inst. *prooemium*: 'Quia sicut ex quatuor elementis omnia corpora conficiuntur, ut terra & aqua & igne & aere, id est, ex viribus horum quatuor elementorum totus mundus gubernatur: ita hic liber comprehendit omnia iura'.

[114] *Gl. Ord.*, gl. *enuncliati* to the *Digest's inscriptio*, before 1,1: 'aequissimae sententiae . . .: illas dulces sententias Iustinianus ex aliis excerpsit, & nobis tradidit legendas'.

[115] Above n. 33.

[116] *Gl. Ord.*, gl. *ius civile ad* Inst. 1,2,1: 'quidquid scriptum habemus de iure, dicitur ius civile . . . Est enim sanctissima res civilis sapientia, quae pretio nummario non est aestimanda'. See also gl. *ius nostrum ad* Inst. 1,2,3: 'id est civile Romanorum . . . Large vocatur ius civile quicquid scriptum habemus de iure generali'.

[117] *Gl. Ord.*, gl. *nisi fallor ad* D. 1,1,1: 'civilis sapientia vera philosophia est'; see also gl. *collecti* to the *Digest's inscriptio*, before 1,1: 'Cui parti philosophiae supponatur: & quidem Ethicae: quia de moribus tractat hoc volumen, sicut alia duo volumina'. As a consequence, it was no longer necessary to study theology before law: gl. *notitia ad* D. 1,1,10.

'holy' text.[118] Its practical value was as evident as its applicability beyond doubt.[119] Hence, the jurists of Bologna saw no reason for discussing the 'validity', i.e. the abstract applicability, of Roman law explicitly. The modern question of the law's validity would have been regarded as heretical; in any case, it did not really make sense. The only relevant questions were those which were addressed by the theory of statutes: namely how to determine the applicability of colliding and conflicting legal sources.[120]

If it was not necessary to discuss the validity of Roman law in abstract, the modern question as to the relation of private law and the state or political domination is ultimately anachronistic with regard to the medieval period. In any event, it would not have made much sense for medieval jurists. Of course, the reason for applying Roman law was not an Emperor's or Prince's command. The legal profession must have been aware of the fact that the *Corpus iuris* had not been promulgated by an Emperor of their time and that it was not backed in any sense by political authority. These jurists knew that they had themselves established the *Corpus iuris* as the textual basis of their learned law. Nevertheless, even Roman law—like all human law—could not be thought to be without some element of domination,[121] which was the basis for its acknowledgement, or recognition, by the law's addressees. Yet, this element of domination was more metaphysical in nature; it related to the person of the Roman *princeps* on the one hand and to the idea of a Holy Roman Empire on the other. Hence, such 'domination' must not be conceived of in modern, mundane terms; it had nothing to do with enforcement and political authority. Rather, it was the intellectual and moral basis of all such secular authority. It was the ultimate foundation of the medieval political, social, and institutional order.[122]

Regarding the application of Roman law in daily legal business, another, more practical factor added to the authority of Roman law, namely the fact that there were simply no satisfactory alternatives to

[118] *Gl. Ord.*, gl. *religiosissimus ad* Inst. *Prooemium*: 'nam ipsae (leges, N.J.) sunt sacrae'.

[119] *Gl. Ord.*, gl. *collecti* to the *Digest's inscriptio* before 1,1.

[120] On this theory see Zimmermann, 'Statuta sunt stricte interpretanda?' and the references below n. 126, all with further references.

[121] *Gl. Ord.*, gl. *Nam & ad* D. 1,3,2: 'nutu divino faciunt principes leges'.

[122] See Stollberg-Rilinger, 'Würde des Gerichts', 194 f. with further references.

the Roman texts.[123] Initially, other laws, such as the *leges Langobardorum*, had also been taught and explained with learned glosses.[124] But such laws were neither perceived as comprehensive nor could they claim an intellectual authority comparable to that of the *Corpus iuris*, which therefore dominated the legal discourse. Here, the authority of Roman law related more to legal knowledge and to the doctrinal categories that are necessary for understanding and formulating matters of law.[125] It followed as a matter of course that statutory law and the more specific commands of local Princes could be applicable alongside and in precedence to Roman law.[126] Their validity was a matter of genuine political domination. Yet, even this differentiation of different types of 'validity' probably amounts to an anachronistic application of later categories. The medieval jurists did not conceptually distinguish doctrine from individual rules; they therefore applied Roman law as a matter of course, where they did not find a local law of primary applicability. Hence, the actual legal practice in a town was typically based on a mix of Roman, local, and Canon law sources. The law's language, in any event, was Latin, and the concepts were taken from the *ius commune*.[127]

(b) The Lothar legend

Later generations, though, could not as easily accept this medieval concept of law. For them, the use of the law as a means of political domination was an increasingly common experience; in this respect, the Catholic Church had become an intellectual and institutional model for the later nation states.[128] As a result, the idea of changing,

[123] Cf. also Wieacker, *Privatrechtsgeschichte*, 70; Engelmann, *Wiedergeburt*, 20 ff.

[124] See de Tocco, *Leges Langobardorum cum argutissimis glosis* (originally 1225).

[125] Cf. also Bellomo, *L'Europa del diritto comune*, 95 f., 166 ff. / *Common Legal Past*, 82 f., 152 ff.; Coing, 'Europäische Privatrechtsgeschichte', 7 ff., 11.

[126] Lange and Kriechbaum, *Römisches Recht im Mittelalter II*, 225 ff., 235 ff.; Coing, *Europäisches Privatrecht I*, 12 f.; Bellomo, *L'Europa del diritto comune*, 91 ff., 96 ff. / *Common Legal Past*, 78 ff., 83 ff.

[127] For a picture of the legal practice in Marseille from the 13th to the 15th centuries, see D. Lord Smail, 'Notaries, Courts, and the Legal Culture', 36 ff.; cf. also Nicolini, 'Autonomia e diritto proprio'.

[128] Berman, *Law and Revolution*, 85 ff., 113 ff.; Reinhard, *Staatsgewalt*, 28, 186 f., 259 ff., 285 f.; Dreier, 'Kanonistik und Konfessionalisierung', 4 ff.; Becker, 'Entstehung der Papstkirche'.

instead of restating, the law by means of legislation evolved.[129] Pope Boniface VIII, for instance, expressly announced his *Liber Sextus* as 'new law'. These ideas were soon used by the Italian and German cities and by the early monarchies in Sicily and England.[130] Accordingly, Thomas Aquinas was defining the law as an *ordinatio*,[131] as a legislative command, while for Baldus statutory law was based on the sovereign's *sic volo sic iubeo*.[132] The idea of later law derogating earlier provisions (*lex posterior derogat legi priori*), which had only been of rather limited applicability in Roman law,[133] and the Canon law prohibition on retroactive law are consequences of this understanding.

Thus, it became standard to rest the law's validity constitutionally on a political legislative command. Since the end of the 15th century, all secular law and thus also Roman law[134] had to be explained on this basis.[135] Now, as such an explanation was difficult to find for the *Corpus iuris*, the idea of imperial legislation was again relied on. It began to be said that the use of the *Digest* had been prescribed by Emperor Lothar III of Supplinburg in 1137.[136] Of course, this story was as wrong, as a matter of historical fact, as the legend of Charlemagne's privilege in the context of the Saxon Mirror.[137] It was a fairy tale invented *ex post* that served to legitimize the increasingly problematic applicability of Roman law. Like the

[129] See, besides the work of Harold Berman, Brynteson, 'Roman Law and Legislation', 421 ff.; Quaritsch, *Staat und Souveränität I*, 132 ff.; Landau, 'Europäische Rechtskultur', 45 ff.; Dreier, 'Kanonistik und Konfessionalisierung', 1, 5; Becker, 'Entstehung der Papstkirche', 277f.

[130] See Keller, 'Veränderung gesellschaftlichen Handelns', 29 ff.; Dilcher, 'Oralität, Verschriftlichung und Wandlungen der Normstruktur', 16 ff.; id., 'Verrechtlichung der Lebensbeziehungen', 95 ff.; Stolleis, 'Condere leges et interpretari', 169 ff.

[131] Aquinas, *Summa theologica II-I, qu.* 90, *art.* 1 and 4: '[Lex] nihil est aliud quam quaedam rationis ordinatio ad bonum commune, ab eo qui curam communitatis habet, promulgate'; see also *qu.* 91, *art.* 1; *qu.* 95, *art.* 2; *qu.* 96, *art.* 4; *qu.* 97, *art.* 1; *qu.* 104, *art.* 1.

[132] '[S]tatuta terrarum ... maiori parte magis consistunt [in] sic volo sic iubeo' (Thus I want, thus I command): Baldus, *Super usibus feudalibus*, cit. after H. Coing, 'Zur Romanistischen Auslegung von Rezeptionsgesetzen', 269.

[133] Modestinus D. 1,5,4. Apparently, the maxim was limited to Imperial constitutions. In the context of civil law (*ius civile*), the derogatory effect of the *lex Aquilia* was not taken to be implied in that statute, but rather expressly stated by the legislator: Ulpian D. 9,2,1 pr.

[134] Krause, 'Kaiserrecht und Rezeption', 126 ff.

[135] Cf. Brunnemann, *Commentarius in Pandectas, ad* 1,1,9 [1].

[136] Cf. Wieacker, *Privatrechtsgeschichte*, 145; Luig, 'Conring', 355, 357 f., 372 f.; Oestmann, 'Lotharische Legende'.

[137] See above at 26.

earlier legend, it came up at a time when the desired applicability of the legal text was believed to be in need of further support.

More remarkably, however, this story seems having been irrelevant for legal argument. We do not usually[138] find it in the major commentaries on Roman law in the 16th and 17th century;[139] instead, the authors telling this story were historical or political writers, like Melanchthon.[140] The leading legal authors of this time apparently did not question the applicability of Roman law. On the contrary, they generally ignored local law[141] and explained the applicability of Roman law on a more pragmatic basis. Matthäus Wesenbeck (1531–1586), for instance, argued that the concept of *ius* (law) derived from *iussum* (command), but that the concept assumed a different meaning when referring to Roman law. In this context, it derived from *iustitia* being its 'ars & doctrina': a learned system of justice to be applied in legal practice.[142] Thus, for Wesenbeck, the *Corpus iuris* expressed eternal principles of justice for private and public law.[143] Other authors, like Brunnemann (1608–1672), didn't even address this question. Clearly, the applicability of Roman law was evident for such authors.[144] And Arnoldus Vinnius (1588–1657), the author of the leading text book on the *Institutes*, simply equated Roman law with the *ius gentium*: 'Hodie jus civile Romanorum quasi gentium quoddam jus commune apud totam fere Europam observatur'.[145]

[138] But see Thieme, 'Statutarrecht und Rezeption', 79 f. Thieme found one reference to this legend in an opinion of 1575, however, not in the context of private law, and only as one of many points of the opponent's argument.

[139] Similarly Luig, 'Conring', 372. Cf., e.g., Wesenbeck, *Paratitla, ad* D. 1,1 [14] ff.; Vinnius, *Commentarius, ad* Inst. 1,2; Huber, *Heedendaegse Rechtsgeleertheyt*, book I, ch. 2.

[140] von Moeller, *Hermann Conring*, 67 ff.

[141] von Stintzing and Landsberg, *Geschichte I, passim*; vol. II, 1; more recently Luig, 'Conring', 370 f.; Coing, 'Die Juristische Fakultät und ihr Lehrprogramm', 30 ff., 49.

[142] Wesenbeck, *Paratitla, ad* D. 1,1 [14]: 'Sed doctrina juris, seu jurisprudentia Romana, à justitia dicitur'. In substance, this argument goes back to the *Glossa ordinaria*: above n. 110.

[143] Wesenbeck, *Paratitla, ad* D. 1,1 [14]: 'ac theses justitiae aequitatisque universales, ad hypotheses civilis vitae, publicas & privatas, rectâ interpretatione accommodat & interflectit'.

[144] Brunnemann, *Commentarius in Pandectas, ad* D. 1,1,1 and 1,1,9; see also id., *Commentarius in Codicem, lib.* I, *tit.* XIV.

[145] Vinnius, *Commentarius, ad* Inst. 1,2,2 [1]: '... utique in quibus causis propriae leges aut consuetudines deficient'. Similarly, some 50 years later, Lauterbach: *Collegium Theoretico-Practicum*, Prolegomena De Praestantia, Autoritate et Libris Juris, § II [5]:

All this shows clearly that the ultimate reason for applying Roman law consisted in the fact that the legal profession treated the *Corpus iuris civilis* as the basic reference text of learned law.[146] Roman law had become a reservoir of legal rules and principles that were easily accessible (at least for lawyers) and that could be seen as universally valid. At the same time the learned *ius commune* had achieved a high degree of autonomy against the political process. The jurists had created the rules of the Roman-Canon civil procedure; despite the existence of written and unwritten particular laws (*ius proprium*), they had ensured a wide field of applicability for the learned *ius commune* in the actual practice before the courts;[147] last but not least, they had modernized and adapted the ancient texts to the needs of their time.[148] On the basis of Justinian's *Corpus iuris*, they had over the centuries created a library of self-referential, authoritative texts such as Accursius' Standard Gloss and the commentaries by Bartolus and Baldus.[149] Altogether, this practice stabilized itself; from the jurists' perspective, there was no need for an ultimate justification like the Lothar legend: professional jurists did not ask for a reason to apply Roman law. And it was not jurists, but rather political writers who refuted this legend in the 17th century. A leading actor in these debates was Hermann Conring. Conring, who had studied medicine and politics, was an internationally well connected and politically engaged writer. Although he had legal interests, he was never professionally active as a doctrinal lawyer. Apparently, he did not care very much for the substantial questions of private law; rather, he fought against the inaccessible and incomprehensible learned science of the *ius commune* and for new laws that should be written in German. Thus, he was ultimately

'Merito ergo suo tantae hodienum [sic!] est autoritatis, ut, quasi Gentium Jus Commune, per totam fere Europam observetur'.

146 Cf. Vinnius, *Commentarius, ad* Inst. 1,2,2 [2]: 'Non quod legis sanciendae causa gentes omnes in unum convenerint: sed quia illud jus propter communem utilitatem tacito consensu gentium approbatum & ab omnes receptum est'.

147 Jansen, '*Ius Commune*', at 3. Details are disputed, and there are significant differences over time and between different courts. For a thorough and detailed analysis of both the normative foundations and the actual practice regarding the application of conflicting legal sources in different German jurisdictions, see Oestmann, *Rechtsvielfalt*, 436 ff., 476 ff., 603 ff. Roman law was long regarded as the most important source of law in that the *Corpus iuris civilis* was the starting point of all legal argument.

148 For the Roman-Dutch law, see Zimmermann, 'Römisch-holländisches Recht', 49 ff.

149 Bellomo, *L'Europa del diritto comune*, 186 f. / *Common Legal Past*, 172 ff.

driven by the idea of truly sovereign domination and by the ideal of a German nation.[150]

Such observations show clearly that the debates concerning the Lothar legend and its refutation must be seen as part of the political discourse; they can only be understood in this context.[151] The Lothar Legend was a political myth, not an answer to a legal problem. Political domination was irrelevant for the *ius commune*: this is true both from the external perspective of historical description—there was never any such domination—and from the internal perspective of legal argument: professional lawyers never relied on such arguments in legal discourse.

(c) *A pattern of wisdom and legality*

Until the 17th century, lawyers had seen no need to explain or justify the applicability of Roman law: they simply applied it, because it was the positive basis of the *ius commune*. Thus, Roman law was generally acknowledged and applied before the courts, if there were no other texts of prior applicability.[152] From the autonomous perspective of the older *ius commune*, the question as to the basis of the Roman law's validity needed no answer; it would be anachronistic to construct any such theory. Political domination, to be sure, was irrelevant.

However, the question did become more urgent in the course of the 17th century, when the learned authors began to pay more attention to the actual practice of the courts. These courts were confronted with so many different legal sources, that they could not simply apply the *Corpus iuris civilis* without further argument.[153] Thus, scholars realized that they could no longer treat the idea of a reception of Roman law as a whole as an evident truism, and that they had to include the positive local law into their doctrinal analysis.[154] According to Schilter, a leading scholar of his generation,

[150] See Conring, *De origine, cap.* XXXV; cf. Stintzing and Landsberg, *Geschichte II*, 172 ff.; Luig, 'Conring', 359 ff., 372 f., 378 ff.

[151] On historiography as a means of constructing an individual or collective identity, see e.g. Angehrn, *Interpretation und Dekonstruktion*, 51 ff., 87 ff., 182 and *passim*; Howell and Prevenier, *Werkstatt des Historikers*, 5 ff.

[152] For references, see above n. 126.

[153] Oestmann, *Rechtsvielfalt*.

[154] See e.g. van Groenewegen, *Tractatus de legibus abrogatis*.

what was required in an actual case was not to prove local law, but conversely to explain the reception of the Roman rule.[155] This changing attitude may be seen, at least in part, as a reaction to the changing political climate and in this sense as an answer of the legal system to the arguments made by writers like Conring. As a result, the formerly largely uniform *ius commune* began to develop into local variations of a more abstract *ius commune*: there was no single *ius commune* anymore, but rather a Roman-Dutch law, a *ius romano-germanicum*, a *ius romano-hispanicum*, a *ius romano-neapolitanum*, a Danish *ius sveco-Romanum*, etc.[156]

In view of this insecure state of the law, Samuel Stryk, the leading German scholar of the time, felt obliged to introduce his *Usus Modernus Pandectarum* (1690) with an extensive treatise on the authority of Roman law and its applicability in German legal practice.[157] However, at this stage a plausible and definitive argument for its applicability could no longer be found. It was now axiomatic that the validity of all law was based on a respective command of the sovereign. In theory, even the validity of customary law depended on approval by the Prince; during the 18th century, the sovereign's political will even became its only legal basis.[158] Yet it was evident that this requirement of a sovereign's command could not be met for the *ius commune*, which had largely preserved its autonomy against political domination. It followed that it was impossible to justify the 'validity' of the *Corpus iuris civilis* on the basis of the prevailing concept of law. In terms of the constitutional doctrine of the 18th century, there was no basis at all to apply Roman law. True, scholars attempted to justify the authority of the

[155] Schilter, *Praxis Juris Romani, exerc.* I, § XII: '... videtur, ut nec Iustiniani promulgatio, ad nos nihil attinens, nos obliget, nec ius illud sub autoritate necessaria, sed probabili tantum ... receptum valet, neque nisi ab observantia, usuque approbantium autoritatem vimque obtineat'.

[156] Coing, 'Europäische Privatrechtsgeschichte', 20; more recently see especially Glenn, *Common Laws*, 22 ff., 105 ff. and *passim*; Glenn, however, assumes that the concurrence of diverse *common laws* was always a characteristic of European law.

[157] Stryk, 'Discursus Praeliminaris de Usu et Auctoritate Juris Romani'; similarly Lauterbach, *Collegium Theoretico-Practicum*, Prolegomena, especially § II De Corpore Juris Civilis.

[158] Garré, *Consuetudo*, 151 ff., 159 f.; Brie, 'Gewohnheitsrecht', 148; Oestmann, *Rechtsvielfalt*, 367 f.

Corpus iuris on the strength of a number of arguments. One such argument was indeed based on domination (*imperium*). It was said that the Emperors or Princes had tacitly approved of the courts' practice. Other arguments related to the tradition and to the practice of the courts (*usus*) or to the extraordinary qualities of Roman law (*ratio* and *certitudo*). Stryk, for instance, explained the applicability of Roman law primarily by its reception in legal science, and secondarily with the tacit approval of this process by the German governments. Yet such arguments were not perceived as convincing anymore. Either they were based on fictions, or they found no basis in the actual constitutional doctrine.[159]

Yet, although leading authors were perfectly aware of this state of the law, they continued to argue on the basis of Justinian's texts.[160] Indeed, even those authors, like Georg Adam Struve, who presented the law as it was applied before the courts, instead of pure Roman theory,[161] did so on the basis of the Roman sources.[162] And even authors, like Mevius, whose focus was not on Roman law anymore, but rather on a local legislation (in the case of Mevius, the statutes of the city of Lübeck), consistently referred to the *Corpus iuris civilis* and to the authorities of the *ius commune*.[163] Individual rules might diverge from Roman law, but the intellectual order of the law, its terminology and doctrinal basis, continued to be based on the Roman sources. For Ulrich Huber there was no doubt that Roman law did not bind the judge and that it had nowhere been received as a whole, instead being accepted only with suitable modifications. Nonetheless, Huber argued Roman law had been received as a 'pattern of wisdom and legality' and as an authoritative reference text among all Christian nations.[164] Accordingly, the Roman *ius*

[159] This is shown in more detail by Luig, 'Geltungsgrund', 819 ff., with further references.

[160] Cf. Thibaut, *System*, vol. I, 11 (§ 13): 'Daß der Grund der recipirten Rechte jetzt wegfalle, oder unsre Lage zweckmäßgere Gesetze erheische, steht *juristisch* der Anwendung derselben nicht entgegen'.

[161] Struve, *Jurisprudentia romano-germanica forensis* (1670); Schilter, *Institutiones iuris ex principiis iuris naturae, gentium & civilis, tum Romani, tum Germanici* (1685); id., *Praxis Juris Romani* (first in 1672, under the title *Exercitationes ad L libros Pandectarum*); Stryk, *Usus modernus*.

[162] See Luig, 'Institutionenlehrbücher', 67 f.

[163] Mevius, *Commentarii in Jus Lubecense, passim*.

[164] Huber, *Heedendaegse Rechtsgeleertheyt*, book I, ch. 2, § 24: 'But because the laws of the State of Rome spread with her ancient empire through the whole of Europe, and

commune continued to provide an overarching intellectual body of legal knowledge, which connected the different and even disparate legal systems of Europe.[165] Again, the anachronistic question, whether the *ius commune* was valid law, and on which rule of recognition or constitutional basis it relied, makes little sense.

4. The idea of textual authorities

After all, European private law has long been developed on the basis of texts that were largely independent of political domination. The *Decretum Gratiani* as well as the Saxon Mirror were written by actors outside the political, governmental sphere of sovereigns, and the authority of the Roman *Corpus iuris civilis* resulted from its recognition by the legal profession. Given these historical findings, it is astonishing to see that the idea of the law and its validity being based on a nation state is taken to be implied within the *concept* of law (rather than in a normative conception of the law) by most jurists today.[166] Of course, there may be good normative reasons to base the law on the authority of the modern state. Yet, it is nevertheless unwise to include this normative connection in the concepts of law and validity. Clearly, these concepts which were not coined before the 19th and 20th centuries[167] are not necessarily adequate for private law developing autonomously from political domination.

Hence, the idea of textual authority may be more adequate for designing a general concept of law. Here, the concept of authority

because they surpass all other known systems of law in sagacity and justice, Roman law kept its force among almost all Christian peoples, so much so that it has been adopted by many of them; not, however, without every free nation taking away or adding what seemed to it good. Among some nations also it has no binding power, but rather serves as a pattern of wisdom and legality, without the judges being actually bound by it'. Similarly Lauterbach, *Collegium Theoretico-Practicum*, Prolegomena, § II [5]: '... reliquae Gentes, quae Jure hoc Romano ex professo non utuntur, ejus nihilominus majestatem communiter tanti faciant, ut illarum LL. rationi & aequitati, licet non autoritati & sanctioni, plurimum tribuant, suasque leges proprias ex illis emendent, acerbas mitigent, obscuras declarent, & deficientes suppleant'.

165 Cf. Zimmermann, 'Das römisch-kanonische ius commune', 10 f.; id., 'Europa und das römische Recht', 252: 'Vielfalt, im Rahmen allerdings einer übergreifenden intellektuellen Einheit'.

166 See above at 2.

167 See Luhmann, 'Geltung des Rechts'.

denotes the abstract, content-independent force of basic legal arguments in legal discourse, i.e. the formal status of textual sources of the law, such as legislation, judicial decisions, or textbooks and commentaries. Normative statements may be understood as arguments that must be taken in consideration,[168] or they can be taken as binding commands. Norms may be given preponderance over other norms on the one hand, or they may be applicable only subsidiarily on the other. And if norms are applicable only subsidiarily, the legal profession may still interpret the norms of primary application narrowly in order to be able to apply the 'better', subsidiary norm; or it may, for instance, interpret special statutes of a political legislator in view of a superior common law, *ius commune*, or global 'background law'.[169]

When jurists make such arguments, they rarely discuss the abstract constitutionality or validity of a norm. Of course, the constitutionality of a provision may often become an important legal matter. Unconstitutional provisions are normally of no legal authority at all. Yet, the question as to the constitutionality of a provision is usually restricted to legislation. Lawyers relying on non-legislative texts therefore normally refrain from questioning the constitutionality of their practice.[170] Rather, they ask whether a norm is applicable in the specific case, or whether another norm is to be given priority. All this could be observed in legal practice

[168] If the law consisted only of normative statements of this sort, it might be described as a law without authorities; see for such a view of the common law Postema, 'Philosophy of the Common Law', 616 ff.; cf. also id., '*A Similibus ad Similia*', 103 ff., 124 ff. However, in actual practice, there *are* authorities also in common law, especially precedents, the American Restatements, and English books of authority, such as *Blackstone, Pollock, Dicey*, or *Chitty*. Even if modern common law is convincingly described as a conventional and institutionalized deliberative practice, this practice is based on textual authorities (whose authority, in turn, is determined by this conventional practice). For a much more complete picture of common-law reasoning, see Eisenberg, 'Legal Reasoning in Common Law'; cf. also Alexander and Sherwin, 'Judges as Rule Makers'.

[169] Cf. *PICC-Commentary*/Michaels, Preamble I [70]; Michaels, 'Umdenken für die UNIDROIT-Prinzipien', comparing the PICC with the American restatements; cf. also *PICC-Commentary*/Scherer, Preamble II [38]: 'backup provisions'; Metzger, *Extra legem, intra ius*, 265 ff.; Smits, 'PECL and the Harmonisation of Private Law in Europe', 580: 'echo of universalism'.

[170] See 29 f., 32 f., 36 above and for an explicit example n. 160. For non-legislative codifications in modern law, see below at 50 ff.

during the *ius commune*, when lawyers had to reconcile and apply a vast mass of colliding and mutually complementing texts;[171] and it can be observed in modern common law, which is clearly no longer an oral tradition.[172] Here, the authorities are primarily the judicial precedents, which are rarely in full consonance, though, and which have been complemented with academic texts of uncertain authority, such as *Blackstone*, *Pollock*, *Dicey*, or *Chitty*, and, in the American context, with the Restatements of the law. All these texts influence the interpretation and application of the political legislator's statutes and constitutional texts such as the Bill of Rights. Interestingly, similar arguments increasingly appear also in the contexts of European private law and of global commercial law.[173]

In the present book, all this shall be comprehensively captured with the concept of a legal text's authority: the abstract authority of a text giving expression to a legal norm consists in the legal profession accepting it as an ultimate source of the law, without requiring further legal reasons to do so. Of course, there may be political, prudential, moral, or other reasons for recognizing such a text as legal authority.[174] But such reasons are not part of the legal system. Their place is rather 'before', or 'outside', the law.[175] Hence, they are usually not part of the legal discourse.

More specifically, the relative authority of a legal text consists in its formal weight in legal argument, where different legal authorities are present and may be in conflict with each other. In such a case, decisions must be made, usually independently of the content of the individual norms in question, as to which of those texts should be

[171] Oestmann, *Rechtsvielfalt*, *passim*; Zimmermann, 'Statuta sunt stricte interpretanda?' See also the references in n. 126 above on the theory of statutes.

[172] But see Simpson, 'Common Law and Legal Theory', 97. This was probably a correct description of the common law until the 16th century. Yet, already in the 18th and 19th centuries, such a theory was no longer plausible for modern English common law (Ibbetson, 'Case-Law and Doctrine', 33 ff.), and it probably sounds absurd for contemporary American common lawyers. True, English common law 'lacks an authoritative authentic text' (Simpson, *loc. cit.*, 88, referring to Pollock). But the present plurality of authoritative texts is different from a truly oral system.

[173] Cf. Wendehorst, 'Private Law Reasoning', 176 ff.; *PICC-Commentary*/Michaels, Preamble I [71] ff., [82] ff., and especially [88] ff., [109] f., [111] ff.; *PICC-Commentary*/Scherer, Preamble II [37] ff., [43] ff., [65] f. and *passim*.

[174] For such reasons, or rather motives, for the recognition of legal texts, see below at 96–136.

[175] See Hart, *Concept of Law*, 107 f.

taken as the ultimate foundation of legal argument.[176] These decisions depend on, and are an expression of, the texts' authority. Indeed, it would be wrong to assume that the legal authority would be a kind of mysterious quality of a text. Rather, authority is assigned to legal texts by those working with them, i.e. by professional lawyers applying and interpreting such texts in the course of legal argument.[177]

Historical evidence has made apparent that it would be unwise to expect the authority of such legal texts to be stable over time. What is more, lawyers cannot always rely on a clear hierarchy between different authorities. As a consequence, the concept of law has often been highly complex and usually in flux. Rather than presupposing a unifying and for this purpose hierarchically structured rule of recognition, lawyers have often found themselves arguing on the basis of legal systems that were characterized by plural, fragmented, and conflicting legal authorities and by organically changing rules of recognition. Indeed, the jurists introducing the new texts of the *Corpus iuris civilis*, the *Decretum Gratiani*, and the Saxon Mirror

[176] See Duve, 'Mit der Autorität gegen die Autoritäten?', 242 ff.: 'relativer Autoritätsbegriff'.

[177] Clearly, such a concept of the law bears similarities with and builds on Hart's *Concept of Law*. What is rejected, though, is first a jurisprudential approach that reduces the law to a system of rules, and secondly the idea of a unifying and hence hierarchically structured rule of recognition (*loc. cit.*, 95, 105 f.). What is more, Hart would probably have rejected the notion of organically changing, not fully consistent rules and processes of recognition; cf., regarding public international law, *loc. cit.*, 233 ff. Thirdly, it may not always be satisfactory to explain legal change on the basis of secondary rules and an unchanging rule of recognition only, and to interpret a change with respect to a legal system's rules of recognition as a revolution (*loc. cit.*, 92 f., 95 f., 116, 118 ff.). Indeed, it would be misleading to conceive of the processes described above at 14 ff. as revolutions, and yet there can be no doubt that these processes entailed changes also with regard to the rules of recognition. From a legal historian's perspective, there are no good reasons to assume a legal system's *empirical* rules of recognition to be immutable over time. At least in the context of constitutional legislation and constitutional change (*loc. cit.*, 149 ff.) and with regard to the first coming into existence of a secondary rule of recognition (*loc. cit.*, 236 f.), this has also been acknowledged by Hart. Thus, in comparison with Hart's formal conventionalism, the concept of law suggested in this book, is based on a more material conventionalism; for such a contrast, see Postema, 'Philosophy of the Common Law', 600 ff., 616. However, what is 'conventional' in such a concept of law is not the deliberative legal practice as such, as Postema argues, but rather the changing authorities of its plural textual foundations. Thus, the concept is more material than Hart's concept, but certainly less material than the deliberative conception of the common law as proposed by authors like Postema.

into medieval law as new legal authorities were even acting—at least implicitly—as proponents of a fundamental legal change which did not only affect the substance of medieval law, but also its rules of recognition.

III. Legislative Codifications and the Legal Profession

It might be argued, though, that all this is merely history, and that the examples are chosen, moreover, from times when no states existed which monopolized the power and the competence to make the law. After all, there are sovereign legislators today which can and do determine the statutes and codifications which must be applied by the courts and therefore exclude non-legislative sources of the law. Again, however, it is doubtful whether such an argument is based on a full understanding of the legal process. Indeed, a closer view reveals that even in more recent times, it was often the legal profession, rather than the political legislator, which ultimately determined the sources of the law and their authority in legal discourse.

An illuminating example of such a development can be found in the early history of the law of the American state of Louisiana after the enactment of the *Code-Napoleon* inspired Louisiana Civil code of 1808. This code was introduced, rather quickly, as a means of defending the civilian Franco-Spanish tradition against the imminent common law.[178] Yet the jurists of Louisiana, both at the bar and on the bench, apparently never accepted this legislation as the ultimate and exclusive source of the law. Rather they regarded it as a kind of restatement of earlier law, and they felt free to continue applying the former sources of the Spanish *ius commune* and other legal sources instead of, or besides, the Civil code.[179] Indeed, lawyers used to work on the basis of self-produced digests of civil law that annotated a reprint of the Civil code with manuscript references to its Roman sources and other civil laws on the same

[178] See Palmer, 'Two Worlds in One', 27 ff.

[179] Kilbourne, Jr., *History of the Louisiana Civil Code*, 62 ff.; Cairns, 'de la Vergne Volume', at V., both with further references; cf. also Fernandez, *From Chaos to Continuity*, 33 f.

subject.[180] Thus, the early codification's authority had been weakened by the classical textual authorities. In 1824/25, this practice even resulted in a legislative reform of the 1808 Civil code, which adapted the codification to the law being applied.[181]

In a similar way, 19th-century Prussian judges continued to decide cases on the basis of Justinian's *Corpus iuris civilis*, although they could (and from a constitutional perspective should) have rather relied on the Prussian Civil code (*Allgemeines Landrecht*, ALR).[182] Even the strength of the Prussian state apparently could not make them change their practices. Indeed, during much of the 19th century, private law was again understood as being largely autonomous against the states' political sphere.[183] Thus, the ALR never achieved a legal status comparable to that of the later German Civil code of the German *Reich* (*Bürgerliches Gesetzbuch*, BGB).[184] Instead of becoming a core subject within the academic *curriculum*, the different German territorial codes were relegated to the practical, non-academic part of legal education;[185] and they received little attention in the legal literature.[186] Judges and academic scholars interpreted the ALR's provisions from the perspective of the Roman *ius commune*; and they never treated it as the comprehensive and exclusive basis of the law, but only as one source among many others.[187]

It was not until the enactment of the BGB that German private lawyers—both in academia and in the judiciary—shifted their perspective on private law from the Roman sources to the new state's

[180] See Moreau Lislet, *Digest*; on these, most recently, Cairns, 'de la Vergne Volume', with further references on other comparable volumes and on the discussion relating to these works.

[181] Kilbourne, *History of the Louisiana Civil Code*, 108 ff., 124 ff.; cf. also Fernandez, *From Chaos to Continuity*, 76 ff., interpreting this development as a battle in the fight against the common law.

[182] Eckert, 'Gesetzesbegriff und Normanwendung', 585 ff.; Kiefer, *Aquilische Haftung*, 191 ff., 225 ff., both with further references on the judicial practice.

[183] See Haferkamp, 'The Science of Private Law', 247 ff., 251, 253 ff.

[184] See Eckert, 'Gesetzesbegriff und Normanwendung', 590: es 'fragt sich ernsthaft, ob die große Kodifikation überhaupt jemals das Ziel der Kodifikatoren erreichte, in der Praxis originär angewendet zu werden'.

[185] For the University of Heidelberg, see Haferkamp, 'von Vangerow', 824 f.

[186] Friedberg, *Eisenacher Konferenz*, 7 ff.

[187] For Prussian judiciary, see the references above n. 182; for academic teaching, see von Savigny, *Landrechtsvorlesung 1824 I*, 6 f.

legislation. And it was only this remarkable shift in perspective that made the BGB the sole basis of positive German law. This is apparent from the extraordinary amount of exegetic literature on the BGB already in existence before 1900.[188] This body of work cannot simply be explained with a Parliament's legislative act: such legislation had also existed in the previous German states. Rather, it ultimately resulted from the decision of the German academic profession at a conference in Eisenach in 1896, to replace the *Corpus iuris* with the BGB as the normative basis of academic teaching and doctrinal research.[189] Of course, this decision may in turn be understood as resulting from a shift in perspective of German lawyers and judges to the new state's political will and legislation.[190] Yet, again, this development can only be understood from within the legal system, as the result of legal discourse; it would be misleading to interpret it as an act of the state taking control of private law.

An even more recent example is the constitutionalization of European private law during the second half of the 20th century. Again, this development cannot adequately be interpreted as the transformation of political decisions into the system of private law. Indeed, the constitutionalization of private law had not been mandated by written constitutions like the German *Grundgesetz*. On the contrary, such a development had not even been thought of by the legislator. Originally, it had been axiomatic, in accordance with the prevailing view of the Constitution of Weimar,[191] that fundamental constitutional rights protected the citizens (only) against the state;[192] what was new in 1949 was only the decision to make the constitutional rights binding also on

[188] See *HKK*/Zimmermann, vor § 1. 'Das Bürgerliche Gesetzbuch ...' [14] with further references. In 1899, a bibliography contained about 4,000 titles of this kind; this was probably more than the total literature ever published on the ALR. Even more remarkably, whereas the literature on the ALR had normally contained references to the *Gemeines Recht*, this was less the case for the new literature: the BGB was, from early on, understood as an autonomous source of the law.

[189] Those decisions at the conference of Eisenach can be found in Friedberg, *Eisenacher Konferenz*, 5 ff., 16 ff.; cf. also *HKK*/Zimmermann, vor § 1. 'Das Bürgerliche Gesetzbuch ...' [15].

[190] See Haferkamp, 'Science', 258 ff., who observes such a shift in perspective after the turn of 1871.

[191] Cf. Anschütz, *Verfassung des Deutschen Reiches*, Art. 117 [1]; 118 [556].

[192] von Mangoldt, 'Schriftlicher Bericht', 5: 'In den Grundrechten sollte also das Verhältnis des Einzelnen zum Staate geregelt werden, damit der Mensch in seiner Würde wieder anerkannt werde'.

the German Parliament.[193] In the new German constitution's first article it was therefore laid down that these rights 'are binding upon the legislator, the administration and the judiciary as immediately applicable law' (Art. 1 III GG). It followed that they were not binding, normally, between fellow citizens.[194] Thus, in the first edition of the first large commentary on the *Grundgesetz*, Hermann von Mangoldt, a leading professor of constitutional law and a politician, who had taken a leading part in the formulation of the *Grundgesetz*, did not even discuss the problem of an indirect effect of fundamental rights; instead he emphasized that the intention of Art. 1 III GG was to clarify that constitutional rights were binding also on the legislator.[195] The problem of an (indirect) effect of constitutional rights between private citizens can only be found in later editions by Friedrich von Klein responding to the discussions after 1948.[196] Thus, the modern doctrine of the 'indirect horizontal effect' of constitutional rights and thus the constitutionalization of private law grew from the conviction of academic lawyers, such as Hans Carl Nipperdey[197] and Günter Dürig,[198] and of the courts[199] that these rights expressed values which, under the social and economic conditions of the 20th century, should also become relevant within the private-law relations of citizens.[200] Authors and courts therefore presented the indirect horizontal effect of constitutional rights rightly as a 'new doctrine' that expressed a change of meaning and function of the constitutional rights'.[201]

[193] Cf. von Mangoldt, 'Schriftlicher Bericht', 7.

[194] There are only few exceptions, where the opposite has explicitly been laid down; cf. Arts. 9 III 2, 20 IV; cf. also Art. 48 II GG.

[195] von Mangoldt, *Grundgesetz*, Art. 1, n. 4.

[196] von Mangoldt and von Klein, *Grundgesetz*, 61 ff. (Vorbemerkungen A II 4).

[197] Nipperdey, 'Gleicher Lohn der Frau'; id., *Grundrechte*; Enneccerus and Nipperdey, *Allgemeiner Teil I*, 91 ff. [§ 15 II.4. and 5.].

[198] Dürig, 'Grundrechte und Zivilrechtsprechung', 175, 176 ff.

[199] See BAGE 1, 185, 191 ff., 193 (3 December 1954; this judgment was apparently strongly influenced by Nipperdey [see n. 197], who was the first President of the Court); BVerfGE 7, 198, 203 ff. (15 January 1958—Lüth) arguing that the constitution's fundamental rights constituted an objective normative order ('objektive Wertordnung') and that they would therefore also be binding on the courts that decided in matters of private law. On the later development of the relevant case law, see Classen, 'Drittwirkung der Grundrechte', 65 ff.

[200] On the debate, see Stern, *Staatsrecht* II/1, 1515 ff.; cf. also Ruffert, *Vorrang der Verfassung*, 8 ff.; Papier, 'Drittwirkung der Grundrechte' [2] ff.

[201] Nipperdey, *Grundrechte*, 15 ff.: 'neue Lehre'; see also BVerfGE 7, 198, 205 (n. 199).

All this shows, again, that it is the legal process itself and not the state's political system that ultimately determines the textual sources of the law by deciding which normative texts must or may be applied in legal argument. This is even more so as far as the relative authority of such texts is concerned. Clearly, this concept is so ambiguous that it is difficult for a Parliament to legislate on the issue. Hence, again, the authority of a text can only be determined by the legal profession, from within the legal process. Of course, the law is always influenced by political decisions. Lawyers do not usually disregard legislators; and the law is always responsive to the political process. The legal system depends on external, political authority; accordingly the law would lose its credibility and authority if lawyers disregarded authoritative legislation and policymaking. The decision of the German legal profession to make the *Reich's* codification the exclusive textual authority of private law discourse is a clear example for this attitude. But it would be misleading to understand the law as simply an expression of the will of political actors or as a function of the political process. The applicability (or validity) and the authority of a legal source are ultimately determined by the legal profession, within the legal process. Thus, in Germany at the turn of the 20th century the concept of private law changed when the BGB replaced the *Corpus iuris* as the main point of reference of legal discourse, and it changed again when it was later 'constitutionalized'. Likewise, the concept of modern private law appears to be in flux as supranational and European legal acts on the one hand, and private law-making on the other, begin to influence the development of private law.[202] In more theoretical terms, this entails that there is no single one rule of recognition or *Grundnorm* of modern private law anymore, which could be identified with the nation state or another monistic political sovereign. Rather we are observing a process of fragmentation and pluralization of different rules of recognition.[203] This will be analysed in more detail in the next chapter.

[202] Cf. Kessedjian, 'La codification privée', 144: '... une modification profonde en cours d'évolution de la force respective des diverses sources du droit'.

[203] See Wendehorst, 'Private Law Reasoning', 168 ff.

Chapter 2

Non-Legislative Codifications in Modern Law

All these observations help to better understand and historically situate non-legislative codifications in the present. The most important of such reference texts are the American Restatements of the law, which have become a major textual authority of the American common law. Today, large parts of the law have been restated, and the Restatements are taken by the participants to the legal discourse as a valid expression of the law. During the last decades, the American restatement approach has also influenced the developments of transnational restatements of the law. The International Institute for the Unification of Private Law (UNIDROIT) has largely applied the terminology and formal style of the American Restatements for its *Principles of International Commercial Contracts*;[1] and a similar approach was taken, on the European level, by the Lando Commission on European Contract Law.[2] Today, the Restatements' formal style is used by the Study Group on a European Civil Code[3] and by the Acquis Group,[4] the main non-legislative actors in the current political process of unifying European private law.

I. The American Restatements of the Law

Historically, the Restatements were a specific answer to peculiar problems of the American common law at the beginning of the 20th

[1] Above at 6.

[2] Zimmermann, 'Comparative Law and the Europeanization of Private Law', 560 ff., 562.

[3] On this group, see below n. 59.

[4] On this group, see below n. 60.

century.[5] 'There is today general dissatisfaction with the administration of justice': this was the introductory sentence of a report of a Committee of 35 leading jurists on the establishment of an American Law Institute.[6] As the report emphasized, this dissatisfaction was not confined to the 'radical section of the community': 'the opinion that the law is unnecessarily uncertain and complex, that many of its rules do not work well in practice, and that its administration often results not in justice, but in injustice, is general among all classes and among persons of widely divergent political and social opinions'.

Indeed, influential American scholars had earlier pronounced similar views[7] arguing for a more scientific and systematic treatment of the law.[8] Similarly, an earlier report, which had been commissioned by the American Bar Association, had shown that already in 1885 about one-half of the cases reaching appellate courts were reversed.[9] Thus, according to the Committee proposing the establishment of the American Law Institute, lawyers felt more and more lost in the mass of published decisions. The common law had become so complex and unclear that its reliability seemed seriously endangered, and an increasing amount of unsystematic and often contradictory statutory legislation substantially contributed to this state of affairs.[10] Altogether, the American legal system was felt to be

[5] On the intellectual and historical background of the founding of the American Law Institute, see LaPiana, 'Founding of the American Law Institute'. More specifically, on the Institute's history, see Hull, 'Restatement and Reform', with detailed references.

[6] ALI, 'Report of the Committee Proposing the Establishment of an American Law Institute', 1.

[7] Pound, 'Dissatisfaction with the Administration of Justice', especially 402 ff. See also, slightly later, Cardozo, *Growth of the Law*, 3 ff.

[8] See especially the speeches of Joseph Beale of Harvard and Wesley N. Hohfeld of Yale that were presented at the 1914 meeting of the Association of American Law Schools: Beale, 'Necessity for a Study of Legal System'; Hohfeld, 'A Vital School of Jurisprudence and Law'. Although Beale had initially opposed the idea of an American Law Institute and although he had earlier criticized the format of the later Restatements ('Dicey's "Conflict of Laws."', 168), he soon actively participated in the Institute and became the reporter of the Conflicts-Restatement (First); see Symeonides, 'First Conflicts Restatement', 41 ff., 47.

[9] ABA, 'Report of the Special Committee Appointed to Consider and Report Whether the Present Delay and Uncertainty in Judicial Administration Can be Lessened, and If So, By What Means', 329 ff.

[10] ALI, 'Report of the Committee Proposing the Establishment of an American Law Institute', 6 ff., 66 ff., 69 ff., 77 f.

standing 'indicted for uncertainty'.[11] Academic treatises, which had for a long time been regarded as sufficient authority for intellectually integrating the common law, had lost their former status. According to the Committee proposing the establishment of the American Law Institute, most of these treatises were of poor quality, as their authors were lost in the collection and examination of the quickly growing case law. Thus, the scholars' contribution to the legal system no longer contained the constructive analysis that was regarded as necessary for unifying and improving the law.[12] At the same time, attempts in the 19th century to systematize and clarify the law by means of civil codes had failed.[13] Thus, the Restatements must be seen in the context of these codification debates.[14] They should authoritatively systematize the law.

Another point of concern was that the formerly unified, 'common' English-American common law was felt to be breaking into parts.[15] Indeed, leading judges in the US Supreme Court had emphasized that the common law was no 'brooding omnipresence in the sky' but would always relate to some sovereign authority.[16] It was obvious that the single states' common laws developed in diverse directions, yet often for no good reason. This was a development, which the legal profession was obviously not prepared to accept. Indeed, scholars had argued that the appropriate subject for legal education and theory was only 'a common law which is not the particular law of any single jurisdiction'.[17] Likewise, the Committee

[11] Cardozo, *Growth of the Law*, 3: 'Our law stands indicted for uncertainty, and the names of weighty witnesses are endorsed upon the bill'.

[12] ALI, 'Report of the Committee Proposing the Establishment of an American Law Institute', 12 ff.

[13] Above, at 16.

[14] Cf. Beale, *Conflict of Laws* I, 43; Cardozo, *Growth of the Law*, 9. For the contemporary discussion Friedman, *History*, 304; Crystal, 'Restatement Movement', 267 ff., 273; LaPiana, 'Founding of the American Law Institute', 1090 ff.; von Mehren, 'Codification and Case Law', 668 f.; Jansen and Michaels, 'Private Law and the State', 387 f., with further references.

[15] On this point, see Gilmore, *Ages of American Law*, 70, 72.

[16] *Southern Pacific Co. v Jensen*, 244 U.S. 205, 222 (1917) (Holmes, J., dissenting). The most prominent authority for this position is the later decision of *Erie Railroad R. R. v Tompkins*, 304 U.S. 64 (1938), which was, however, decided after the foundation of the American Law Institute in 1923.

[17] Beale, 'Necessity for a Study of Legal System', 37; cf. also Symeonides, 'First Conflicts Restatement', 56 ff.

proposing the establishment of the American Law Institute felt that the common law should in principle develop homogenously and as a unity.[18]

1. Making legal authority

The Restatements were designed as a means of overcoming this unsatisfactory state of the legal system while at the same time preserving the flexibility of the common law.[19] They were meant to 'make certain much that is now uncertain and to simplify unnecessary complexities, but also to promote those changes which will tend better to adapt the laws to the needs of life'. Hence, the Restatements should be 'at once analytical, critical and constructive'.[20] It followed, first, that the Restatements should have an intellectual order that made them easily accessible. However, they should not be as rigidly systematized as European codifications; in this respect, the Restatements are a counter-model to the European codifications.[21] Secondly, the founders of the American Law Institute were of the strong opinion that the Restatements should not be adopted by statute:[22] the Restatements were meant to clarify and structure, yet not to ossify the law. Judges were therefore not assumed to be formally bound by the Restatements; rather they were to retain discretion whether to follow them in a specific case. This would allow the Restatements to be much more detailed and precise than a European codification could be.

[18] ALI, 'Report of the Committee Proposing the Establishment of an American Law Institute', 8 f., 85 ff. A different picture is drawn, in this respect, by Hesselink, 'Choices Made by the Lando Commission', 77 f., who neglects, however, these central historical sources.

[19] For an overview, see Michaels, 'Restatements'.

[20] ALI, 'Report of the Committee Proposing the Establishment of an American Law Institute', 14.

[21] Cf. also ALI, 'Report of the Committee Proposing the Establishment of an American Law Institute', 28. Continental observers, accordingly, emphasize this difference between codifications and the Restatements; see Zekoll, 'Law Institute', 112 ff. Nevertheless, it is disputed, within the American context, whether the Restatements were in effect more a bulwark against codification, or too similar in approach and structure to civil-law codes; cf. Adams, 'Blaming the Mirror', 226 ff.; Crystal, 'Restatement Movement', *passim*, both with further references.

[22] ALI, 'Report of the Committee Proposing the Establishment of an American Law Institute', 19 ff., 23 ff.

Nevertheless, the Restatements were from early on designed to become authoritative texts in themselves. Although they should be 'less than a code', they were clearly meant to be 'more than a treatise'.[23] From the very beginning of the project, it was clear that the Restatements, 'even though ... not ... formally adopted by legislatures' should be given 'such authority as is now accorded a prior decision of the highest court of the jurisdiction'.[24] The general understanding was that the Restatements could otherwise not achieve what was regarded as their most important purpose: that they made the law accessible to a professional lawyer without the need for consulting further authority.[25]

In view of this programme, the Restatements have been a remarkable success. Their status as a highly authoritative source of the law, even if remarkably rarely discussed explicitly, cannot be doubted. Already by 1934, the American Law Institute could show that the Restatements had been applied as authorities in hundreds of judicial decisions.[26] Their use as an ultimate source of the law[27] by the courts soon became pervasive;[28] and the Restatements are widely taken as the basic reference texts for the purpose of academic teaching.[29] Indeed, leading textbook authors had actively participated in the restatement process; from early on, they characterized the Restatements' authority as comparable to 'a statement by the highest court of a state ... In other words it is presumably a true statement of the law'.[30] Thus, today, '[b]y and large, if the Restatement states the rule, that is the end' of legal argument:[31] the Restatements are treated as a legal authority for which no further

[23] Cardozo, *Growth of the Law*, 9 and ff., 16 f.

[24] ALI, 'Report of the Committee Proposing the Establishment of an American Law Institute', 25; see also *loc. cit.*, 29.

[25] On the early debates within the American Law Institute, see Cardozo, *Growth of the Law*, 10, 16; cf. also Frank, 'Law Institute', 617.

[26] ALI, *Restatement in the Courts*, 1934.

[27] There is no comprehensive analysis; for examples, see Eisenberg, 'Concept of National Law', 1251 ff. A somewhat more complete review of the largely uncritically receptive reaction of the courts to a new Restatement can be found in Maggs, 'Ipse Dixit', 512 f., 517 ff.

[28] von Mehren, *Law in the United States*, 21 f.; Frank, 'Law Institute', 638 ff.; Zekoll, 'Law Institute', 115 ff.

[29] Rheinstein, 'Leader Groups', 692 f.

[30] Cf. Beale, *Conflict of Laws* I, 43.

[31] Snyder, 'Private Lawmaking', 381 (and f.) with further references.

support is necessary. Thus, courts apparently applied the Restatement (Second) of Contracts like a statute, i.e. without further argument, even in cases where this amounted to a deviation from earlier law.[32] Indeed, the Institute has become an object of pressure group lobbying;[33] this shows that the Restatements have achieved a degree of legal authority which is comparable to that of Parliamentarian legislation.

American writers have always emphasized that the Restatements must not be regarded as strictly binding; they do not have 'the force of a code'.[34] Courts are of course free to deviate from a restatement's particular provision; and if a restatement introduces a substantially new rule, this will not always be accepted in all jurisdictions. A telling and well-known example can be seen in the history of American product liability. Here, § 402A of the Restatement (Second) of the Law of Torts introduced a strict products liability regime, although this had previously been the law only in a very small number of states.[35] Nevertheless, the rule was soon regarded as good law in most American jurisdictions.[36] Yet, when the Institute introduced a more restrictive approach in the Restatement (Third) of Torts: Products Liability, this was widely criticized by academic writers and has not been consistently applied by the courts.[37]

Nevertheless, even in those areas where the Restatements did not actually unify the law in substance, they have at least achieved a high degree of intellectual unity.[38] From early on, the American Law Institute had published 'Annotations' that described the single state's law in terms of compliance with, or divergence from, the respective restatement's provisions;[39] in the course of the century

[32] Maggs, 'Ipse Dixit', 527 ff., 530 f.

[33] Cf. Wolfram, 'Bismarck's Sausages', 820 ff.; Barker, 'Lobbying and the American Law Institute'; Frank, 'Law Institute', 628 ff.; see also the Student Note, 'Just What You'd Expect', 2367.

[34] Beale, *Conflict of Laws* I, 43.

[35] Wechsler, 'Restatements and Legal Change', 188 ff.; Zekoll, 'Law Institute', 113 ff.

[36] Schwartz, Kelly and Partlett, *Prosser, Wade and Schwartz's Torts*, 736 f., with further references on the debate.

[37] Vandall and Vandall, 'Accurate Restatement'; Kysar, 'Expectation of Consumers'.

[38] Cf. Rheinstein, 'Leader Groups', 692 f.; Frank, 'Law Institute', 639: 'the visions of the founders have been realized'. It should be taken into account, though, that John P. Frank used to be a leading member of the American Law Institute.

[39] Cf. e.g. ALI, *Contracts. Colorado Annotations* (1936).

such annotations were produced for most states and nearly all restatements. Moreover, in some early instances, the Restatements' reporters even wrote textbooks that were designed as a commentary to the relevant restatement.[40] Thus, the American Restatements of the Law achieved a status that is comparable to that of the Roman *Corpus iuris civilis* as the main reference text of the *ius commune*.[41] In most states, they are recognized as non-legislative and supra-jurisdictional sources of the law. As a result, they have become the intellectual backbone of what may be conceived of as a national American common law.[42] Intellectually and to a large degree also in terms of substance, the Restatements continue to unify and integrate the different American common laws into one national legal system. While it is true that during the last decades there have been signs of their authority being in decline,[43] for most of the 20th century they have contributed constructively and innovatively to the law's development.

2. Tradition and innovation

A central question had from early on been whether the Restatements should be purely descriptive or also prescriptive in approach.[44]

[40] See especially Beale, *Conflict of Laws*; cf. also Williston and Thompson, *Contracts* (3rd ed.). Although Williston largely retained the original systematic order of his textbook (on which the restatement was based, however), he regularly based the exposition of a problem or definition on the relevant provision in the Restatement or at least referred, in the first footnote of each paragraph, to such a relevant provision.

[41] The comparison is anything but new; cf., though sceptically, Holmes, Letter to Harold Laski, 15 February 1923: 'You can't evoke genius by announcing a *corpus iuris*': *Holmes-Laski Letters I*, 481 f. Indeed, the idea of an American *corpus iuris* had been present in the public discourse since 1910; cf. LaPiana, 'Founding of the American Law Institute', 1107, with further references.

[42] Eisenberg, 'Concept of National Law', 1232 ff. and *passim*. Although Eisenberg does not see the Restatements as the only source of American national common law, he throughout assigns a special status to them.

[43] Cf. Bernstein, 'Restatement Redux', 1667 ff. Looking at product liability, in particular, Bernstein doubts, on the one hand, whether Restatements are still necessary, as there are alternative new technological possibilities of achieving legal certainty. On the other hand, Bernstein questions whether the desired unity of the law is still a realistic aim as American law has indeed become strongly politicized.

[44] Zekoll, 'Law Institute', 112 ff.; Frank, 'Law Institute', 617 f.; cf. also Metzger, *Extra legem, intra ius*, 140 ff.

Whereas some authors criticized the Restatements for being too conservative and describing the law as it was instead of the law as it should be developed,[45] other critics accused its drafters for taking too much of a political approach presenting desired rules instead of the actual state of the law.[46] The fundamental question had already been a subject of the debates during the American Law Institute's foundation;[47] and it was also addressed in the report of the Committee of 35. This report presented a clear programme which was based on the feeling that 'law must be stable, and yet it cannot stand still'.[48] Hence, the approach should be basically descriptive, but this should not preclude prescriptive and even innovative elements from the restatement.[49]

Clearly, prescriptive decisions had to be made where the Restatements were to lay down a clear rule, even though the question of the law was reasonably disputed.[50] Indeed, even a *prima vista* purely doctrinal issue, such as the assignment of a particular question to the heading of 'duty of care' or 'breach of duty' may be political in effect, as it determines whether the question is decided by the judge or by the jury.[51] What is more, the American Law Institute has always seen the Restatements as a means of promoting

[45] See Cohen, 'Transcendental Nonsense', 833 f.: 'The "Restatement of the Law" ... is the last long-drawn-out gasp of a dying tradition'; Gilmore, *Ages of American Law*, 73 f.; Friedman, *History*, 304 f.

[46] Recent debate has focused on the standard of products liability; for an overview of the discussions during the drafting-process, see Vandall, 'Constructing a Roof Before the Foundation is Prepared', 261: 'wish list from manufacturing America'. A good overview and further references can be found in the anonymous Student Note, 'Just What You'd Expect', 2374 ff., 2376, 2378 f. For the more recent debate after the Restatement's publication, see Vandall and Vandall, 'Accurate Restatement'; Kysar, 'Expectation of Consumers'.

[47] See Hull, 'Restatement and Reform', who shows, convincingly, that a 'reformist plan' was from early on part of the Institute's agenda.

[48] Cardozo, *Growth of the Law*, 2, citing the initial sentence of Pound, *Legal History*, 1.

[49] ALI, 'Report of the Committee Proposing the Establishment of an American Law Institute', 14 ff.: the Restatements 'should be at once analytical, critical and constructive'.

[50] ALI, 'Report of the Committee Proposing the Establishment of an American Law Institute', 15.

[51] Stapleton, 'Controlling the Future by Restatement', 264 f. and *passim*.

legal change:[52] if it was possible to reasonably predict the future development of the law, this should be laid down in the rules. Only in disputed 'matters of general public concern and discussion' was a decision of the a-political, non-governmental Institute regarded as inappropriate; therefore, taxation and fiscal matters were seen to be outside the Institute's 'competence'.[53]

This is not the appropriate place for a detailed discussion on whether the Restatements have in actual fact followed a more conservative, descriptive or a more innovative, prescriptive approach.[54] On the one hand, the approach of the American Law Institute has significantly changed over the years: modern Restatements present themselves more as suggestions for the law's future development by judges than the original Restatements (first).[55] On the other hand, such questions are difficult to measure objectively; hence, they will remain a matter of judgment and political debate. In the present context, it is worth emphasizing, however, that representatives of the Institute have argued, not unconvincingly, that the Restatements' success depended not least on their blurring the distinction between description and prescription: between the law as it is and the law as it ought to be. As Herbert Wechsler, speaking as the Institute's President, put it: 'if we ask ourselves what courts will do in fact ... can we divorce our answers

[52] ALI, 'Certificate of Incorporation', at <http://www.ali.org/doc/charter.pdf>: 'The particular business and objects of the society are educational, and are to promote the clarification and simplification of the law *and its better adaptation to social needs*, to secure the better administration of justice, and to encourage and carry on scholarly and scientific legal work' (emphasis added).

[53] ALI, 'Report of the Committee Proposing the Establishment of an American Law Institute', 15 f.: 'Changes which do not fall under the ban of this limitation, and which will carry out more efficiently ends generally accepted as desirable are within the province of the restatement to suggest'.

[54] Cf. Adams, 'Blaming the Mirror', 242 ff.; Frank, 'Law Institute', 624 f.; Zekoll, 'Law Institute', 112 ff. For a detailed analysis and evaluation of the different Restatements of the first series see DeMott, 'First Restatement of Agency', especially 31 ff.; Movsesian, 'Williston'; Kelley, 'Reform by Descriptive Theory'; Kull, 'Restitution and Reform'; Symeonides, 'First Conflicts Restatement'. The general impression given by these studies is that the first Restatements were mildly reformatory (Kelley, *loc. cit.*, 106 f.). They stabilized the respective subjects doctrinally on the basis of a traditional, more or less pragmatic concept of law, which was clearly never purely formalistic. Moreover, all of these Restatements included some more innovative 'progressive' rules that implied a change or reform of the prevailing law.

[55] Cf. also Michaels, 'Restatements'.

wholly from our view of what they ought to do . . .?'[56] Indeed, the American Law Institute could never have become a promoter of legal change if its activity was not regarded by the American legal profession as a—by and large—fair description of the law's development.

II. Non-Legislative Codifications in Europe

All these observations help to explain the present European Common Frame of Reference (CFR) process. This process must be seen both as an attempt by politicians in the European Union to unify and control private law[57]—a process, which is open-ended and in the present context of no particular interest—and, at the same time, as a continuation of the Lando process of unifying private law by means of scholarly, non-legislative codifications. The Lando Commission's *Principles of European Contract Law* (PECL), the first of these modern non-legislative codifications of European private law, have indeed been well-received, and the Lando Commission has found successor groups, such as the European Group on Tort Law, which presented its *Principles on European Tort Law* in 2005,[58] the Study Group on a European Civil Code (Study Group ECC),[59] and the Research Group on EC Private Law (Acquis Group).[60] Whereas the Study Group ECC is currently publishing a broad range of *Principles of European Law*,[61] which are supposedly based on a comparison of the

[56] Wechsler, 'Restatements and Legal Change', 190. For an analysis of the Restatement of Torts (First) on such a basis, see Kelley, 'Reform by Descriptive Theory', especially 122 ff.

[57] See above at 14 f.

[58] European Group on Tort Law, *Principles of European Tort Law*; on these Principles, Zimmermann, 'Comparison and Points of Contact'; Jansen, 'Principles of European Tort Law'; id., 'State of Art of European Tort Law'; Wagner, 'Harmonizing European Tort Law'; Schmidt-Kessel, *Reform des Schadenersatzrechts I*.

[59] On that Group, see von Bar, 'Die Study Group on a European Civil Code'; Wurmnest, 'Privatrechtsvereinheitlichung in Europa', 732 ff.

[60] <http://www.acquis-group.org>. The Group was founded in 2002 on the basis that the European *acquis communautaire* had not been taken into account by the Lando Commission and by the Study Group ECC.

[61] Published thus far: Study Group ECC/von Bar, *Benevolent Intervention*; Study Group ECC/Hesselink *et al., Commercial Agency*; Study Group ECC/Barendrecht *et al., Service Contracts*; Study Group ECC/Drobnig, *Personal Security*; Study Group ECC/Lilleholt *et al., Lease of Goods*; Study Group ECC/Hondius *et al., Sales*.

national private laws in Europe,[62] the Acquis Group has formulated in its *Acquis Principles* a systematizing compilation of the European Union's *acquis communautaire*:[63] a body of private law, which is usually not taken into account by the Study Group ECC.[64] What is more, these two groups have together prepared an 'academic' *Draft Common Frame of Reference* (DCFR):[65] a text, which is on the one hand meant to be a draft for a 'political' CFR, but on the other hand presents itself as a non-legislative codification of its own authority.

1. The *Principles of European Contract Law*

At present, the PECL are the only one of those texts, which has already had a chance of standing the test of recognition in legal practice; and leading observers, such as Reinhard Zimmermann and Jan Smits, have praised them as a success.[66] Indeed, the PECL have significantly contributed to the current process of unifying European contract law. Nevertheless, an evaluation on the success of such an international legal instrument is a matter of personal judgment, and it is remarkable that the success of the Vienna Convention on the International Sale of Goods (CISG) has been viewed more critically,[67] although the CISG has been used by many courts in a

[62] The comparative basis of these principles, however, is often very weak; for the Study Group's Principles on *Benevolent Intervention*, see Jansen, '*Negotiorum Gestio* und *Benevolent Intervention in Another's Affairs*'. Similarly, the principles on service contracts find no basis in any national legal system.

[63] The Research Group on the Existing EC Private Law (ed.), *Acquis Principles. Contract I*. For more detail, see Jansen and Zimmermann, 'Restating the Acquis communautaire?'; cf. also below at 90 ff., 92 f.

[64] An exception, though, are the Principles on *Sales*, which are largely based on the Directive 1999/44/EC of the European Parliament and of the Council of 25 May 1999 on certain aspects of the sale of consumer goods and associated guarantees.

[65] von Bar, Clive and Schulte-Nölke (eds), *DCFR Outline Edition*. For an evaluation of the DCFR's *Interim Outline Edition* of 2008 (which has not been changed in great substance), see Eidenmüller, Faust, Grigoleit, Jansen, Wagner and Zimmermann, 'Policy Choices and Codification Problems'.

[66] Zimmermann, 'Comparative Law and the Europeanization of Private Law', 563; Smits, 'PECL and the Harmonisation of Private Law in Europe', 572 f., 576 f., 580 ff. It should be taken into account, though, that Reinhard Zimmermann was an active Member of the third Working Team of the Lando Commission.

[67] See especially, for the United States, Reimann, 'The CISG in the United States'; for a recent overview with regard to the actual practice, see Ferrari *et al.* (eds), *Draft UNCITRAL Digest*.

great number of cases, and although it has had a significant impact on the international unification of contract law, too, and not least in Europe.

Clearly, such judgments depend on relevant expectations. Whereas it could be hoped that the CISG might become the normal instrument for international trade, nothing like this could be expected for the PECL. Indeed, being a soft-law instrument, which is not backed by the political authority of a state, the PECL are not normally acknowledged as 'law' applicable under choice-of-law rules; this is especially true in Europe.[68] What is more, the PECL were added, or superimposed, onto well-administered national legal systems that are mostly codified and that all have a strong national legal tradition supported by an influential national legal profession. This sharply distinguishes the present situation in Europe from the state of American law in the first half of the 20th century: European legal systems cannot be consolidated or stabilized by the PECL; rather these Principles may be perceived, from an internal, national perspective, as an external irritation. Thus, expectations were lowered from the outset: any influence on a national legal system, which is more than insignificant in effect, must be judged, from the PECL's perspective, as a success.

2. An echo of universalism

If such influence can in fact be perceived today, this may be taken as an indication that there are jurists who feel a need for a European civil code or a comparable, non-legislative reference text. Indeed, this feeling motivated the Lando Commission, a group of comparative law scholars from different European countries,[69] when it began its work in 1982 independently of any governmental mandate.[70] Today, the same motivation can be observed not only

[68] Art. 3 Rome Convention (EC Convention on the Law Applicable to Contractual Obligations (1998) OJ C 27/24); now Art. 3 Regulation (EC) No 593/2008 of the European Parliament and of the Council of 17 June 2008 on the law applicable to contractual obligations (Rome I), (2008) OJ L 177/6; on the discussion of the question with regard to the PICC, see *PICC-Commentary*/Michaels, Preamble I [51] ff. Thus, the Principles can only be incorporated into a contract as if they were standard terms.

[69] Lando, 'Preface', xii f.

[70] Lando, 'Preface', xi. The project had already been proposed by Ole Lando in 1976.

among the working groups, which continue the Lando process of unifying European private law by means of non-legislative 'restatements', but also among political legislators, scholars, and—in some Member States of the European Union—even among judges. Indeed—despite their evident lack of political or 'democratic' legitimacy—the PECL have been recognized, even by traditional national scholars, as a 'source of law' in a broad sense;[71] and they have even been treated as authoritative reference texts by European courts.[72] Remarkable developments, in this respect, are reported from Spain, where the PECL are used by the *Tribunal Supremo* and also by lower courts as a driver for change and as an authoritative reference text in a process of modernizing contract law.[73] Similarly, though less spectacularly, the PECL are also beginning to influence actual legal practice in the Netherlands[74] and before the European Court of Justice, where some Advocates General have based their opinions on these Principles.[75] Similar developments can be observed in academia. Here, the PECL are today not seen only as an expression and result of comparative research; moreover, they have become an 'object of European scholarship' in themselves.[76] They are a reference text for a new European legal scholarship treating the PECL as a textual authority in themselves.[77]

[71] See, e.g., Canaris, 'UNIDROIT Principles und PECL im System der Rechtsquellen', 13 ff., 29 ff.: 'Rechtsgewinnungsquelle'; Canaris uses the UNIDROIT *Principles* and the PECL as a basis for introducing a contractual remedy for disgorging profits, although there is no legislative basis for such a remedy in the German BGB. He does not, however, treat the Principles as an ultimate legal authority, which could be used without further justification in legal argument.

[72] Zimmermann, *PECL als Ausdruck und Gegenstand Europäischer Rechtswissenschaft*, 2003, 49 ff., with further references.

[73] See Vendrell Cervantes, 'Application of the PECL', analysing 12 decisions of the *Tribunal Supremo* and nine decisions of other courts, all of them but one between 2005 and 2007.

[74] See Busch, 'PECL before the Supreme Court of the Netherlands'.

[75] See Trstenjak, 'Der Gemeinsame Referenzrahmen und der Europäische Gerichtshof'.

[76] Zimmermann, *PECL als Ausdruck und Gegenstand Europäischer Rechtswissenschaft*; cf. also id., '*Ius Commune* and the PECL', 33 ff.; id., 'PECL: Contemporary Manifestation of the Old, and Possible Foundations for a New, European Scholarship of Private Law'.

[77] Busch and Schelhaas (eds), *PECL and Dutch Law*; Antoniolli and Veneziano (eds), *PECL and Italian Law*; see also MacQueen and Zimmermann (eds), *European Contract Law*.

The reasons for such developments are easy to see. On the one hand, there is a growing feeling that the nationalized state of private law in Europe is unsatisfactory. True, private law principles often rest on political decisions, and the modern codifications have been conceived of as an expression of a people's identity.[78] But, as in the United States, many of the differences between the national European systems of contract law cannot be explained on the basis of diverging political values or as expressing national identities. Often, they are simply a result of historical accident. Non-legislative codifications may be used as a means of overcoming this type of intellectually irritating difference. To treat European principles as authoritative may lead to a slow convergence of the national legal systems.[79] Thus, legislators often want to overcome an alleged parochial state of national law and therefore wish to draft statutes and codifications in a way that matches the 'European state of the art'. They may thus be prepared to accept principles of European law as a model. This could be observed already in the context of the German *Schuldrechtsreform* (reform of the law of obligations, 2001/2002),[80] and it is apparently happening again in the course of the present reform of the French *Code civil*. In fact, the formulation of national legislative acts is increasingly guided by constitutional, European or other types of supranational law. As a result, modern legislation has become part of the internal legal process.[81] In such complex legal dynamics, non-legislatively carried-out codifications may indeed gain the status of authoritative texts. In constitutional terms, there are fewer restrictions on legislators than on judges about which texts to treat as authoritative; and non-legislative

[78] This point is elaborated in more detail in Jansen, *Binnenmarkt*, 19.

[79] Zimmermann, 'Comparative Law and the Europeanization of Private Law', 563; Smits, 'PECL and the Harmonisation of Private Law', 572 f., 576 f., 580 ff.

[80] This was even more remarkable as the PECL had been published only two years before and as the rules on prescription that were taken as a legislative model had not even been officially published; see *BT-Drucksache* 14/6040 (14 May 2001), 80, 86, 89, 92 f., 131, 133 ff., 177, 179, 181 f., 186, 188, 196, 209, 212, 217 f., 220, 223, 238, 240, 244, 268 (CISG), 92, 103, 129, 131, 164 f., 214 (PECL); *BT-Drucksache* 14/7052 (9 October 2001), 174 f. (CISG), 178 (PECL). Nevertheless, influential authors had already introduced these Principles into the critical discussion of the first draft of the reform as supra-national textual authorities; see U. Huber, 'Das geplante Recht der Leistungsstörungen'.

[81] See Wendehorst, 'Private Law Reasoning', 148 ff.

law-making has become a normal phenomenon of modern law, especially on the supranational level. Here, non-legislative codifications, like the PECL, very much look like an official piece of legislation. Indeed, they consist of rules that are not formulated to convince other participants to the legal discourse, but to be applied by their addressees.[82]

On the other hand, many codifications have become 'prison cells' of private law in the course of the 19th and 20th centuries.[83] In some European countries, influential lawyers and courts increasingly regard the traditional rules of their national codification as unsatisfactory, and yet this legislation is the basis of their private law. In such a situation, the legal professions may look for other sources of the law to overcome the traditional limitations of their codifications. It is not surprising that they listen to an 'echo of universalism'[84] having recourse to European principles as soft law, if those principles look attractive and if they have been assigned sufficient authority in European legal discourse; this explains the recent developments in Spain.[85] However, such developments should not be over-emphasized. In the present day, cases where the PECL have in fact been the legal basis for a judicial change of the law are still exceptional. Clearly, there are great differences between the various legal systems. The practice of Spanish courts, for example, would today be unthinkable in Germany or France.

3. Some results

All in all, the present authority of the PECL in Europe cannot be compared with the authority of the American Restatements in the United States. Normally, the European Principles are not used by the courts as an ultimate textual authority. Nonetheless, these developments make apparent that the authority of a non-legislative codification of European private law may well increase in the

[82] Art. 1:101 (1) PECL; see Michaels, 'Privatautonomie und Privatkodifikation', 591; similarly for the DCFR von Bar, Clive and Schulte-Nölke (eds), *DCFR Outline Edition*, Introduction [6] ff.

[83] The metaphor is old: Wüstendörfer, 'Die deutsche Rechtswissenschaft am Wendepunkt', 224.

[84] Smits, 'PECL and the Harmonisation of Private Law', 580.

[85] Vendrell Cervantes, 'Application of the PECL', 534 ff., with further references.

future.[86] Clearly, the Study Group ECC and the Acquis Group intend the DCFR to become such a textual authority for European private law.[87] They have actively supported a process of recognition by already making a first outline of the DCFR publicly accessible[88] and by promoting it at conferences.[89] Both groups can count on the fact that there is no legal competence for the European Union to legislate comprehensively in matters of private law.[90] At the same time, their 'academic' DCFR will, most probably, remain, for the time being, the only non-legislative codification of the European law of obligations.[91]

This is not to say, however, that the DCFR will in fact become a textual authority in itself. That status can only be achieved by sufficient recognition in the eyes of the European legal professions. Of course, it is far too early for a conclusive judgment about the impact of the DCFR on European private law.[92] History cannot be preempted. Yet it is probably fair to say that non-legislative codifications of European private law will face greater obstacles in this respect than the American Restatements: not least because the DCFR presently receives a rather cool greeting from the legal

[86] Concurring Hesselink, 'CFR as a Source of European Private Law', 923 ff.

[87] Schulte-Nölke, 'Contract Law or Law of Obligations?', 50; cf. also Pfeiffer, 'Von den PECL zum DCFR', 705 f.

[88] Cf. above n. 65.

[89] It is probably no coincidence that the two main conferences on the first outline of the DCFR were held in Osnabrück (17 to 19 April 2008) and Münster (3 and 4 July 2008), where the Study Group ECC and Acquis Group or leading members of the groups are based. Other large conferences, open to the general public, were held at Trier (6 and 7 March 2008) and Barcelona (6 and 7 June 2008).

[90] For more detail see Hähnchen, 'Rechtsform des CFR', with a discussion of different possible bases of competence and different legal forms (such as directive, regulation etc.) for the CFR. On the one hand, there is no legal basis for a binding European instrument comprehensively codifying or restating European private law, yet, on the other hand, it does not seem to be politically wise for European politicians to discuss further competences for the European Union.

[91] But see the *Principles of European Tort Law*, which have been prepared by the European Group on Tort Law: above n. 58 with further references.

[92] Cf. the discussion in Schmidt-Kessel (ed.), *Der gemeinsame Referenzrahmen*: Röthel, 'Der Referenzrahmen als Modellgesetz?'; Riesenhuber, 'Systembildung durch den CFR'; Leible, 'Auswirkungen des CFR auf eine gemeinschaftsrechtskonforme Auslegung'; Trstenjak, 'Der Gemeinsame Referenzrahmen und der Europäische Gerichtshof'. Most of these contributions, however, do not clearly distinguish the non-legislative DCFR from the political CFR, since the authors were expecting the DCFR to develop soon into a political CFR.

professions of Europe, which are disappointed by its many substantial deficiencies.[93] Perhaps more importantly, the present parochial state of national European laws still appears to be more an intellectual than a practical problem.[94] There is no general feeling of a crisis of the law's administration in Europe. Most European legal systems are based on long-established codifications that have become the basic reference texts of the different national legal discourses; accordingly the DCFR can only become one concurring or conflicting basic text besides others. Relying on a European text of authority will therefore most likely remain exceptional. At present, the PECL have Europeanized contract law only at the level of scholarly discourse; in most Member States they have not reached actual legal practice. In fact, unlike the American Restatements, it will be difficult to regard the PECL or the DCFR as a 'secondary source of the law':[95] why should one look into one of those texts for information of the content of one's own well-administered and fully commented on codified law? Hence, the DCFR cannot accomplish what has been argued to be the main purpose of a codification: a reduction of the law's complexity.[96] Rather, it will increase the law's complexity by adding to the legal system a further basic reference text, one which may be in conflict with national codifications on the one hand and with the European Union's legislation on the other.

III. The UNIDROIT *Principles of International Commercial Contracts*

A picture of present non-legislative codifications would not be complete without a reference to UNIDROIT's *Principles of International*

[93] See, for Germany, Eidenmüller, Faust, Grigoleit, Jansen, Wagner and Zimmermann, 'Policy Choices and Codification Problems'; cf. also *Palandt*/Heinrichs, Einleitung 1 [33], and the contributions by Faust, Eidenmüller, Wagner, and Wendehorst in Schulze *et al.* (eds), *Der akademische Entwurf für einen Gemeinsamen Referenzrahmen*; for the United Kingdom, see Whittaker, '"Draft Common Frame of Reference". An Assessment'; id. 'A Framework of Principle for European Contract Law?'.

[94] Jansen, *Binnenmarkt*, 7 ff. and *passim*; cf. also Michaels, 'Restatements', at 4.

[95] Michaels, 'Restatements', at 4; cf. also with regard to the PICC, *PICC-Commentary*/Michaels, Preamble I [3] f., with further references on the current debate.

[96] Kroppenberg, 'Der gescheiterte Codex', 117.

Commercial Contracts (PICC), which were first published in 1994 and then in a revised and enlarged version again in 2004.[97] The purpose of these principles corresponds with the agenda of the American Law Institute, the Lando Commission, and its European successors in that the PICC are meant to become a textual basis for a new *ius commune*.[98] Yet, whereas the American Restatements on the one hand and the PECL or the DCFR on the other formulate restatements of the law in a specific part of the world, the PICC claim to be a universal, or uniform, reference text for a specific sector of society, namely for international trade.[99]

UNIDROIT[100] was originally a foundation of the League of Nations. It was established in 1926, as an independent, intergovernmental organization; and it was later re-established on the basis of a multilateral agreement (the UNIDROIT Statute),[101] to which at present 63 states from all over the world and with different economic, political, and cultural backgrounds have acceded.[102] All these states are represented in the Institute's General Assembly. This organ, despite being the Institute's final decision maker,[103] is quite distant from the actual daily work.[104] Thus, the most important body is the Governing Council,[105] which consists, apart from the President and one *ex officio* representative of the International Court of Justice, of 25 elected members:[106] judges and academics, but also

[97] For an overview, see Zimmermann, 'Unidroit-Grundregeln'.

[98] See, expressly, Bonell, *International Restatement*, 1 ff., 3; cf. also *loc. cit.*, 9 ff.

[99] PICC Preamble (*Purpose of the Principles*): '(1) These Principles set forth general rules for international commercial contracts; see Bonell, *International Restatement*, 68 ff.; *PICC-Commentary*/Michaels, Preamble I [21] ff.; [25] ff.

[100] See Art. 1 (1) of the Statute of UNIDROIT (available at <http://www.unidroit.org/mm/statute-e.pdf>): 'The purposes of the International Institute for the Unification of Private Law are to examine ways of harmonising and coordinating the private law of States and of groups of States, and to prepare gradually for the adoption by the various States of uniform rules of private law'.

[101] See n. 100.

[102] For the history of the PICC and of UNIDROIT, see *PICC-Commentary*/Vogenauer, Introduction [14] ff.

[103] See Arts. 16 ff. UNIDROIT Statute (n. 100). Many of the General Assembly's decisions need to be approved by the Member States, however.

[104] Indeed, the General Assembly does not do much more than 'approv[ing] the Work Programme every three years': Art. 5 (3) UNIDROIT Statute (n. 100).

[105] See Arts. 11–14, 15 (2) UNIDROIT Statute (n. 100).

[106] Art. 6 UNIDROIT Statute (n. 100).

civil servants and other practitioners.[107] It is this rather independent body which finally approves of final drafts for uniform law instruments.[108] However, such instruments will of course not become good uniform law if they are not subsequently endorsed by the Member States.

1. A UNIDROIT Restatement of global law?

However, such participation of the Member States did not take place in the case of the PICC. Whereas the usual legal instruments of UNIDROIT are international conventions or model laws (*lois-type*),[109] these forms were considered inappropriate for a unification of the law of commercial contracts. Preference was given to a non-legislative reference text, which should be modelled after the American Restatements.[110] The main motive was that the PICC would not have to be adopted by individual states, if they were drafted as a non-binding instrument.[111] Hence, the rules could be formulated without a view to future political negotiations and compromise with the representatives of national governments. What is more, the instrument could be easily revised at a later stage.

The PICC were designed as a restatement of international commercial contracts on the basis of the contract laws of the world's major jurisdictions and existing international instruments in the area of contract law, such as the CISG.[112] The project of drafting such an instrument had already been envisaged in 1968 by Mario Matteucci, who at this time served as the Institute's Secretary-General and later became its President.[113] However, the development remained slow

[107] *PICC-Commentary*/Vogenauer, Introduction [14].

[108] Arts. 1(2)(a), 14(3) UNIDROIT Statute (n. 100). According to Art. 14(5), it is also the Governing Council's task to consider the appropriate diplomatic steps to convince the Member States to adopt such instruments.

[109] See *PICC-Commentary*/Vogenauer, Introduction [7] ff., discussing different 'tools of harmonization' and their respective advantages and disadvantages.

[110] For discussion, see Bonell, *International Restatement*, 1 ff., 14 ff.; *PICC-Commentary*/ Vogenauer, Introduction [12] f.; see also Basedow, 'Die UNIDROIT-Prinzipien', 1 ff.; id., 'Uniform Law Conventions and the UNIDROIT Principles', 129 f.

[111] Governing Council of UNIDROIT, 'Introduction to the 1994 Edition', xiv f.

[112] For more details about the PICC's sources *PICC-Commentary*/Vogenauer, Introduction [21] f.

[113] Bonell, *International Restatement*, 27, with references.

until a special Working Group was established for this project in 1980.[114] This Group was mainly composed of comparative law scholars, who represented the world's different legal systems.[115] It worked largely independently of the Institute and its organs: the Working Group did not adhere to formal consultation mechanisms with stakeholders and it never allowed for participation of representatives of the Member States' governments.[116] Only a few disputes from within the Group were ever submitted to the Governing Council.

It is a result of this rather autonomous formulation of the PICC, that the Council felt itself unable to formally adopt them as its own instrument. Rather, the Council decided, in May 1994, in the light of controversy among its members,[117] that it 'would not formally approve the Principles but rather authorise their publication'; at the same time the Council recommended its 'widest possible distribution' in practice.[118] Thus, formally, the PICC cannot be seen as an instrument of UNIDROIT. They lack a political *sic volo sic iubeo* from the Institute's side[119] and they are therefore not fully backed by the Institute's political authority. Nevertheless, the Principles have the Governing Council's *nihil obstat* and the Institute's institutional support. Thus, they are even officially published under the Institute's name, as if they had been formally approved.

The lack of formal approval corresponds to the claim of the PICC to be of persuasive authority, rather than formally binding.[120] *Prima vista*, such a claim makes perfect sense, and it corresponds to the American Law Institute's claim of authority for its Restatements.[121] Yet, whereas the American Restatements could at least

[114] See for all Bonell, *International Restatement*, 27 ff.; *PICC-Commentary*/Vogenauer, Introduction [16] ff., both with further references.

[115] For the individual participants of the Group, see Bonell, *International Restatement*, 29 f., 36 f.; for the second Working Group established in 1997, see *loc. cit.*, 40, 43. See also *loc. cit.*, 33 ff. for a long list of other jurists, who collaborated with the first Working Group, and 41, 43 f. for observers and advisors contributing to the work of the second Group.

[116] *PICC-Commentary*/Vogenauer, Introduction [20].

[117] See (1994) *UNIDROIT Proceedings and Papers*, CD (73) 18, pp. 11 ff.

[118] (1994) *UNIDROIT Proceedings and Papers*, CD (73) 18, p. 22.

[119] Cf. above at 35 and below at 85 ff.

[120] Governing Council of UNIDROIT, 'Introduction to the 1994 Edition', xv; see also Bonell, *International Restatement*, 25.

[121] Above at 54.

make a plausible claim of being a genuine, i.e. by and large descriptive, restatement of common principles of American common law,[122] such a claim seems more difficult to maintain for the PECL, and it seems even less convincing for the PICC. Indeed, whereas the PECL formulate rules for a European society, which is—despite the different languages and national identities—culturally, politically, and economically more or less homogenous, the PICC were originally meant to bridge capitalist and socialist legal systems; today they must be acceptable for Western, Asian, and Islamic business, and for both developed and developing countries. Thus, as there are probably not sufficient commonalities for a genuine restatement,[123] an important aspect of the PICC must be seen to be proposing new law for international commerce. Many of its rules are innovative, and they claim to be addressing the needs of international trade more appropriately than the different national legal systems.[124]

In this context, innovation does not relate only to more technical matters, such as problems originating from the use of different languages or from the fact that contract partners are situated in different time zones. Substantial innovation can also be found in foundational principles of the law, such as the *favor contractus*, which informs many of the PICC's rules by giving preference to a re-interpretation, rather than an avoidance of the contract.[125] There can be no serious doubt that the Working Group often followed a 'best-solution approach'.[126] Yet, for such a proposal, one would normally expect reasons to be given. However, no such reasoning can be found in the PICC. Its official Comments are explanations of the rules, not justifications of a particular solution or policy. What is

[122] Above at 56 ff.

[123] See e.g. Furmston, 'UNIDROIT Principles and International Commercial Arbitration', 205; Basedow, 'Die UNIDROIT-Prinzipien', 3, 15 ff.

[124] See Bonell, *International Restatement*, 11 f., 24, 48 ff., describing the PICC as 'a mixture of both tradition and innovation' (24).

[125] Bonell, *International Restatement*, 50 ff., 102 ff. Examples are Arts. 6.2.3, 7.1.4, and 7.3.1 PICC, which favour keeping a contract alive despite hardship or breach of contractual obligations. These provisions cannot be regarded as an expression of contract law values that are globally recognized; see the Notes to Art. 6:111 PECL; *PICC-Commentary*/Schelhaas, Art. 7.1.4 [2].

[126] Bonell, *International Restatement*, 31 ff., 45 ff. and *passim*.

more, they do not reveal to what degree the provisions in question are actually understood as descriptive or prescriptive.[127] As in the case of the American Restatements (first), the strategy was apparently to blur the difference between norms and fact, between stating new and describing existing law.[128]

2. Making a global contract law

If the objective of the PICC had been to become the standard authority for international commercial contracts, especially in arbitration, its success is difficult to evaluate objectively. This is largely due to the fact that different groups of actors involved in the legal administration of international commercial law apparently developed different attitudes to this instrument. Thus, whereas the Governing Council of UNIDROIT recently claimed that the 'success in practice of the UNIDROIT Principles ... surpassed the most optimistic expectations',[129] a more distanced and neutral commentator emphasized that 'business people and practitioners have ... been slow to embrace the PICC'.[130] Indeed, the majority of national lawyers are probably still not familiar with the Principles; and most national systems of international private law do not allow for a choice of the PICC, because these Principles do not meet the requirement of nation states' 'law'.[131] As a consequence, there is still little case law which was decided on the basis of the PICC.[132]

[127] See *PICC-Commentary*/Michaels, Preamble I [3] f.

[128] See Basedow, 'Die UNIDROIT-Prinzipien', 132: 'Die traditionelle Grenze zwischen Recht und Tatsachen muß verwischt und die positivistische Vorstellung, daß ... normative Texte nur dann Bindungswirkung entfalten können, wenn sie in der verfassungsrechtlichen vorgesehenen Weise zustandegekommen sind, muß überwunden werden'.

[129] Governing Council of UNIDROIT, 'Introduction to the 2004 Edition', viii.

[130] *PICC-Commentary*/Vogenauer, Introduction [41].

[131] For a thorough comparative overview, see *PICC-Commentary*/Michaels, Preamble I [51] ff., also with references to contrary scholarly opinions, which have, however, only rarely convinced the respective courts.

[132] For an overview see Bonell, *UNIDROIT Principles in Practice*; the record is updated at <http://www.unilex.info/dynasite.cfm?dssid=2377&dsmid=13617>. Another reason is, of course, that most arbitration awards are not published for reasons of confidentiality. Bonell estimates that 'the total number of awards referring in one way or another to the UNIDROIT Principles amounts to an average of 15 per year': *loc. cit.*, xii.

Indeed, choosing the PICC or only a non-national legal standard continues to be exceptional.[133] This may be a sobering finding, at least if one assumes that choice of law is normally well-considered and that the PICC are addressed, first of all, to the international business community.[134]

Despite this reluctance on the practitioners' side, however, the PICC have today become a well acknowledged instrument of international arbitration. From an international arbitrator's perspective, 'the PICC are the most comprehensive and regularly updated statement of internationally recognized legal rules applicable to international commercial contracts'.[135] They may therefore be regarded as an appropriate legal instrument for deciding disputes of international commerce. Indeed, there is evidence that arbitrators are increasingly inclined to apply the Principles if the parties' choice of law allows them to do so.[136] Of course, the parties' intentions will always be given priority. Nonetheless, there is abundant case law on arbitration tribunals and national courts taking the PICC as an evidence of transnational law in those cases where the parties had chosen the *lex mercatoria* or 'general principles'.[137] Of course, in such a case a tribunal must assess whether the specific provision of the PICC indeed reflects a 'common core of current global contract law'.[138] Yet, this is a somewhat fictitious notion as there is neither a well-defined body of global commercial

[133] This point is emphasized by *PICC-Commentary*/Vogenauer, Introduction [40] f.; see also Oser, *A Governing Law?*, 28 f.; Dasser, 'Mouse or Monster?', 139 ff. In fact, the actual number of courts' decisions and reported arbitration awards applying the PICC may even be in decline; see the record at <http://www.unilex.info/dynasite.cfm?dssid=2377&dsmid=13618&x=1>, which reports only eight cases for 2008 (as of 12 November 2009).

[134] Cf. PICC Preamble (*Purpose of the Principles*):

'(1) These Principles set forth general rules for international commercial contracts.
(2) They shall be applied when the parties have agreed that their contract be governed by them.
(3) They may be applied . . . '. See also the Comments 4 to the Preamble.

[135] *PICC-Commentary*/Scherer, Preamble II [27].

[136] Bortolotti, 'The UNIDROIT Principles', 142.

[137] *PICC-Commentary*/Scherer, Preamble II [18], with further references; cf. also [38]; Bortolotti, 'The UNIDROIT Principles', 150 f.; Oser, *A Governing Law?*, 30 f., 49 ff.; *PICC-Commentary*/Michaels, Preamble I [65] ff., with further references.

[138] *PICC-Commentary*/Scherer, Preamble II [18].

law nor a sufficiently broad common core of national laws on international contracts.[139] At the same time, it is normally anything but evident what the parties exactly wished to refer to when they referred to the *lex mercatoria* or 'general principles'. Thus, it is not surprising to see arbitrators in such cases falling back on the PICC.

Furthermore, arbitration tribunals have often applied the PICC as a neutral law or default law in case of an absence of a choice of law,[140] especially where arbitration involves a state;[141] and the PICC are also used as an instrument to supplement an incomplete *lex contractus*.[142] What is more, as the PICC have been formulated independently of national governmental influence, they are apparently seen as a neutral standard of transnational justice and as an expression of a global legal consensus.[143] Indeed, arbitrators even relied on the PICC when they had been asked to decide *ex aequo et bono* or as *amiables compositeurs*.[144] Perhaps even more importantly, the PICC have been used by arbitrators as a 'conceptual matrix' for analysing and applying domestic and uniform law,[145] they may be applied as 'a set of backup provisions',[146] and they are taken as a standard for validating, or controlling, decisions that have been reached under domestic law.[147] Even if the rules actually applied in such cases are still those of domestic law, and if the recourse to the PICC may in a formal sense be regarded as an *obiter dictum*,[148] they have thus become an expression of what is regarded as a transnational standard of contractual justice. It follows, according to

[139] Cf. Dasser, 'Mouse or Monster?', 132 ff.

[140] Marella, 'Choice of Law in Third-Millennium Arbitrations', 1156 ff.; *PICC-Commentary*/Scherer, Preamble II [27], both with ample further references.

[141] *PICC-Commentary*/Scherer, Preamble II [35].

[142] *PICC-Commentary*/Scherer, Preamble II [38].

[143] Cf. Brödermann, 'The Growing Importance of the UNIDROIT Principles', 756 ff.; Oser, *A Governing Law?*, 57 ff., 154; more reluctantly Bortolotti, 'The UNIDROIT Principles', 143 ff.

[144] *PICC-Commentary*/Scherer, Preamble II [64] ff. with references.

[145] Marella, 'Choice of Law in Third-Millennium Arbitrations', 1167 ff., 1173 with examples.

[146] *PICC-Commentary*/Scherer, Preamble II [60].

[147] *PICC-Commentary*/Scherer, Preamble II [55] f.; Marella, 'Choice of Law in Third-Millennium Arbitrations', 1169, with examples, where the PICC were used for giving 'transnational status' to decisions reached under domestic law.

[148] This point is emphasized by *PICC-Commentary*/Scherer, Preamble II [57]; *PICC-Commentary*/Vogenauer, Introduction [40]; cf. also *PICC-Commentary*/Vogenauer, Art. 1,7 [23] ff.

some observers, that the PICC are even changing the value basis of international commercial contract law.[149]

All this reveals again a remarkable similarity with the use of Justinian's *Corpus iuris* during the *ius commune.*[150] Clearly, jurists must give priority to particular legislation, be it because the parties have chosen to do so, or because there is specific statutory law backed by the political authority of a town or guild or by a modern parliamentarian legislator.[151] But the non-legislative reference text is nonetheless treated as an authoritative legal standard. It is therefore applied subsidiarily and it informs the interpretation of a particular law. Indeed, the parallel with the status of the *Corpus iuris* is confirmed by the fact that the PICC have proved extremely influential on legislative reforms of contract laws in many parts of the world.[152] Although the PICC are no model law, such a use was clearly intended by its authors when the PICC went 'beyond the boundaries of party autonomy' in their new edition of 2004.[153] This function was originally considered supplemental only; yet, today, it may have become a main aspect of the PICC in the actual global reality.[154] In 2007, the use of the Principles was also recommended by UNCITRAL;[155] and the PICC are increasingly regarded in scholarly discourse as a major textual authority of global commercial contract law.[156] Today, they are seen as 'General Principles of Law': as an instrument for the interpretation and supplementation of uniform and national law.[157]

[149] Berger, 'UNIDROIT Principles and the new *lex mercatoria*'.

[150] Concurring Michaels, 'Umdenken für die UNIDROIT-Prinzipien'.

[151] Above at 33 f.

[152] *PICC-Commentary*/Michaels, Preamble I [118] ff. with a thorough overview; cf. also the contributions to Cashin Ritaine and Lein (eds), *The UNIDROIT Principles 2004*.

[153] Bonell, *International Restatement*, 78 ff. Examples are rules of three-person relationships, such as the assignment of rights, and rules on limitation periods, which are normally beyond the parties' autonomy.

[154] *PICC-Commentary*/Michaels, Preamble I [118].

[155] 'The United Nations Commission on International Trade Law,...(c)ommends the use of the Unidroit Principles 2004, as appropriate, for their intended purposes'; see *PICC-Commentary*/Michaels, Preamble I [99].

[156] Cf. Heidemann, *Methodology of Uniform Contract Law*, 143 ff. and *passim*: 'source of law'.

[157] Basedow, 'Uniform Law Conventions and the UNIDROIT Principles', 133 ff., 135; Burkart, *Interpretatives Zusammenwirken*, 209–253. More reluctantly, though with regret, Ferrari, in: Schwenzer (ed.), *Schlechtriem/Schwenzer*, Art. 7 [59] ff. For national

It is therefore not surprising that the PICC have become the object of a genuine doctrinal *Commentary on the UNIDROIT Principles of International Commercial Contracts*, edited in 2009 by Stefan Vogenauer and Jan Kleinheisterkamp. Since the days of the commentaries to the *Digest*, this is probably the first major non-official commentary on a non-legislative reference text;[158] and in the same way as those earlier commentaries treated the Roman texts as the actual law, this modern commentary treats its reference text as if it were binding legislation.[159] The authors of this commentary, mostly international legal scholars, but also some arbitrators, are impartial representatives of the legal profession in that none of them was involved in drafting the PICC or otherwise has a particular personal interest in promoting their use. Yet, in effect, this is precisely, what they do by elevating the PICC to the status of an authoritative textual basis of global contract law and by furthering the application of the Principles in legal practice. Thus, the claim that the contributors to this commentary 'did not subscribe to a uniform agenda'[160] may easily be misunderstood. The commentary is not just a piece of disinterested academic work. Its authors do more than objectively describe the PICC's doctrinal structure and compare it with other legal systems. Rather, they significantly contribute to the making of a global commercial contract law by complementing the PICC's text with a body of exegetic and comparative doctrinal learning[161] and also with practical recommendations as to how the PICC should be used in legal practice.[162] Hence,

law see the references in n. 71 above; *PICC-Commentary*/Michaels, Preamble I [88] ff., [100] ff., [111] ff., with further references.

[158] The early textbooks on the American Restatements (above n. 40) were written by the authors of the respective Restatements; they therefore had more the character of 'official' explanations.

[159] *PICC-Commentary*/Vogenauer and Kleinheisterkamp, Preface, viii: 'for the purposes of this commentary we treat the Principles as we would treat a binding contract law . . . '.

[160] *PICC-Commentary*/Vogenauer and Kleinheisterkamp, Preface, viii.

[161] Thus, the commentators make interpretative use of the drafting history of the provisions (since about 2000, the materials have been generally accessible on the webpage of UNIDROIT <http://www.unidroit.org>, among the Institute's annually ordered Documents, under the heading 'Study L'); and they explain, mostly on the basis of broad comparative learning, whether the provisions are in fact an expression of a global consensus or rather a specific national rule or even an innovative new solution.

[162] *PICC-Commentary*/Vogenauer and Kleinheisterkamp, Preface, viii.

its authors must be seen as agents of a new global commercial *ius commune*.

Thus, not unlike the standard glosses to the medieval reference texts, the commentary transforms the rather abstract textual authority of the PICC into an applicable system of rules. As a result, it is not an overstatement saying that there is today again a transnational system of commercial contract law.[163] Its textual basis was formulated by UNIDROIT, yet the law is actually made by the legal profession. The legal profession recognizes the text as a standard for national legislation and it fleshes it out doctrinally into a comprehensive body of law. In short: the legal profession makes the PICC the textual basis of a transnational commercial contract law.

IV. Some Results

It would be a mistake simply to equate the American Restatements, the PECL, and the PICC in their being both transjurisdictional and non-legislative restatements of private law. After all, there are important differences, not only as to the social and legal background of these texts, but also with regard to their function and effect on legal practice. Thus, the impact and authority of the American Restatements can only be understood in the historical context of American common law at the beginning of the 20th century. They were generally accepted as an appropriate answer from the legal profession to what was perceived as a profound crisis in the common law. The PICC are singular in filling in a textual vacuum of global law, such a textual vacuum having become rare in modern law. And the PECL are more an expression of legal idealism than an answer to practical legal needs.

Thus, it is perhaps not surprising that only the American Restatements actually succeed in *making* legal authority. The authority of the PECL and of the PICC was not immediately brought into effect by their authors, but developed *ex post*, and—in the case of the PICC—in a way which significantly differed from

[163] Cf. Metzger, *Extra legem, intra ius*, 554.

their authors' original intentions.[164] Hence, the authority of these texts can clearly not be equated. Whereas the American Restatements were not only recognized as legally authoritative by academic lawyers, but also by the judiciary and at the bar, the PECL's authority is limited to the scholarly legal discourse. The PICC's authority is again of different kind. As far as it reaches, namely in the field of global commercial contract law, it is significantly stronger than the authority of the PECL. Here, the PICC are not only recognized as authoritative among scholars; they are also *applied* in practice by arbitrators. Still, their authority has reached neither the different national legal professions nor the global business community: actors, who still prefer national solutions for choice-of-law agreements.

[164] Michaels, 'Umdenken für die UNIDROIT-Prinzipien'.

PART II

ANALYSIS

Chapter 3

Textual Authorities: a Classification

The texts presented in the two previous chapters were formulated and recognized as textual foundations of the law at different times, on different continents, and in strongly divergent legal cultures. It is all the more remarkable, therefore, that there are—despite the many important differences, of course—rather obvious structural similarities. Thus, lawyers have again and again acknowledged non-legislative textual authorities besides the 'normal' statutory law that was backed by some political domination. What is more, there are significant parallels between the use of the American Restatements, the PICC, and the PECL today and the legal practice during the times of the *ius commune*. Indeed, it has often been emphasized and it was shown above[1] that the authority of the *Corpus iuris civilis* strongly varied in time and space. Sometimes the Roman texts were used as immediately applicable law, whereas at other times and places, they were not more than a basis text for teaching purposes and a common reference for scholarly discourse. Exactly the same can be observed with the modern non-legislative codifications.

Even if it is the legal profession, rather than the political process, which ultimately determines the legal authority of legal texts,[2] the law has always been, and of course continues to be, responsive to political, social, and cultural circumstances. Thus, the PECL may be seen as the legal system's response to the fundamental political and economic changes of Europe resulting from the political integration of Europe in the second half of the 20th century; here—as so often—the law may assume a leading role in a political process. The

[1] See 28–41.

[2] Cf. also Luhmann, *Recht der Gesellschaft*, 414 ff. / *Law as a Social System*, 362 ff.; Duve, 'Mit der Autorität gegen die Autoritäten?', 242 ff.

medieval establishment of non-legislative texts of authority was a response to the fundamental social and cultural changes following the Papal revolution; and likewise the PICC respond to the economic globalization and the development of a global law of commercial contracts. Indeed, whereas national legislative codifications, such as the French *Code civil*, the Italian *Codice civile*, or the German *Bürgerliches Gesetzbuch*, have mostly been an expression of socio-political consolidation, non-legislative codifications may be seen—with some reservation, of course, which is always appropriate for historical generalizations—as an answer of the legal system to fundamental social, political, or economic changes. Legal systems may themselves establish or even formulate basic reference texts which are necessary for the law's administration, if the political sector proves unable, for whatever reason, to do so. This is evident in the case of the medieval textual authorities, but it can likewise be seen in the case of the modern texts.

It should not be inferred, however, that non-legislative codifications are typically a means of legal change. On the contrary: all the modern restatements discussed in the second chapter are rather conservative in substance. Indeed, the transjurisdictional character of most of the texts discussed in this book shows clearly that private law may be independent from political and social changes. Indeed, such processes always had and usually have local or regional aspects. Here, private law may develop its own specific normative rationality that is independent of such local processes; this becomes especially important in times of rapid social change. Thus, the American Restatements have been plausibly described as a means of protecting and strengthening an old idea of American law which by large parts of the legal profession was felt to be threatened,[3] when on the one hand the codification movement failed and left the practical desire for legal certainty unfulfilled, and when on the other hand the critical movement of realist lawyers fundamentally questioned the legal process.

From a jurisprudential point of view, these observations cast doubt on the 20th-century attempts to reconstruct the validity of private law on the basis of a single unifying and hence typically

[3] Cf. Gilmore, *Ages of American Law*, 72 ff.

state-oriented *Grundnorm* or rule of recognition.[4] True, such models may well capture what lawyers believe—or pretend to believe—to be the intellectual or constitutional basis of private law. From a purely logical, analytical point of view, such a model may even be defensible as long as it is possible, at least in theory, to reconstruct strict hierarchies between different texts of authority and to distinguish plausibly between the law on the one hand and the law's application and non-legal regulation on the other hand. Yet, as the discussion of the 'validity' of the *Corpus iuris civilis* as a textual basis of the *ius commune* has shown, there may be important differences between the constitutional assumptions and the actual practice of professional jurists.[5]

Of course, the authority of a state's legislation is today normally beyond dispute and the sources of private law may even relate exclusively to the state's domination. However, this would be rather exceptional.[6] It follows that a more adequate model of the implicit constitutional basis of private law must usually consist of a complex system of different reference texts that are acknowledged as the authoritative bases of private law. For an American lawyer, this system at least consists of the relevant state's common and statutory law, the relevant Federal common and statutory law, and finally of the non-legislative Restatements of the American Law Institute.[7] For European lawyers, such a system is based on national codifications, statutory legislation, and on human rights, as acknowledged in the national constitutions and in international discourse; this system is complemented with the European Treaties and the quasi-state legislation of the European Union,[8] as well as with the judicial authorities of all these systems, and, finally—perhaps—with international non-legislative authorities, such as the PECL and the PICC.

[4] See above at 2 f., 41ff. Not all proponents of such models related the law to the state; this is especially true for H.L.A. Hart. However, as has been seen above, the idea of a unifying rule of recognition is most plausible in legal systems which are controlled by the modern state.

[5] Above at 35ff., 39 f.

[6] Cf. also Vogenauer, 'Sources of Law and Legal Method in Comparative Law', 881 ff.

[7] Eisenberg, 'Concept of National Law'.

[8] MacCormick, 'The Maastricht-Urteil', 262 ff. describing the state of law in Europe as '... pluralistic rather than monistic and interactive rather than hierarchical ... distinct but interacting systems of law'.

What is more, models of the legal system which are based on the formal distinction between the law backed by the state's domination (legislation and judge-made law) on the one hand, and non-legislative legal writing on the other cannot adequately account for the fact that non-legislative texts may assume similar or even greater authority than legislation in actual legal practice. Indeed, nor can they account for the fact that the authority of all legislation ultimately depends on its reception in professional discourse.[9] As has been seen above, private law is constituted by the texts which are recognized by the legal profession as the basic sources of private law;[10] and the legal profession may even recognize non-political, state-independent actors like the American Law Institute as 'little legislators'.[11] The purpose of this chapter is therefore to formulate, as a systematic summary of the previous two chapters and as a conceptual basis for the following final chapter, a more adequate, ideal-typical[12] classification of different forms of textual legal authorities. This classification rests on an abstract conceptual distinction of political domination, or legislative authority, on the one hand and non-legislative, or professional, authority on the other hand. This distinction, however, is analytical rather than descriptive in nature. It must therefore not be paralleled with the distinction between legislating on and applying the law. Indeed, it has been seen in the previous chapters that the legislation / application distinction does not provide an adequate description of complex legal reality. Rather, there are different forms of legislative and of non-legislative, professional authorities. It will be seen that the ideas of political domination and non-legislative professional authority are realized by these textual authorities in varying degree. For example, some forms of parliamentarian legislation are much more an expression of political domination than others; and in most legal systems, the authority of

[9] Cf. Snyder, 'Private Lawmaking', 403 ff.

[10] Eisenberg, 'Concept of National Law', 1231 ff., 1246 ff., discussing some ambiguity in Hart's concept of law; cf. also Snyder, 'Private Lawmaking', 403 ff., who emphasizes that non-legislative rules may be mandatory (410 ff.).

[11] Snyder, 'Private Lawmaking', 376.

[12] The concept of an ideal type (*Idealtypus*) is taken here in its orginial, Weberian sense; see Weber, *Wirtschaft und Gesellschaft,* 1 ff., 9 f.; id., '"Objektivität" sozialwissenschaftlicher und sozialpolitischer Erkenntnis', 190 ff.

judicial decisions oscillates between binding precedent, or domination, and persuasive authority, or professionalism.

I. Political Domination

1. Legislation

Legislative authority, or domination, is the sovereign's power legitimately to determine the law according to its free political choice.[13] Thus, for Ulpian, the Emperor's will was the law;[14] and, in the same spirit, Baldus later argued that the modern statutory law of his time was not based on rational argument or principles of natural justice, but on the sovereigns' will and command alone.[15] Modern constitutional systems seem to have constrained such unlimited power. It is no longer the Parliament's will as such that is binding in law, but rather the Parliament's will as far as it has been expressed in the appropriate legal form. A typical example is a statute introducing new policy.

Seen from a different perspective, however, modern parliaments appear even less constrained than pre-modern Kings and Princes in forming their political will. Pre-parliamentarian legislation was expected to include a formal justification of the specific provisions, usually in the form of a preamble:[16] a practice that has been readopted, in the 20th century, by the totalitarian regimes of Germany[17] and—somewhat irritatingly—also by the European Union.[18] In contrast,

[13] Weber, 'Die drei Typen der legitimen Herrschaft'; cf. also id., *Wirtschaft und Gesellschaft*, 28 f., 122 ff.; for the English terminology, id., *Economy and Society* I, 53 f., 212 ff.: 'domination' is different from 'power', as it is defined 'as the probability that ... commands ... will be obeyed by a given group of persons'; it is normally based on 'the belief in *legitimacy*'.

[14] Ulpian D. 1,4,1 pr.: 'Quod principi placuit, legis habet vigorem'; see above at 1.

[15] See above at 35.

[16] See Immel, 'Typologie der Gesetzgebung', 26 ff.; Fögen, *Lied vom Gesetz*, 2007, 9 ff.; cf. also Rethorn, 'Funktionen von Präambeln', 298 ff.

[17] Fögen, *Lied vom Gesetz*, 15 ff.

[18] Art. 253 (now 296) EC. For critique, see Fögen, *Lied vom Gesetz*, 23: 'Es (the *prooemium*) ist ein rückständiges Lied, das absolutistischen und totalitären Singsang nachahmt und fortsetzt. ... Es ist ein intrigantes Lied, weil es den Völkern Europas vormacht, was die Völker Europas wollen'.

no such obligation or practice exists in modern parliamentarian systems, like England, Germany, or France. From a legal (rather than a political) point of view, democratic sovereigns are not expected to offer good reasons or explanations for their legislation.[19] They may well feel entitled to make the law on the basis of the majority's free decision. Within the limits of a constitution or other superior law, such legislation transforms the sovereign's political will into a binding legal command. It is binding not for its inherent rationality, but for the sole reason that the political legislator is constitutionally empowered to make the law according to its arbitrary choice.

2. Codifications

Modern codifications provide for comprehensive and therefore systematic legislation over a substantial part of the law. Seen from a formal, constitutional perspective, such codifications may be regarded as an expression of political domination in the same sense as statutory legislation. Modern codifications are of course based on the sovereign's will; they replace former law with a new textual basis; and often there is even a strong political will for having such a codification.[20] Yet, as has been seen above, the normative substance of a codification is normally not determined by parliaments and governments. Codifications are typically drafted in the spirit of a largely declaratory restatement of the law.[21] Usually, therefore, the legislator relies on professional advice and often even adds non-legislative, professional authority to a new code.[22] If governments or parliaments decide to change the law in substance or to introduce

[19] Cf. Waldhoff, 'Begründungspflichten des parlamentarischen Gesetzgebers', 329 ff., with further references on the actual discussion.

[20] For the present debate about a codification of European private law, see the European Parliament's 'Resolution on action to bring into line the private law of the Member States', A2–157/89 [1989] OJ C158/400; 'Resolution on the harmonization of certain sectors of the private law of the Member States', A3-0329/94 [1994] OJ C205/518. See also, from 2000, the 'Resolution on the Commission's Annual Work Programme 2000', B5-0228/2000, the 'Resolution on the Commission's work programme for 2000', B5-0229/2000, and the 'Resolution on the Commission's annual legislative programme for 2000' B5-0230/2000, all [2000] OJ C377/323.

[21] Above at 17f.

[22] See below at 104.

some new legal policy, this is done more easily, and more appropriately, outside of the codification, in some special statute, regulation, or directive.[23] Accordingly, it seems that the English Law Commission has always been working on the assumption that an eventual codification of the law must be preceded by substantial legal reform.[24] Thus, with regard to the law's substance, codifications cannot be regarded as a full expression of political domination.

3. Judicial decisions

Legislators are not the only actors who are vested with the state's authority to make the law. Judges, too, may similarly exert some sort of domination; this is true despite the fact that judicial decisions present themselves as interpretations and applications of the existing law. In every case where judges are given discretion in deciding a case, and where their decisions will have the force of binding precedent, they are vested with law-making authority. Of course, this authority cannot be put on an equal footing with the legislator's authority. Whereas legislators are bound only by constitutional and, perhaps, international law, judges are bound by the whole legal system. What is more, even in cases that are not fully determined by legislation and precedent, judges are normally expected to give legal, rather than political or moral, reasons for their decisions.[25] They are not permitted to develop the law on the basis of politically contested policies. Yet, although the weight of a judicial decision in legal discourse largely depends on its professional qualities, the formal authority of judicial decisions is not limited to professional argument. Between the parties, judicial decisions are strictly binding as an expression of the state's domination; and as far as there is a strict rule of precedent, judicial decisions are also binding on other courts and thus generate abstract legal rules. This is sufficient reason for placing and analysing judicial decisions in the context of political domination rather than in the context of professional authority.

[23] Noll, *Gesetzgebungslehre*, 214 ff., distinguishing 'gestaltende' and 'kodifizierende Gesetzgebung'; Basedow, 'Transjurisdictional Codification', 976.

[24] A. Braun, 'English codification debate', at 4, with further references.

[25] Langenbucher, *Richterrecht*, 22 ff.; Zimmermann and Jansen, 'Quieta Movere', 305 f.

Nevertheless, it is important to realize that the Janus-faced authority of judicial decisions combines elements of domination and professional authority.

What is more, judges have again and again introduced new policies into the legal system; often, indeed, they feel free to do so and understand themselves as promoters of legal and even social change. This is especially the case in legal systems where judges are democratically elected or appointed on political terms. In such systems, judicial interventions may even impose rules that could never have been the outcome of the political process; a famous historical example is the 'invention' of judicial review by the US Supreme Court in *Marbury v Madison*.[26] Today European lawyers are similarly witnessing the European Court of Justice (ECJ) fashioning 'a judicially enforceable constitution out of international treaty law ...':[27] Indeed, the ECJ has become a powerful 'motor of European integration', when it established—against the express intention of the Member States—private enforcement of European law by introducing the direct effect of directives and by making the Member States liable against their citizens for violations of European law. Political scientists therefore regard the court as an important *political* actor in the process of unifying Europe.[28]

II. Non-Legislative, Professional Authorities

Whereas legislative authority can be characterized as domination, i.e. the sovereign's power to make the law according to its free political choice, non-legislative authority in the law does not contain such an element of arbitrariness. Non-legislative authority is essentially derivative in character: being representative in nature, it depends on and derives from some kind of legislation or else pre-existing legal

[26] 5 U.S. 137; see Friedman, *History*, 79 ff., 86 ff.

[27] Stone Sweet, *Governing with Judges*, 153–193: 'The European Court of Justice ... is the most powerful and influential supranational court in world history' (153). 'In today's multi-tiered European polity, the sovereignty of the legislature, and the primacy of national executives, are dead. In concert or in rivalry, European legislators govern with judges' (193); see also Haltern, *Europarecht* [594] ff.

[28] Stone Sweet, *Governing with Judges*, especially 153 ff.; id., *Judicial Construction of Europe*, especially 64 ff.

authority.[29] Hence, legal actors without a claim to the state's domination normally present their work not as making but as describing or representing the existing law. Yet, it would be misleading to characterize non-legislative authority as purely 'descriptive' in nature: if it were, it would be no authority at all.

Nonetheless, an important difference between domination and non-legislative, professional authority consists in domination being prospective in that it can typically be captured by a formal rule of recognition which, for instance, makes future legislation or judgments binding upon their addressees.[30] In contrast, non-legislative authority is essentially retrospective. The non-legislative, professional authority of a legal text derives exclusively from its subsequent recognition in the legal process; it cannot be determined in advance.

1. Doctrine

Doctrinal books of authority, such as treatises and commentaries, may be taken as an ideal-typical example of non-legislative professional authority. Even if such books present themselves as an explanation of the legislation to which they relate, their authority depends solely on the status which is assigned to them by the participants to the legal discourse. Doctrinal authority is created autopoietically by the legal profession. Nevertheless, such authority may be remarkably strong. Since the days of Accursius' Standard Gloss to the *Corpus iuris civilis*, lawyers have again and again equated doctrinal books of authority with the law.[31] Indeed, for centuries many courts equated the gloss with the law;[32] and until the 18th century, a *communis opinio doctorum* was generally regarded as an argument sufficient in itself to justify a legal decision.[33] Similarly,

[29] Ernst, 'Gelehrtes Recht', 10 f., 15 ff. and *passim*.

[30] But see the observations above at 45 ff. with regard to the changing authority of legislative codifications in the 19th and 20th centuries.

[31] On the autopoietical inner-legal creation of authority in the form of *communis opinio*, see Drosdeck, *Die herrschende Meinung*, 78 ff., 89 ff., 99 ff., 111 ff., 134 ff.; cf. also Duve, 'Mit der Autorität gegen die Autoritäten?'.

[32] Weimar, 'Accursius', 19.

[33] J. Schröder, 'Communis opinio', 405. See also Koschaker, *Europa und das römische Recht*, 99 ff.; Duve, 'Mit der Autorität gegen die Autoritäten?', 243 ff.

the German commentary published under the name of *Palandt* is today taken by many lower court judges to be stating the law.[34]

Doctrinal writers do not usually explicitly propose or justify a new norm or legal principle. Instead, their business is normally to describe, represent, or reconstruct norms already existing in the legal system. Indeed, the 'descriptive meaning (beschreibender Sinn)' of the normative propositions of legal science has puzzled legal thinkers during much of the 20th century.[35] Thus, H.L.A. Hart compared doctrinal work plausibly with the translation of commands that are issued in a foreign language.[36] But doctrinal writers never simply describe one legal command or provision after another; rather, they integrate and reconstruct a complex body of legislative or judicial norms within an orderly intellectual system.[37] Hence, a doctrinal treatise or commentary usually contains much more than a mere 'translation' of legislation.[38] It enriches the law with structure, coherence, and meaning.[39] Usually, it also contains normative conclusions that may be plausible, but cannot be achieved by means of logical deduction alone.[40] Doctrine should therefore be characterized, more satisfactorily, as a precarious mix of descriptive, conceptual, and normative elements.[41] Hence, authority matters: doctrinal treatises and commentaries have often influenced and changed the law, and they continue to do so.

2. Compilations

Doctrinal works, however, are not the only texts of non-legislative authority in the law. Another form of non-legislatively authoritative legal text is a compilation: a rearrangement of individual statutory norms of independent prior authority. Compilations put a number of individual, historically and intellectually unrelated expressions of

[34] See below 121 ff.

[35] Kelsen, *Reine Rechtslehre*, 77 / *Pure Theory*, 75; on this theory see especially Golding, 'Kelsen', 357 ff., 361 ff. See also Funke, *Allgemeine Rechtslehre*, 212, 220 f., with further references on earlier authors, such as Bierling und Somló making similar points.

[36] Hart, 'Kelsen Visited', 287 ff., 293 f.

[37] Hart, 'Kelsen Visited', 294 f.; Golding, 'Kelsen', 361 ff., 365 f.

[38] Cf. Golding, 'Kelsen', 365.

[39] See Herberger, 'Rangstufen der Rechtsdogmatik', 69 ff.

[40] Cf. also Ernst, 'Gelehrtes Recht', 28 ff.

[41] Jansen, 'Dogmatik', 753 ff.

the sovereign's will or other texts of authority into an orderly system, yet without any thorough doctrinal 'translation'. Nevertheless, such a compilation may achieve a significance that goes far beyond making the law more easily accessible: compilations may fundamentally reshape a legal system. A remarkable example was the *Decretum Gratiani*, which became the foundation of Canon law despite being written as a private scholar's non-legislative compilation.[42]

By making decisions about which norms are to be put into the compilatory text and which norms are to be excluded, compilations determine what counts as important in a legal system and what is still regarded as good law on the one hand, and which norms no longer need to be taken into consideration on the other. What is more, compilations mutually relate formerly unrelated norms; they thus put isolated provisions into a legal context, and they add a basic intellectual structure to a legal system. All this unavoidably influences the meaning of the individual norms that are collected in the compilatory text. Finally, compilations cannot achieve coherence without making normative decisions—explicitly or implicitly—in the many inevitable cases of contradictions and tensions that characterize a historically grown body of unrelated statutory norms. All this could clearly be seen in the case of the *Decretum Gratiani*,[43] and it can be seen, today, in the Acquis Group's *Acquis Principles*.[44]

Compilations have not only been produced by scholars, independently of a political mandate, but often also by legislative authorities. Thus, Justinian compiled the doctrinal authorities of classical Roman law and the decisions of the Roman Emperors into his *Digest* and his *Codex* respectively. He thereby wished to ensure that the legal discourse was based on one single authoritative text under his political control. Thus, he connected the political authority of his person with the non-legislative, 'academic' authority of the leading jurists of classical Roman law.[45] Today, too, legal compilations are rarely made outside the political sector of

[42] Above at 21ff.

[43] For details see Thier, 'Dynamische Schriftlichkeit', 15 ff., 27 ff.

[44] Cf. Jansen and Zimmermann, 'Restating the Acquis communautaire?', 520 ff.

[45] Jansen, 'Traditionsbegründung', 543; Wallinga, *Tanta / ΔΕΔΩΚΕΝ*, 103 ff.

the states' administrations.[46] Yet, a more recent example of a non-legislative compilation is the Acquis Group's *Acquis Principles*,[47] which put the inconsistent body of EU law into a new, systematic order.

3. Restatements

A final, third type of non-legislatively, professionally authoritative texts is the 'restatement' in a wide, generic sense: non-legislative statements of norms that purport to be largely a description (or re-statement) of pre-existing, though inconsistently ordered, law. As has been seen above, such restatements are not a unique feature of the American legal system. At the end of the 20th century, the idea has been transplanted to Europe and to a global level;[48] earlier examples were the Saxon Mirror and similar medieval law books.[49] By presenting the law as a more or less coherent system of rules, such restatements, too, are unavoidably constructive in nature; this is especially relevant for transnational restatements of the law that intend to overcome the present differences between different national legal systems.[50]

Restatements are genuinely non-legislative codifications. They comprehensively lay down the rules of a large body of the law; and they do this, usually, in a form that is more structured and consistent than the previous law. At times, it may be difficult to draw a clear distinction between a restatement and a modern compilation. For example, the Acquis Group understands its Principles not as a compilation, but as a restatement.[51] Now, there is of course no 'official' definition of the concept of a restatement, yet there are important differences between the *Acquis Principles* and the American Restatements and other restatements such as the PECL and the

[46] For some recent legislative compilations, see Basedow, 'Transjurisdictional Codification', 974 f.

[47] The Research Group on the Existing EC Private Law (ed.), *Acquis Principles. Contract I*; see Jansen and Zimmermann, 'Restating the Acquis communautaire?'.

[48] Above at 59 ff., 66 ff.

[49] Above at 23 ff.

[50] See, for the PECL, Smits, 'PECL and the Harmonisation of Private Law in Europe', 580 ff.; for the PICC, above at 67, 69 f.

[51] Ajani and Schulte-Nölke, 'The Principles of the Existing EC Contract Law'.

PICC. Those differences may help to clarify the idea of a modern restatement. Thus, while restatements typically claim to elaborate the common principles of *different* legal systems or jurisdictions, the *Acquis Principles* are designed to provide a coherent reconstruction, or systematic revision, of a body of law that has been created by one and the same sovereign. What is more, while the *Acquis Principles'* formulation of individual norms is often very close to the wording of the original European directive, restatements usually offer new formulations; they never base the formulation of norms on the wording of one single legislator.

Like compilations, restatements have to make normative choices with regard to private-law values.[52] Nevertheless, they typically lack legal argument, and—unlike compilations, which typically incorporate legislative authorities—restatements often don't even cite authorities. Historical examples are the Saxon Mirror and the first series of the American Restatements; the same observation can today be made in the case of the PICC.[53] Indeed, the authority of such a text may even include elements of quasi-legislative domination. Restatements may be binding *ratione imperii*, if the legal profession regards their author(s) as empowered legitimately to make the law.[54] This attitude may be taken as an explanation for the more recent controversy concerning the question of whether UNIDROIT was entitled to give its authorizing *nihil obstat* to the PICC,[55] or whether the European institutions could authoritatively publish a 'political' CFR in a non-legislative form.[56]

[52] See, for the PECL, Hesselink, 'Choices Made by the Lando Commission', 107–124.

[53] *PICC-Commentary*/Vogenauer, Introduction [21], [23], [27]. The PECL, in contrast, do contain references to national legal systems in their comparative notes; these are meant to support the principles' claim to be restating the law.

[54] See below at 135.

[55] See for such critique Raeschke-Kessler, 'Should an Arbitrator apply the UNIDROIT-Principles?', 172 f.; Kessedjian, 'Un exercice de rénovation des sources du droit', 651 f. Contra Bonell, *International Restatement*, 38.

[56] Cf. von Bar and Schulte-Nölke, 'Gemeinsamer Referenzrahmen', 168; Hähnchen, 'Rechtsform des CFR'; Jansen, 'Traditionsbegründung', 542 with further references.

III. Conclusion

After all, there are few instances of pure domination or of pure professional authority in actual legal practice. The authority of a legal text usually results from elements of both domination and of professional quality. Only legislation on the one hand and purely doctrinal work on the other do not include complementary authority elements; and the authority of judicial decisions is truly Janus-faced. Thus, domination and professional authority are ideal-typological notions: conceptual tools that may be helpful for analysing and understanding the legal process, but should not be misunderstood as concepts depicting or representing the legal reality.

Chapter 4

The Making of Legal Authority

On the basis of previous observations and clarifications, the final chapter of this book shall address the question of how legal authority is made. More specifically, it shall be asked how non-legislative reference texts can achieve such a high degree of authority that the participants in legal discourse may rely on such texts as an ultimate source of the law. Even if a full answer to this question is not possible, because the legal authority of an individual reference text is always the result of an individual historical process of recognition that cannot be fully explained on the basis of abstract theory alone, and because such processes are often connected with social struggle for influence, wealth, and reputation,[1] it may be possible, nevertheless, to identify and better understand some factors contributing to the authority of a legal reference text.

I. Profession-Related Factors

Now, in specifically addressing the question as to the factors explaining the recognition of a legal reference-text's authority, one theory that has often been used for explaining the authority of Roman law during the *ius commune*[2] must be rejected from the outset. Legal authority cannot be explained by a text's being used in academia and academic teaching. Such a theory simply begs the question why the text was treated as authority in the law schools: for instance, the professors' reasons for using such texts for teaching

[1] For the medieval *ius commune,* see Kantorowicz, 'Kingship under the Impact of Scientific Jurisprudence', 90 ff.; Görich, 'Fragen zum Kontext der roncalischen Gesetze', 318 ff.; for the modern 'lex mercatoria' Dezalay and Garth, *Dealing in Virtue.*

[2] See e.g. Coing, 'Europäische Privatrechtsgeschichte', 7 ff.

purposes, and the motives of students to accept such a practice by attending this kind of lecture and the universities where professors taught on such a basis.

Clearly, the authority of a text never depends on its intrinsic qualities alone: both text-related and profession-related factors contribute to its force. Replacing, or only enriching, former legal authority with a new basic reference text is always 'costly' for the legal profession. Lawyers will have to make themselves acquainted with the new texts and with their intellectual structure. They will not be eager to do so if there is a shared feeling that their legal system works smoothly. Hence, a new reference text of legal authority will normally not be accepted if there is no need for such a change of the law. This explains the neglect of the PECL in the legal practice of many European legal systems. As long as the parochial state of private law in Europe is regarded more as an intellectual than as a practical problem, local lawyers will normally see no reason to rely on European Principles.

1. Defects in the law's administration

It follows that the perception of some kind of legal crisis or defects in the administration of the law will normally be present when a legal profession accepts a new text as an authoritative source of law. This could not only be seen with the American Restatements, which were the legal profession's answer to what was perceived of as a profound crisis of American common law,[3] but also with the *Corpus iuris civilis* and with the Saxon Mirror. The main reason for treating the *Corpus iuris* as a text of authority was probably that there was simply not enough law, and that there was no textual alternative that could be taken as a comprehensive basis of a rational legal science.[4] Similarly, the Saxon Mirror made it possible to transform the formerly oral Saxon law into a more reliable and rational written system.[5] Likewise, modern non-legislative codifications are written as bridges between diverging legal systems.[6] Thus, the PICC respond

[3] Above at 50 ff. [4] Above at 28 ff. [5] Above at 23 ff.

[6] Kessedjian, 'La codification privée', 142 f., comparing the PECL and the PICC with the American Restatements; cf. also, for the PECL, Hesselink, 'Choices Made by the Lando Commission', 126 f.

to an alleged need for a written body of genuinely transnational legal rules.[7] Their success can partly be explained by the fact that influential actors in the transnational administration of law see practical advantages in bridging their national legal systems with a truly transnational system of rules.[8] Again, these Principles remedy the evident lack of a textual basis for the growing global law of commercial contracts.

2. The legal profession's social identity

Another important profession-related factor contributing to the acceptance of a text as legal authority is apparently the social identity of the legal profession. The relevant text must be understood as representing the social entity with which the legal profession identifies.[9] Thus, Justinian's *Corpus iuris civilis* could only become the main textual authority of the *ius commune* because medieval lawyers identified the text with their idea of a Roman Empire unifying the Christian people;[10] the legend of Charlemagne's privilege[11] presented the Saxon Mirror as a specific belonging of the Saxon people; and the *Code civil* and the German BGB are famous examples of successful legislative codifications that were seen as 'cathedrals of national splendour'.[12] Similarly, an important factor contributing to the success of the American Restatements was that American scholars had never paid much attention to local state law.[13] As a

[7] See Bonell, *International Restatement*, 11: 'The present state of international contract law is far from satisfactory'.

[8] Cf. *PICC-Commentary*/Scherer, Preamble II [18]: 'Arbitrators dislike working in a vacuum ...'.

[9] See Kroppenberg, 'Mythos Kodifikation', also on the mythological narratives accompanying codifications until the present day.

[10] Calasso, 'diritto comune', 49 f., 66 f. and *passim*; Koschaker, *Europa und das römische Recht*, 69 ff.; Kantorowicz, 'Kingship under the Impact of Scientific Jurisprudence', 100 ff. But see Fögen, 'Römisches Recht und Rombilder', 59 ff., 82: '... dieses Recht brauchte kein Rom (this law did not need Rome)'.

[11] Above at 26 f.

[12] Windscheid, 'Das römische Recht in Deutschland', 48: 'Dom nationaler Herrlichkeit'. The historical literature on this point is extensive; see, among others, Wieacker, 'Der Kampf um die Nationalgesetzbücher', 84 ff.; Dölemeier, 'Kodifikationsbewegung', 1421, 1427, 1564, 1575, 1602; Jansen, *Binnenmarkt*, 19 f.

[13] Cf. Eisenberg, 'Concept of National Law', 1237 ff.; Rheinstein, 'Leader Groups', 691 ff.

result, the legal profession engaged in a national US-American legal discourse, which has been described as a 'product of a cultural aspiration to be an American nation with an American culture and an American law'.[14]

Similar ideas today inspire the European CFR process, which is based on the desire, especially among some legal scholars and politicians, to create a symbol of a European cultural identity and legal unification;[15] correspondingly, the recognition of the PECL and even of a legislative ('political') CFR as sources of law will depend on a sufficient degree of a 'uniform European mentality' among European lawyers.[16] Even in the transnational context of global law, the PICC appear to be supported by a comparable social-identity factor. Here, the profession does not identify locally with a nation, but rather with an international business community. Indeed, this may be one main reason for the frequent claim that the PICC represent a new 'lex mercatoria'.[17]

It would be clearly wrong, however, to assume that the feeling of a legal profession's identity was always an essential factor determining the recognition and rejection of textual authorities. Thus, American lawyers continued to apply English common-law sources after the Independence, even though these sources were badly tarnished as the king's law. Here, no other legal authorities were available (at least in the English language); hence, there was no feasible alternative to continuing the common-law tradition.[18] Nevertheless, the

[14] Eisenberg, 'Concept of National Law', 1242 (and f.). Cf. also Metzger, *Extra legem, intra ius*, 146 f., emphasizing in this context the strong influence of federal constitutional law on private law.

[15] See Fauvarque-Cosson, 'Faut-il un Code civil européen?', 471; Lurga, *Vereinheitlichung des Vertragsrechts*, 128 f.; Jansen, *Binnenmarkt*, 20 f., with further references.

[16] Smits, 'PECL and the Harmonisation of Private Law in Europe', 584, emphasizing, rightly, that 'harmonisation of law is always a matter of both a common text *and* a common practice' (590).

[17] Cf. the PICC, Preamble (3); Berger, 'UNIDROIT Principles and the new *lex mercatoria*'; more references in *PICC-Commentary*/Michaels, Preamble I [64] f. Thus, in 1995, when the PICC had just appeared, the Institute of International Business Law and Practice organized a conference on the topic 'UNIDROIT Principles for International Commercial Contracts: A New Lex Mercatoria?': Institute of International Business Law and Practice (ed.), *A New Lex Mercatoria?*, 1995. But see now Bonell, *International Restatement*, 208 ff.; Michaels, *loc. cit.* [9].

[18] On the discussions among American lawyers, see Friedman, *History*, 65 ff.

importance of a legal profession's identity can be seen, very clearly, as a weighty factor also explaining the failure of codifications. One example is the rather weak authority of the 19th-century German codifications.[19] Indeed, one of the factors contributing to the legal profession's reluctance towards a full recognition of the Prussian ALR (*Allgemeines Landrecht für die Preußischen Staaten*) apparently consisted in the fact that the leading scholars of the Historical School identified more with a German nation than with the Prussian state.[20] This was no German peculiarity. For example, the cool attitude of the Louisiana legal profession towards the civil code of 1808 apparently resulted from their identification with their strong Spanish tradition.[21]

II. Text-Related Factors

Whereas profession-related authority-factors depend on the state of a legal system, on the political circumstances, and on the cultural self-understanding of the legal profession, text-related factors concern the qualities of the text as such, for example its rationality and legitimacy. A remarkably conscious and thoughtful discussion of such factors can be found in the report of the Committee of 35 leading jurists on the establishment of an American Law Institute,[22] which therefore deserves some closer attention. These authors emphasized three main factors, namely authorship, procedure, and

[19] Above at 46 f.

[20] See von Savigny, *Vom Beruf unserer Zeit*, 136, 161: 'wir wollen ... Gemeinschaft der Nation und Concentration ihrer wissenschaftlichen Bestrebungen auf dasselbe Object. Für diesen Zweck verlangen sie (die Freunde eines Gesetzbuchs, N.J.) ein Gesetzbuch, was aber die gewünschte Einheit nur für die Hälfte von Deutschland hervorbringen, die andere Hälfte dagegen schärfer als vorher absondern würde. Ich sehe das rechte Mittel in einer organisch fortschreitenden Rechtswissenschaft, die der ganzen Nation gemein seyn kann'; cf. also id., *Landrechtsvorlesung 1824 I*, 10 f.; Puchta, *Cursus der Institutionen I*, 23, 27: 'So entspricht dem deutschen Volk ein deutsches Recht, wie eine deutsche Sprache, als Eigenthum aller Stämme und Zweige, in die es sich theilt. ... wenn die nationale Einheit mächtig genug ist, wird es ihr ... gelingen, die zufällige politische Trennung zu überwinden'. Cf. Haferkamp, 'Science', 254.

[21] See above at 45 f.; Kilbourne, Jr., *History of the Louisiana Civil Code*, 108 ff.

[22] ALI, 'Report of the Committee Proposing the Establishment of an American Law Institute'.

form. It will be seen that all these factors are indeed important aspects of a reference text's authority. They are decisive for the attitude of a legal profession with regard to the legitimacy, the reliability, and the usefulness of a reference text. Yet, it will be seen that none of these authority factors is indispensable. Such factors only contribute, in varying degree and combinations, to the legal profession accepting a text as authority; and a text may even become authoritative if one or the other of these factors is largely absent.

1. Representation, authorship, and procedure

The American Law Institute has never been a democratic institution; rather, it was constructed as a strongly elitist organization.[23] Nonetheless, the Institute was designed, from early on, to represent the American legal profession as a whole.[24] It was felt that the Restatements could only achieve the desirable degree of authority if they were 'generally recognized as a work carried on by the legal profession in fulfillment [sic] of an obligation to the American people'.[25] Established institutions, such as the American Bar Association or the American Association of Law Schools were regarded as insufficiently representative of the legal profession as a whole for being entrusted with the restatements project.[26] Indeed, the Institute's success must be attributed to a large degree on the founding members' bringing together the different, and traditionally hostile, legal professions.[27] Thus, when the Institute was founded at a meeting on 23 February 1923, the New York Times could describe it as 'probably the most distinguished gathering of the legal profession in the history of the country':[28] the Institute's incorporators were William H. Taft, the former President of the United States and at that time Chief Justice, and Charles E. Hughes, a former

[23] Snyder, 'Private Lawmaking', 434.

[24] ALI, 'Report of the Committee Proposing the Establishment of an American Law Institute', 29 ff., 34, 37 ff.; see also Frank, 'Law Institute', 615 ff.

[25] ALI, 'Report of the Committee Proposing the Establishment of an American Law Institute', 29.

[26] ALI, 'Report of the Committee Proposing the Establishment of an American Law Institute', 30 ff.

[27] Cf. Hull, 'Restatement and Reform'.

[28] N.Y. Times, 24 February 1923, 10, as cited by Hull, 'Restatement and Reform', 86.

member of the Supreme Court and a judge of high reputation (he later became Chief Justice). The leading members of the Institute were powerful politicians,[29] high-ranking administrative lawyers,[30] influential judges (among them Benjamin Cardozo, Learned Hand, and also the sceptical Oliver Wendell Holmes[31]), well-known academics, such as Roscoe Pound, and John H. Wigmore, and the leading representatives of the American Bar. Even to the present day, membership of the American Law Institute is regarded as an exceptional honour, and the Institute has long been said to represent an elite of the American legal profession.[32]

Related to the American Law Institute's commitment to representation was an emphasis on procedure.[33] The Restatements should be drafted in a way that made them 'represent the considered legal judgment, not merely of the Reporter, nor even of his Advisers, but of the profession throughout the country'.[34] Hence, the 'legislative' process should be transparent and allow for the participation of anyone from the wider legal world. Before a reporter's proposal is presented to the Institute's members at an annual meeting, it will be discussed by the Committee of Advisors, the Membership Consultative Group, and by the Council.[35] What is more, the 'Discussion Drafts' and 'Tentative Drafts' are made public to allow for a general critical discussion and thus for a discursive participation of those who are interested in the project. At the same time, the Institute has always been alive to the risks of professional lobbying. The Institute and most of its members regard political influence of

[29] Besides Taft, e.g. John W. Davis, a Solicitor General of the United States, U.S. Ambassador to the UK and Democratic Party nominee for President in 1924.

[30] Thus, George W. Wickersham, the Institute's first President, had been Attorney General under President Taft, and Elihu Root, the Honorary President of the Institute, had served as the Secretary of the State under President Roosevelt.

[31] Holmes, Letter to Harold Laski, 15 February 1923, in: *Holmes-Laski Letters I*, 481 f.

[32] Frank, 'Law Institute', 617 ff., 625 ff. In 1923, membership totalled 308; it has increased meanwhile to more than 3,000 members: *loc. cit.*, 625 f.; see also the Institute's homepage: <http://www.ali.org/index.cfm?fuseaction=about.membership>. During the last decades, however, the declining reputation of doctrinal scholarship in American legal academia has resulted in an under-representation of the best-known American scholars in the ALI.

[33] ALI, 'Report of the Committee Proposing the Establishment of an American Law Institute', 48 ff.

[34] Frank, 'Law Institute', 620.

[35] Zekoll, 'Law Institute', 109 ff.

interest groups as inappropriate and take efforts to make sure that individual pressure groups cannot successfully influence the content of a restatement.[36] As a result, despite the Institute's lack of democratic legitimization, it has succeeded in presenting its products as the considered views of the legal profession as a whole.

All this indicates that fair representation and procedural values have become important authority factors for non-legislative codifications as well. True, no such elements were present in earlier authoritative reference texts. Yet these texts are much older than the idea of replacing, or complementing, substantial standards of justice with democratic ideals and the idea of procedural legitimacy.[37] In more recent times, both these ideas have apparently been acknowledged more generally. They were present in the context of the UNIDROIT-Principles and also in the CFR process. Thus, the authority of the PICC is backed by the reputation and standing of the UNIDROIT-Institute, which presents itself—somewhat misleadingly and perhaps even illegitimately[38]—as the Principles' author.[39] What is more, emphasis has always been placed on the fact that the Working Group drafting the PICC was composed of scholars from different countries and, more importantly, from the different legal traditions of the world.[40] When the PICC were revised, representatives of international arbitration organizations were invited as 'observers' to attend and actively participate in the drafting process.[41] And in the current process of revision and

[36] Frank, 'Law Institute', 628 ff.; Zekoll, 'Law Institute', 117 ff.

[37] See, among others, Rawls, *Theory of Justice*, 74 ff., 104, 173f.; Habermas, *Faktizität und Geltung*, 151 ff., 187 ff., 367 ff. and *passim*.

[38] See Kessedjian, 'Un exercice de rénovation des sources du droit', 643, 646 f.: 'Qui est l'auteur de cet ouvrage? La réponse est à la foi simple et malaisée à donner.... Organisation internationale intergouvernementale, l'Unidroit donne son *imprimatur* à un ouvrage qui porte son nom mais qui a été élaboré par des membres de la doctrine'. See also p. 655 f. and above at 93, n. 55 for further references on the discussion.

[39] In actual legal practice today, the PICC are usually seen as an official legal product of UNIDROIT; cf. Marella, 'Choice of Law in Third-Millennium Arbitrations', 1141; Brödermann, 'The Growing Importance of the UNIDROIT Principles', 757; Basedow, 'Die UNIDROIT-Prinzipien', 1: 'Im Mai 1994 hat der Governing Council von UNIDROIT die UNIDROIT-Prinzipien ... angenommen ...'; similarly id., 'Uniform Law Conventions and the UNIDROIT Principles', 129.

[40] *PICC-Commentary*/Vogenauer, Introduction [18], [24].

[41] Bonell, *International Restatement*, 41; *PICC-Commentary*/Vogenauer, 'Introduction' [26], [44].

supplementation of the PICC, all the drafts and discussion papers are made available to the general public.[42]

Similarly, the Lando Commission,[43] the Study Group ECC,[44] and the Acquis Group[45] sought to represent the different European nations in their membership, and the latter two groups relied on democratic procedures for making their decisions.[46] What is more, first drafts of the rules of these two groups have been discussed with political 'stakeholders' at conferences, which were organized by the European Commission.[47] Thus, the procedural ideals of adequate representation, transparency, and discursive participation were implicitly acknowledged as important authority factors. True, the actual processes may have suffered from shortcomings in this respect. For example, there could never be a genuinely public discussion before the DCFR's publication, as the drafts were never made public.[48] But such shortcomings are irrelevant for the normative statement that fair representation and the procedural values of transparency and discursive participation are today generally regarded as important authority factors also for non-legislative codifications. These factors are increasingly treated as decisive for a text's legitimacy, and legal authority can never be independent of legitimacy. Nonetheless, these factors are clearly not indispensable. The Lando Commission never made its discussions and drafts public and yet its authority among European scholars is not significantly weaker than that of the PICC.

[42] See <http://www.unidroit.org/english/workprogramme/study050/main.htm>.

[43] Lando, 'Preface', xii f.

[44] Study Group ECC/von Bar, *Benevolent Intervention*, vii f.

[45] Dannemann, 'Introduction', xxvi.

[46] Study Group ECC/von Bar, *Benevolent Intervention*, vii f.; Dannemann, 'Introduction', xxv ff. The smaller Lando Commission has apparently worked on a more discursive, consensual basis.

[47] Commission (EC), 'European Contract Law and the Revision of the Acquis: the way forward', COM(2004) 651 final, 11 October 2004, at 3.1.2 and 3.2.3; Commission (EC), 'First Annual Progress Report on European Contract Law and the Acquis Review', COM(2005) 456 final, 23 September 2005, *passim*; Staudenmayer, 'Weitere Schritte im Europäischen Vertragsrecht', 104; cf. also Dannemann, 'Introduction', xxvii.

[48] For a critique, see von Bar and Schulte-Nölke, 'Gemeinsamer Referenzrahmen', 166 ff.; Schmidt-Kessel, 'Auf dem Weg zum Gemeinsamen Referenzrahmen', 6 f.; Jansen, 'Traditionsbegründung', 544 with further references.

In the discussions preceding the American Law Institute, representation and procedure alone were never regarded as sufficient for establishing authoritative authorship. Furthermore, emphasis was put on professional excellence and reputation. The reporters preparing the Restatements were—and still are today—the leading doctrinal scholars in the relevant field of the law;[49] and they are advised by experienced members of the different legal professions.[50] Indeed, this emphasis on professional excellence is an old, well-established means of establishing legal authority. Justinian expressly relied on it in his *Institutes*, which he claimed as being based on the work of leading Roman lawyers, especially Gaius on the one hand, and on the compilatory craftsmanship of the leading contemporary jurists Tribonian, Theophilus, and Dorotheus on the other.[51] Likewise, each *lex* in the *Digest* is introduced with the classical author's name and a reference to the specific book from which the text was taken.[52] For later generations, this was a reason to conclude that Justinian had prepared texts of outstanding legal quality and justice;[53] this factor substantially contributed to the *Digest's* authority among medieval jurists.[54] Likewise, national codification projects have always relied on the prestigious advice of prominent members of the legal profession; the UNIDROIT-Institute has emphasized the reputation of the members of its Governing Council and of the jurists involved in the preparation of the PICC;[55] and the European Union even established a 'Network of Excellence' for preparing an academic draft for a political CFR.[56] Clearly, the excellence and reputation of the authors of such a text shall guarantee its professional reliability.

[49] ALI, 'Report of the Committee Proposing the Establishment of an American Law Institute', 54 f.; Frank, 'Law Institute', 618 f.: 'whenever possible ... the foremost legal scholar in the country on the topic'; Zekoll, 'Law Institute', 109.

[50] Frank, 'Law Institute', 620; Zekoll, 'Law Institute', 110.

[51] See Inst. Const. Imperatoriam, 3, 6.

[52] See D. Const. Tanta, 13, 19, 21, 23 f.

[53] See above at 32, n. 114.

[54] Above at 31 ff.

[55] *PICC-Commentary*/Vogenauer, Introduction [14]; Bonell, *International Restatement*, 29 f., 33 ff., 36 f., 40 f., 43 f.; cf. also Kessedjian, 'Un exercice de rénovation des sources du droit', 644 f. Contrast the more reluctant presentation by Lando, 'Preface', xii f.

[56] See <http://www.copecl.org>.

Again, however, professional excellence is apparently neither necessary for a non-legislative reference text to achieve legal authority, nor is it regarded as the most important factor. As far as we know, neither Eike von Repgow, the author of the Saxon Mirror, nor Gratian, the author(s) of the *Decretum Gratiani*, had particular reputations as excellent jurists. And today no one is asking whether the unnumbered doctoral students working in the Study Group ECC really represent the legal elite of Europe. A legal text's authority may be independent of the authority of its author(s). Yet, it is noteworthy that the decline of the American Restatements' authority during the last decades corresponds to the declining reputation of doctrinal scholarship in American legal academia. Today, American scholars of the highest reputation are no longer engaged in the traditional doctrinal work which is the daily business of the American Law Institute; hence, the leading law schools are not contributing to its reputation as strongly as they used to.

2. Form I: coherence and order

Even more important than representation and procedure was, according to the American Law Institute's Committee of 35, the 'question of form'. Indeed this question was 'of the first importance'. To achieve the desired intellectual unity of the law, a textbook-like treatment of the law was deemed unsatisfactory: the Restatements should avoid a 'mixture of statement of present law, historical description and discussion of legal theory which is characteristic of the law treatise'.[57] Instead, it was decided that there should be a normative 'statement of the principles of the law'. The rules should be drafted 'with the care and precision of a well-drawn statute', and with 'the mental attitude ... of those who desire to express the law in statutory form'. Even in cases of reasonable uncertainty, the Restatements should therefore lay down a single, decisive rule of the law;[58] this is what the Restatements actually do,

[57] ALI, 'Report of the Committee Proposing the Establishment of an American Law Institute', 20.

[58] ALI, 'Report of the Committee Proposing the Establishment of an American Law Institute', 15.

even in the present day. A similar approach has been taken by the UNIDROIT-Institute: the PICC present the amorphous and inconsistent law of international commercial contracts in the form of a continental codification.[59] Again, much emphasis was placed on drafting rules that are easily applicable for practical lawyers.[60]

True, in an American Restatement, as in the PICC or in the PECL, the statements of the rules are accompanied by explanatory Comments and Illustrations; yet, these Comments have always been separated from the rule 'by typographical or other device'.[61] In the Restatements, the rules were from early on printed in bold letters; and they are separated from the commenting text (see Figure 3 below; a similar picture is presented by the PICC: Appendix, Figure 7).[62] Clearly, these commenting explanations were designed to be of lesser importance. Indeed, what is 'applied' in practical legal discourse today, are the black-letter rules, rather than the accompanying Comments. What is more, the American Law Institute decided that there should be no reference to common law authorities in the Restatements' first series (the reporter's notes are a later development), because the Restatements should be more than a considered statement on the basis of legal pros and cons.[63] Hence, the American Restatements mostly have been and often are 'authoritative without authorities'.[64] Remarkably, the same is true, again, for the PICC, where the official Comments 'systematically refrain from referring to national laws'.[65]

All this brings to our attention the important fact that the authority of a basic reference text does not necessarily depend on the persuasiveness of the arguments offered; this distinguishes such texts

[59] Bonell, *International Restatement*, 61.

[60] Bonell, *International Restatement*, ix, 23, 62 ff.

[61] See for all ALI, 'Report of the Committee Proposing the Establishment of an American Law Institute', 19 f.

[62] The Lando Commission, however, has not set its Rules in bold letters, but rather in italics.

[63] Williston, 'The Restatement of Contracts', 777: '(i)t seemed that the Restatement would be more likely to achieve an authority of its own ... if exact rules were clearly stated without argument'.

[64] Frank, 'Law Institute', 621, on the first series of the American Restatements. See also below at 126 ff.

[65] Governing Council of UNIDROIT, 'Introduction to the 1994 Edition', xv. See for this point below at 132.

from doctrinal articles and from judicial decisions.[66] Indeed, both compilations and restatements are largely void of legal argument. If such texts are authoritative *imperio rationis*, what is meant by 'ratio' cannot therefore be the 'forceless force of the better argument',[67] or only the ideas of a 'best solution' or 'superior quality' of rules.[68] Rather, it is the coherence and structure of the text and the accessibility of individual rules. To base the law on convincing argument may be an ideal of legal and especially doctrinal discourse, and it should, of course, be a guiding directive for those preparing a restatement of the law. But the quality of arguments cannot ultimately determine the authority of basic reference texts if the function of such texts consists in ending otherwise unlimited normative controversy. Reference texts of legal authority are necessary for the very reason that most normative propositions may reasonably be disputed. Thus, both legislative and non-legislative reference texts provide for a premise of normative argument that cannot normally be questioned. Their function consists in replacing (normative) argument with (legal) authority.[69]

The relevance and effects of a legal text's form have probably been underestimated in modern law; this has been the complaint of the few authors who have analysed such questions in more detail.[70] Many modern lawyers think that the content of a text is much more important than its form.[71] Even the working groups drafting the modern international restatements have placed significantly less

[66] Cf., with regard to judicial decisions, Postema, 'Philosophy of the Common Law', 592 ff., 601 ff. Other authors, however, have argued that the authority of judicial decisions does not, and should not, depend on the persuasiveness of arguments alone; cf. Alexander and Sherwin, 'Judges as Rule Makers'. However, the force of arguments given will often determine the weight of precedents, even in systems that acknowledge a formal rule of precedent.

[67] Habermas, 'Wahrheitstheorien', especially 161: 'zwangloser Zwang des besseren Arguments'.

[68] But see *PICC-Commentary*/Vogenauer, Introduction [23]; *PICC-Commentary*/Michaels, Preamble I [6].

[69] Kroppenberg, 'Der gescheiterte Codex', 117.

[70] Summers, *Form and Function*, 7, 24 ff. True, there is an intensive discussion on legal formalism, but this discussion primarily concerns formal arguments in the law, rather than the form of legal texts.

[71] Thus, the principle of freedom of form determines the discussion of European private law; see Art. 2:101 PECL; Art. 1:303 ACQP; Kötz, *Europäisches Vertragsrecht I*, 118 ff.

effort on the question of form than the American Law Institute for its Restatements.[72] However, the assumption that form is less important than substance is doubted not only by the findings of other disciplines,[73] but also by a view on the citation practice of courts. Of course, the authority which has been assigned to the PECL[74] and to the PICC,[75] may be explained—*prima vista* plausibly—with the current processes of Europeanizing or globalizing the national legal systems in Europe.[76] But other texts, such as the *International Encyclopedia of Comparative Law*, or the works of the Common-Core Group,[77] have never achieved a comparable status as European or global texts of reference.[78] This is so even though these works arguably rest on a far broader comparative basis and contain much more material and references to national authorities, and although a common view holds that the authority of transnational principles of contract law depends on and is therefore limited to their 'restatement function'.[79] Likewise, although monographs are often much more thorough in their doctrinal argument, German courts usually rely on commentaries as doctrinal authorities; citing a monograph would be exceptional, especially in lower courts.[80] Thus, the form of a text is apparently an important factor contributing to its authority in legal discourse.

[72] Cf. Bonell, *International Restatement*, 61 ff., who discusses under the heading of 'formal presentation' mainly problems of structure and language. No considerations about the formal presentation can be found in Lando, 'Preface'.

[73] See Oesterreicher, 'Autorität der Form'. See also the other contributions to Oesterreicher *et al.* (eds), *Autorität der Form* and below at 117 ff. on the semantics of formal presentation.

[74] Above at 60 ff.

[75] Above at 71 ff.

[76] Zimmermann, 'Comparative Law and the Europeanization of Private Law', 542 f., 563 f.

[77] Zimmermann and Whittaker, *Good Faith*; Gordley, *Enforceability of Promises*; Bussani and Palmer, *Pure Economic Loss*; Werro and Palmer, *Boundaries of Strict Liability*; Kieninger *et al., Security Rights in Movable Property*; Sefton-Green, *Mistake, Fraud and Duties to Inform*; Graziadei *et al., Commercial Trusts*; Pozzo, *Property and Environment*; Möllers and Heinemann, *The Enforcement of Competition Law*.

[78] In this respect I rely on personal information by Mauro Bussani, one of the two co-directors of the Common-Core Group.

[79] *PICC-Commentary*/Michaels, Preamble I [3] f., [70], [101], [112].

[80] Thus, a representative sample of the Federal Supreme Court's judgments (taken from vols. 5, 25, 45, 65, 85, 105, 125, 145, and 165) showed 1,574 references to commentaries, but only 318 to monographs (including PhD theses). Of these monographs, most are cited in areas of the law for which no commentaries existed, or in cases

The natural function of form is usually seen to present a specific legal content. For lawyers, form is a 'purposive systematic arrangement of the unit as a whole'. Questions of formal presentation should therefore be discussed from a purely functional perspective, central aspects being the clarity, transparency, and accessibility of relevant normative information.[81] Thus, legal literature should be structured in a way that makes the individual statements and arguments easily accessible. Similarly, legislation should be drafted in a prescriptive language and in the form of general, precise, and definite provisions, which identify and clearly relate to individual norms.[82] Both legislative and non-legislative codifications should apply a coherent terminology; and they should be structured as a system of short articles, which allows for a convenient, easy reference.[83] Convenience and clarity are the main formal qualities of legal texts and they significantly contribute to their use and authority in legal practice.[84]

Thus, the remarkable authority of the *Decretum Gratiani* resulted primarily from the fact that it presented an easily accessible reconstruction of Canon law, which was both comprehensive and consistent.[85] Similarly, the success of the American Restatements was largely due to the fact that they presented the common law in the form of a consistent and well-ordered system of rather short, easily applicable norms. The same is true for the PICC which present the

where the court discusses an old and strong line of criticism against its jurisprudence. In such a case, especially, where such criticism ultimately results in a deviation from former case law, the court apparently wishes to present the opinion of the academic profession as a whole; therefore it often refers to more than 20 monographs and articles for one single argument. Furthermore, references to articles in journals mostly concern actual questions (838 out of 1,404 citations altogether), which were not then settled in the commentaries. Details of this analysis are on file with the author.

[81] Cf. Summers, *Form and Function*, 6 ff., 40 ff., 47 ff., 77 ff.

[82] Summers, *Form and Function*, 15, 21, 138 ff., 143 ff., 155 ff., 161 ff., 190 ff.; Lötscher, 'Gesetze als Texte', 189 ff., 195 ff.

[83] Summers, *Form and Function*, 320 ff., though without consideration of non-legislative codifications.

[84] Cf., with regard to the failure of the *Codex Theodosianus*, Kroppenberg, 'Der gescheiterte Codex', 118 ff. Kroppenberg argues, convincingly, that this legislation's failure resulted from the fact that it did not meet the formal requirements of a codification: a comprehensive, clear, and well-structured text that unifies the law by including everything that is valid and excluding former, dead norms.

[85] Helmholz, *Classical Canon Law*, 7 f.

amorphous international commercial law in the form of a systematic codification.[86] Indeed, non-legislative codifications can only gain legal authority if they can be understood as a conveniently applicable expression of the law. Hence, formal order, consistency, and system are essential. Conversely, the authority of modern legislation may be decreasing, as it is perceived by the legal profession to be increasingly incoherent.[87]

It should not be overlooked, though, that this factor, despite its great importance, allows for exceptions as well. For example, the *Digest* did not even come close to the formal standards of a modern codification. Neither were they drafted in a prescriptive language nor in the form of general, precise, and definite provisions. Rather, they compiled excerpts from scholarly literature: learned explanations of the edict and discussions of individual cases. Those texts represented the Roman scholarly debate in its full complexity and with many of its scholarly controversies; hence, tensions and even contradictions between different fragments could not be avoided. What is more, the *Digest* was originally not even well-structured. As there was no numbering of the different *leges* and fragments, medieval scholars had to cite these texts by their initial words. True, the *Digest* was not without important formal qualities, especially if seen from the perspective of a medieval lawyer. There was at least some order, which was ultimately based on the Roman edict: the different titles usually treat different actions. Moreover, the texts were based on a generally consistent, technical terminology and—by and large—on coherent legal principle. Thus, despite their formal shortcomings, it was possible to use the *Digest* as a textual reference for legal discourse. Nevertheless, the *Digest's* authority cannot be explained with its formal quality. Clearly, other factors proved decisive. The *Corpus iuris* became authoritative, in the

[86] Above at 106.

[87] Cf. Flume, 'Vom Beruf unserer Zeit für Gesetzgebung', 1429: a provision which was incoherently placed into the codification, should be treated as non-existent ('pro non scripto'); Ernst, 'Gelehrtes Recht', 32; Lübbe-Wolf, 'Expropriation der Jurisprudenz?', 288; Fleischer, 'Gesellschafts- und Kapitalmarktrecht', 62. Conversely, a convincing, widely accepted doctrinal foundation for legislation may add to its authority; cf. Behrends, 'Bündnis zwischen Gesetz und Dogmatik', 9, 24 and *passim*; Herberger, 'Rangstufen der Rechtsdogmatik', 77 ff.

absence of a textual alternative, because of the strong profession-related factors supporting its use.[88]

3. Form II: staging authority

Besides this instrumental function of creating consistency and order, the form of a legal text may also assume a quasi-rhetorical dimension, which results from the fact that it adds a graphical or typographical structure to the text. And indeed, form does much more than simply present legal content: form symbolically stages and thus institutionalizes legal normativity. Legal authorities are social institutions[89] and therefore normally need to create symbols of themselves in order to become part of the social and legal reality.[90] Hence, the distinction between law and non-law, between valid legislation and mere politics, is usually constructed by formal criteria.[91] Thus, the legislative character of a text depends primarily on formal rules identifying the competent legislator, on formal procedural requirements in Parliament, and on formal requirements for the promulgation of the text. Similarly, a judgment will normally be identified by purely formal criteria that institutionally identify courts and distinguish judgments from other judicial communications.

Even more remarkably, however, form may, in itself, create legal obligation. Thus, in early Roman law, form was even a kind of ritual; it was the form in itself—the solemn formulation of the appropriate words—and not the will of parties or legislators, which brought about the legal effect ('Wirkform'[92]): 'form', it has been said, 'is the oldest norm'.[93] Of course, to look for anything comparable to such archaic features of former law in modern legal systems may at first appear inappropriate. Modern law is supposedly rational; it is based on the will

[88] Above 29 ff., 41 f., 96 f.

[89] See MacCormick, *Institutions of Law*, 22 ff., 33 ff.; Tamanaha, *General Jurisprudence*, 137 ff.

[90] Cf. Rehberg, 'Institutionen als symbolische Ordnungen', 58 ff.

[91] Summers, *Form and Function*, 18 f.; cf. also Luhmann, 'Geltung des Rechts', 278 and ff., describing the law's validity as a symbol of the legal system's unity.

[92] See Dulckeit, 'Lehre vom Rechtsgeschäft', 160 ff.: 'die Form ist hier ... der alleinige und allein wirkende rechtsgeschäftliche Inhalt selbst'.

[93] For discussion, see Zimmermann, *The Law of Obligations*, 82 ff.; Oestmann, 'Zwillingsschwester der Freiheit', 24 ff., both with further references.

of parties and legislators, rather than on the irrational belief in solemn *hocus pocus*. It is remarkable, though, that the modern political institutions, on which the law's validity was long assumed to rest, have never made do without symbolically staging their authority.[94] States and governments create symbols of themselves and of their power and legitimacy in parliaments[95] and parliamentarian architecture,[96] in military parades, and in constitutions.[97] A president's oath of office is no less a ceremonial ritual than the medieval enthroning of a king:[98] it demonstrates and creates loyalty and authority. Thus, when the US President Obama was inaugurated, he used the Bible on which President Lincoln had sworn; thereby, Obama made himself symbolically bound to God and to the former President's legacy.[99] Similarly, meetings of the heads of states are often put on stage with great effort: shaking hands, especially of hostile actors, will regularly be a performance in front of an international television audience; and it may be of high symbolic relevance if heads of states meet in private.[100] Thus, when the Soviet President Gorbachev invited the German Chancellor Kohl to his private land residence, to which no foreign head of state had been before, this was perceived by Kohl himself and by the general public as a symbolic creation of an intimate and trustful personal relationship. Indeed, this meeting marked the beginning of a totally new political relationship between the Soviet Union and the new Germany.[101] The informal knitwear worn by those statesmen at this occasion has therefore become a symbol in the collective historical memory; it is exhibited in the German historical Museum *Haus der Geschichte*.

Likewise, modern courts and court procedures apparently cannot do without symbols and ceremony staging the institution's dignity and authority. In fact the dress codes, imposed by virtually all legal systems today on their lawyers and judges, are remarkably similar to

[94] Rehberg, 'Institutionen als symbolische Ordnungen', 62 ff.

[95] Patzelt, 'Symbolizität und Stabilität'.

[96] Oberreuter, 'Institution und Inszenierung'; Patzelt, 'Symbolizität und Stabilität', 624 ff.

[97] Gebhardt, 'Verfassung und Symbolizität'.

[98] See Althoff, *Macht der Rituale*, 85 ff., 173 ff.

[99] See *The Washington Post*, 21 January 2009, p. A01: 'Obama Sworn in as 44th President of the US', and 'A Historic Inauguration Draws Throngs to the Mall'; *Süddeutsche Zeitung*, 21 January 2009, p. 3: 'Ein Mann, ein Versprechen'.

[100] Althoff, *Macht der Rituale*, 92.

[101] Kohl, *Erinnerungen, 1990–1994*, 172 ff.; *Frankfurter Allgemeine Zeitung*, 18 July 1990, p. 3: 'Ein Gefühl, als könnte man Berge versetzen'; *Süddeutsche Zeitung*, 18 July 1990, p. 3: 'Das gewaltige Gefühl der Erleichterung'.

those of the *Reichskammergericht* and *Oberhofrat*.[102] What is more, these dress codes are disputed, which shows that important symbolic interests are at stake.[103] Similarly, as far as legal authority cannot derive from the state alone, it needs to be vindicated. Other participants in the legal discourse must be motivated to accept a text's authority; yet in the absence of any absolute authority, there can be no cogent legal reason for such recognition. Analysing the form of such texts as a means of symbolically presenting them as an authoritative legal institution may therefore be helpful for better understanding the legal process.

(a) Typographical authority: the example of standard glosses

One group of texts to be analysed from such a perspective are the standard glosses (*glossae ordinariae*) to the main medieval books of authority and especially to the medieval law books.[104] Of these standard glosses the oldest one was Accursius' *Magna Glossa*, or *Glossa Ordinaria*, to the *Corpus iuris civilis* (see Figure 1 below). This Gloss was presented, perhaps somewhat unjustifiedly,[105] as a collection and summary of the achievements of early medieval scholarship on Roman law, and it was one of the first works in European history that presented the law as an exegetic science. Indeed, the idea to find rational and legitimate solutions for normative conflicts on the basis of authoritative texts on the one hand and of exegetic method on the other was a central aspect of the legal and theological reform movement of the first half of the 12th century.[106]

[102] See Stollberg-Rilinger, 'Würde des Gerichts', 192 ff., 201 ff.; cf. for Germany today § 20 Rechtsanwalts-Berufsordnung (as of 1 March 2006).

[103] See BVerfGE 28, 21 ff. on the constitutionality of a duty to wear a gown; more recently, on the question of whether there is a duty to wear a white tie under the gown (only the duty of wearing a gown is mentioned in § 20 Rechtsanwalts-Berufsordnung) OLG Braunschweig, (1995) *NJW* 2113 f. (27 April 1995); VG Berlin, (2007) *NJW* 793 f. (19 July 2006): statutory duties to wear such a tie in Lower Saxony viz. Berlin; OLG München, (2006) *NJW* 3079 f. (14 July 2006): customary duty to wear such a tie in Bavaria; cf. also LG Mannheim, 4 Qs 52/08 (27 January 2009), all decisions with further references.

[104] See already above at 22 (Standard Gloss to the *Decretum*), 25 (*Buch's Gloss* to the Saxon Mirror), 37 (Standard Gloss to the *Corpus iuris civilis*).

[105] Accursius did not present a complete picture of his predecessors' and contemporaries' discussions. In large parts his Gloss was an improved version of the earlier *apparatus* of Johannes Bassianus and Azo; thus, it was a summary of one specific legal school. Glosses, written elsewhere, were only exceptionally included; see Jakobs, *Magna Glossa*, 283 ff. and *passim*, with further references.

[106] Jansen, 'Das gelehrte Recht', 161 ff., with further references.

This idea became a central aspect of a broader historical process of rationalizing, pacifying, and legalizing medieval society.[107]

One notable result of this conception of normativity was that legal and theological language became descriptive.[108] This was a development whose importance cannot be overstated. Formerly, the law had been treated within the context of ethics and politics; hence, it was discussed in the always disputed moral categories of 'right' and 'wrong'. Now, however, the 'ought' of a legal proposition was based on an external legislative, or else objective, textual, authority, on which the legal profession's interpretative claims depended. It followed that normative propositions about the law could be presented, in objective language, as 'true' (or 'false'); hence, they were open to rational argument. Until the 20th century, scholars, such as Kelsen, have been puzzled by the fact resulting thereof: that legal doctrine formulates its normative propositions in a 'descriptive sense'.[109] The 'declaratory' theory of legal argument and judicial decision making, as it was many centuries later formulated by Blackstone,[110] Savigny,[111] Dworkin,[112] or Canaris,[113] is an expression of those assumptions. Indeed, it is no coincidence that the common lawyer Blackstone's argument was based on a rather civilian conception of a 'legal science', defined by method and authoritative sources.[114]

For this modern textual approach to the law, the medieval jurists and theologians had to establish authoritative texts on the one hand,

[107] Cf. Wieacker, *Privatrechtsgeschichte*, 97-203; cf. especially 131 f., 151 f., 190 ff. See also Dilcher, 'Verrechtlichung der Lebensbeziehungen', 96 ff., with further references on this theory, which may be traced back to the writings of Max Weber.

[108] This peculiarity of doctrinal propositions can already be observed in Roman law, where the doctrinal language of the *Digest* and the *Institutes* was largely descriptive, as well. The reason here, however, was not that legal science was understood as exegetic in nature: in fact, exegetic arguments are rare in the *Digest*. The reason was rather that the Roman *iurisconsulti* understood their profession as *describing* the prerequisites of actions that had been laid down in authoritative texts, such as the *edict*. Thus, it was the reification of legal entities which allowed for a descriptive and thus rational approach to the law.

[109] See above at 90.

[110] Blackstone, *Commentaries I*, 69 f.

[111] von Savigny, *System I*, 13 ff., 45 ff., 83 ff.; see also Windscheid, *Pandektenrecht I*, 50 ff. (§ 20). For an analysis of the basic ideas of those authors, see Brockmöller, *Entstehung der Rechtstheorie*, 89 ff., 91, 93, 108 ff.

[112] Dworkin, *Taking Rights Seriously*, 81 ff.; id., 'No Right Answer?'

[113] Canaris, *Systemdenken und Systembegriff*, 67 ff.

[114] This conception of legal science is even the main topic of the introduction to Blackstone's *Commentaries* (vol. I, 4 f. and *passim*).

and they had to present their normative claims as being correct interpretations of those texts on the other. Yet establishing a textual authority was not possible on the basis of rational argument alone. It was not uncommon, therefore, to put textual authority spectacularly on stage, for example by physically presenting to a court the books of authority, on which an actor relied. Thus, in one of the most famous heresy processes of the 12th century, the accused Gilbert of Poitiers, one of the most famous academics of his time, made his people carry piles of books into the court.[115] He wanted to put on stage the fact that he relied on the authorities of the church fathers, and he wanted to make these authorities visible to the court.[116]

Another—perhaps less spectacular but certainly no less efficient—means of staging authority was to publish the authoritative texts (the Holy Scripture, the *Corpus iuris civilis*, and the authoritative legal compilations of the Catholic Church) together with a standardized marginal gloss (see Figure 1). Here, the main text was typically written in larger letters, and it was often illustrated with beautiful, expensive miniatures emphasizing its special dignity and authority. More importantly, the central text was typographically enclosed by a gloss: a collection of little comments, which were related through references to specific words of the central text. These glosses, usually written in smaller letters that were specifically designed to remain readable even in small size,[117] explained the main text's meaning or discussed specific problems that related to a specific part of the text. They thus collected and defined the generally acknowledged doctrinal knowledge of their time.

[115] Gottfried von Auxerre, 'De condemnatione errorum Gilberti Porretani', 587, 589: 'magnorum voluminum corpora per clericos suos Pictaviensis fecisset afferri'.

[116] '(O)rthodoxorum patrum ... in corpore librorum integras attulerat ... auctoritates': Otto von Freising, *Ottonis Gesta Friderici I. imperatoris, lib.* I, *cap.* LVIII. See Jansen, 'Das gelehrte Recht', 160 f., with further references.

[117] Mazal, *Geschichte der Buchkultur 3/1*, 213 f. Letters of divergent size are no invention of later book-printers. Hence, it is misleading to explain the specific typographical presentation of the printed standard glosses as a means of replacing colour in structuring the complex legal texts (see for such a thesis Röhl, 'Bilder in gedruckten Rechtsbüchern', 332). Indeed, all main aspects of the typographical organization of printed books were practised already in medieval handwritten books; see Raible, 'Semiotik der Textgestalt', 8 ff.; Chartier, *Lesewelten*, 34 f.

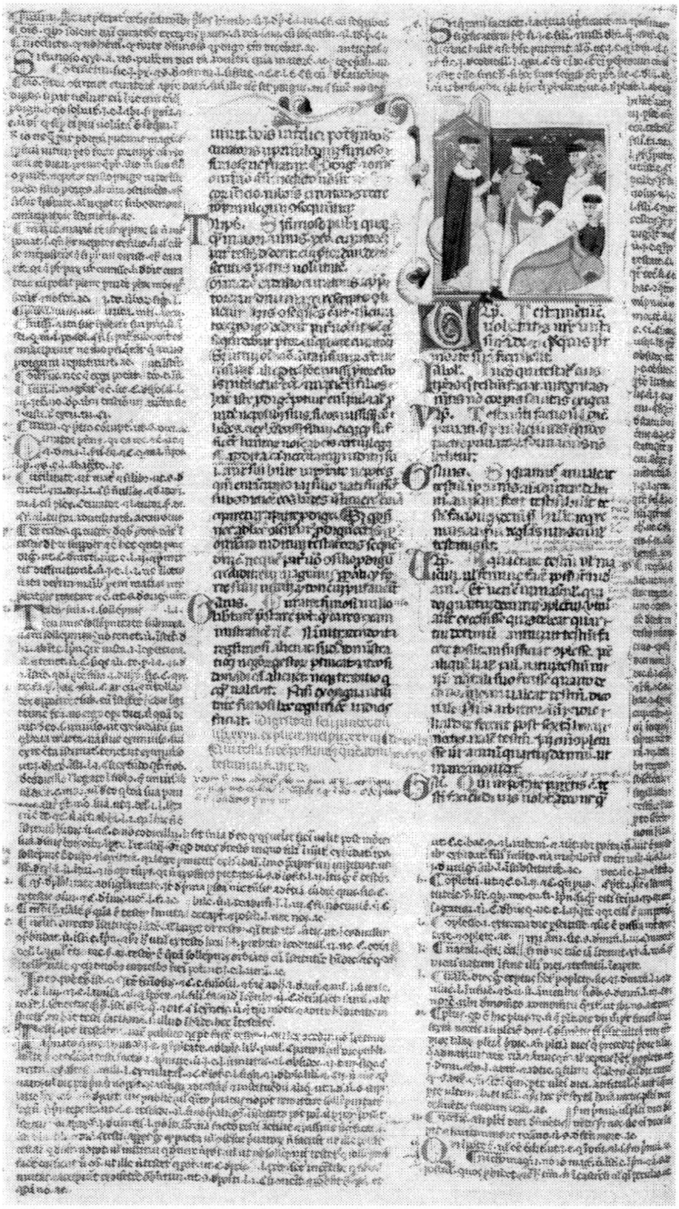

Figure 1. *Corpus iuris civilis* (*Digesta*) with *Glossa ordinaria*[118]

[118] *Digest (Infortiatum)*, Italian manuscript, ca. 1270-80, Free Library of Philadelphia (Shelfmark: Lewis E 244), *fol.* 50 v.

The textual form of the glosses developed out of medieval academic teaching and scholarly discourse.[119] Indeed, the first glosses may have been little annotations written by students of law or theology, not very different from a modern student writing the meaning of a word at the margin or between the lines of a Latin text.[120] The form of the glosses was maintained, however, when the individual glosses developed into large, more systematic and standardized *apparatus*, as we see them in the standard glosses. However, at this stage, producing a gloss had become quite difficult, both in handwriting and in print. Indeed, the modern 'critical' editions of the *Glossa ordinaria* to the Bible have for this reason omitted the *Glossa interlinearis* which was written in between the text's lines.[121] It would have been much easier, for instance, to put the glosses into footnotes below the text or to present the learned comments in the form of a continuous lemmatic commentary with brief phrases of the authoritative text (*lemmata*) inserted, or in the form of an edition of the authoritative text with comments interposed between the text's different paragraphs. These latter forms were not unknown to the medieval scholars; they had been used by the commentators of late antiquity,[122] with whose writings the medieval scholars were familiar.[123] Clearly, the form of the gloss was consciously chosen and the typographical organization of the text must be seen as having meaning. Indeed, one of the main actors in the movement leading to the canonization of the Bible's Standard Gloss was the very same Gilbert of Poitiers, whose good sense for staging textual authority has just been seen.[124]

[119] On the intellectual background and the developments of this practice, see Baldwin, *The Scholastic Culture*, 61, 72 ff.; cf. also, on the pre-Accursian glosses, Dolezalek, '*Libri magistrorum*', with further references.

[120] The word 'gloss' or *glossa* derives from the Greek γλῶσσα and originally means 'explanation of a word or phrase which is difficult to understand'.

[121] Cf. Smalley, 'Glossa ordinaria', 454; Graf Reventlow, *Epochen der Bibelauslegung II*, 149.

[122] See Schulz, *Roman Legal Science*, 183 f.; a more detailed discussion is found in id., *Geschichte der römischen Rechtswissenschaft*, 225 f., with a discussion also of non-legal commentaries.

[123] This is especially true for theology; see on the form of the *Glossa Ordinaria* to the Holy Scripture, Gibson, 'The Glossed Bible', ix.

[124] See Mazal, *Geschichte der Buchkultur 3/1*, 91 f.; Smalley, 'Glossa ordinaria', 453 f.

Of course, such a 'reading' of written texts may surprise many modern readers, and especially jurists. Yet, there can be no doubt today that the visual presentation of a text may be specifically designed to transport additional meaning. Of particular importance is the typographical organization of the one-dimensional text in the two dimensions of the written or printed page. Here, it is general knowledge today that typography may visually create different values of, and relations between, different bodies of text; it may thus represent hierarchical structures of domination.[125] Remarkably, in the case of the medieval glosses, such reading gains further plausibility from the fact that the glosses to legal texts significantly differ in their presentation from the Standard Gloss to the Holy Scripture. From the 12th century onwards, this latter Gloss usually combined a set of marginal glosses with a *Glossa interlinearis*, written in between the Bible text's lines (see Appendix, Figure 5);[126] at the same time, interlinear glosses, which had previously also been used by lawyers, disappeared in the legal context.

In medieval society, the authority of the Holy Scripture was beyond doubt. It did not need to be vindicated by the Gloss. Rather, this text depicted in its complex typographical structure the richness of the Lord's words and the close intellectual connection between the true theological learning and the Holy Words.[127] In contrast, the presentation of the marginal glosses to the legal texts established a relation of hierarchy between the authoritative central text and the body of scholarly learning, which referred to and depended on the central text. This is the first impression of even a modern reader, and the medieval culture was both much more visual and more hierarchical than the modern world. What is more,

[125] See Wehle, *Typographische Kultur*, 119 ff., 168 ff.; Raible, 'Semiotik der Textgestalt'. On antique lemmatic commentaries, which may be seen as predecessors of the medieval glosses, see Cancik, 'Der Text als Bild', 85 ff.

[126] Smalley, 'Glossa ordinaria', 452–456; Gibson, 'The Glossed Bible', viii; cf. also Mazal, *Geschichte der Buchkultur 3/1*, 91 f.; Graf Reventlow, *Epochen der Bibelauslegung II*, 147 ff., on the history of the Standard Gloss to the Bible. This presentation can no longer be found in modern editions; yet it can be seen in the marvellous first print of the Holy Scripture with its Gloss by the printer Adolph Rusch (*Biblia Latina cum Glossa Ordinaria*, Straßburg 1480 f.; see Appendix, Figure 5) and in many later editions until the 17th century; on all those editions, see Froehlich, 'The Printed Gloss'.

[127] Smalley, 'Glossa ordinaria', 454: 'graphische und sachliche Einheit'.

the form of the marginal gloss represented a dialectical relation of mutually stabilizing processes of recognition between the central text and its gloss. The gloss derived its explanatory authority and legitimacy from the main text to which it was related; yet, at the same time, the main text was presented as authoritative in its being the object of the gloss. It was thus staged as the centre of normative meaning, from which the legitimacy of other normative propositions derived.

What is more, in sharp contrast to the Bible's Standard Gloss, this presentation established a clear separation between the central text and the marginal gloss. This separation represented an institutional distinction between the law and its scholarly description, which is taken for granted by most modern lawyers, which is of the utmost importance for Western legal thinking, but which is, nevertheless, anything but naturally given or evident. Law is a human artefact, and it is constantly developed by the participants to the legal discourse. Hence, the idea of a sharp, categorical distinction between the law and its description has always contained an element of legal fiction. On the one hand, the *Corpus iuris* derived its meaning, at least in large parts, from the gloss and from later commentaries. Medieval lawyers gave expression to this fact by the short formula: 'quid non agnoscit glossa, non agnoscit curia': courts would only acknowledge an interpretation of the *Corpus iuris* if it could be found in the Gloss. On the other hand, codifications, as has been seen above, were usually written as largely descriptive restatements of the law in force.[128] Nonetheless, this distinction proved decisive with regard to the social function of law. It transformed the legal process into a rational discourse; and it helped separate the legal discourse institutionally from politics and morality. Lawyers acknowledging this distinction will understand that they must not arbitrarily develop the law on the basis of politically contested policy. They will recognize the law's intrinsic rationality on the one hand and normally accept the decisions of the political legislator on the other hand.

The *Glossa ordinaria* institutionalized this distinction as a social fact. Both typographically and in its descriptive language, the Gloss presented itself as a mere explanation of the main text's meaning.

[128] See above at 17 f.

Conversely, the central legislative text appeared as a statement, rather than as a description of the law. Thus, the *Glossa ordinaria* presented this distinction as an evident matter of fact and thereby helped jurists forget about its fictional character: was it not evident that there was a sharp distinction between the law in the centre of the text and its peripheral explanatory description? No longer could the status of a legal proposition be doubted. If it was to be found in the centre, then it was the law; if it was at the margin it could only be a description, or explanation, of the law. Fictions must be plausible if they are going to work; and nothing could create greater plausibility than typographically symbolizing this distinction. It put onto the readers' stage both the institutional separation of these texts and their mutual dependence with regard to authority and meaning, which was essential for both texts' legitimacy and recognition. This is probably the reason why—despite the immense cost of producing such a book[129]—medieval publishers rarely produced copies of the *Corpus iuris civilis* without the *Glossa ordinaria*; this practice was continued until the 17th century. Notably, the same happened with the *Decretum Gratiani* and its Gloss by Johannes Teutonicus and Bartholomaeus of Brescia[130] and with the Saxon Mirror.[131] Indeed, *Buch's Gloss* to the Saxon Mirror immediately raised the formal status of this text from an instrument which could be only used for proving customary law, to a generally acknowledged textual source of the *ius commune*, which had to be applied by the courts without further proof.[132]

In the medieval legal glosses, the function of formal presentation to symbolize and thus establish authority and meaning is manifest. Presenting the central text as authoritative added to its authority; and presenting scholarly literature as an explanatory gloss helped maintain the fiction of the declaratory approach to the law. Remarkably, this mechanism worked for both sides. The *Corpus iuris* became the main source of authority for the *ius commune*; and

[129] Bellomo, *L'Europa de diritto comune*, 75 ff. / *The Common Legal Past*, 63 ff. Thus, for producing one volume of the *Digestum vetus* (ca. one third of the Digest), the skin of about 100 sheep was needed; and an experienced writer needed one year for copying the Roman text and another year for the accompanying Gloss; cf. Soetermeer, 'Exemplar und Pecia', 483.

[130] See above at 22.

[131] Kannowski, *Buch'sche Glosse*, 18 ff.

[132] Kroeschell, 'Rechtsaufzeichnung und Rechtswirklichkeit', 379 f.

the Gloss became its principal doctrinal authority. From the middle of the 13th century onwards, it was regarded as the starting point of every interpretation of the *Corpus iuris* and it was often even recognized as a formal source of the law.[133] Remarkably, the same was true for the other standard glosses. The Saxon Mirror and its Gloss were soon perceived as a unity; and *Buch's Gloss* was recognized, in the same way as the standard glosses to the *Corpus iuris* and the *Decretum*, as a source of the law.[134] All this must be taken as a confirmation that the authority of these texts was created, at least in part, by their formal presentation as an eminent text's gloss.

(b) A German commentary

Modern legislation no longer needs the same kind of formal presentation. During the 20th century, it has been beyond doubt that their authority deriving from the state's domination is sufficient for making the legal profession apply the legislator's statutory law. Law gazettes, accordingly, may be printed simply and cheaply. It is not necessary specifically to present the dignity or authority of a state's legislation.

The non-legislative authority of modern academic writing, however, is more problematic. Doctrine enriches the law with structure, coherence, and meaning; hence, authority matters. The inner-legal, self-referential process of creating books of authority can therefore be observed even today.[135] This process significantly reduces the complexity of the law: instead of researching all relevant arguments and weighing their mutual force, a judge may simply rely on the opinion of one or two authoritative authors. Now, in German law, the most influential form of doctrinal writing is the commentary;[136] and among those commentaries to the civil code, the best established is the *Palandt* (Figure 2). In many courts it is the only commentary of which every judge has a copy on his or her desk; nearly every lawyer owns a volume of this book (about 50,000 copies are sold annually) and in most federal states (*Länder*), it is officially admitted as an aid in the Second *Staatsexamen* (state exam).

[133] Cf. Weimar, 'Accursius', 19.
[134] Kannowski, *Buch'sche Glosse*, 18 ff. with references.
[135] See above at 89 f.
[136] See above n. 80.

555 ***Unwirksamkeit einer Vertragsstrafe.*** **Eine Vereinbarung, durch die sich der Vermieter eine Vertragsstrafe vom Mieter versprechen lässt, ist unwirksam.**

1 **Anwendbar:** nur bei Wohnraum (Einf 88 v § 535), auch gem § 549 II, III, für alle Verpfl, insbes auch Räumg (allgM). – **Vertragsstrafe:** §§ 339 ff, auch VertrStrafVerspr Dritter (MüKo/Bieber Rn 4); fingierte Gebühren für Mahng u Bearbeitg od übermäß Verzugszins (AG Bln-Schönebg ZMR **99**, 489). Auch eine Verfallklausel kann einer VertrStrafe gleichzusetzen sein (BGH NJW **60**, 1568). SchadErsPauschalen fallen nur ausnahmsw unter § 555 (MüKo/Bieber Rn 4 mwN, str), zB die Pauschalabgeltg in Höhe von einer Monatsmiete bei vorzeit Mietaufhebg, auch im FormularVertr (Karlsr NJW-RR **00**, 1538 nimmt Verstoß gg §§ 305 c I, 307 I an), jedenfalls, wenn darin der MietVertr auf Wunsch des Mieters aufgehoben wird (Hbg ZMR **90**, 270 mwN;
2 umstr). – **Wirkung:** Nichtigk der VertrStrafe (§ 134); der MietVertr wird davon nicht berührt.

Kapitel 2. Die Miete

Unterkapitel 1. Vereinbarungen über die Miete

556 ***Vereinbarungen über Betriebskosten.*** (1) [1] **Die Vertragsparteien können vereinbaren, dass der Mieter Betriebskosten trägt.** [2] **Betriebskosten sind die Kosten, die dem Eigentümer oder Erbbauberechtigten durch das Eigentum oder das Erbbaurecht am Grundstück oder durch den bestimmungsmäßigen Gebrauch des Gebäudes, der Nebengebäude, Anlagen, Einrichtungen und des Grundstücks laufend entstehen.** [3] **Für die Aufstellung der Betriebskosten gilt die Betriebskostenverordnung vom 25. November 2003 (BGBl. I S. 2346, 2347) fort.** [4] **Die Bundesregierung wird ermächtigt, durch Rechtsverordnung ohne Zustimmung des Bundesrates Vorschriften über die Aufstellung der Betriebskosten zu erlassen.**

(2) [1] **Die Vertragsparteien können vorbehaltlich anderweitiger Vorschriften vereinbaren, dass Betriebskosten als Pauschale oder als Vorauszahlung ausgewiesen werden.** [2] **Vorauszahlungen für Betriebskosten dürfen nur in angemessener Höhe vereinbart werden.**

(3) [1] **Über die Vorauszahlungen für Betriebskosten ist jährlich abzurechnen; dabei ist der Grundsatz der Wirtschaftlichkeit zu beachten.** [2] **Die Abrechnung ist dem Mieter spätestens bis zum Ablauf des zwölften Monats nach Ende des Abrechnungszeitraums mitzuteilen.** [3] **Nach Ablauf dieser Frist ist die Geltendmachung einer Nachforderung durch den Vermieter ausgeschlossen, es sei denn, der Vermieter hat die verspätete Geltendmachung nicht zu vertreten.** [4] **Der Vermieter ist zu Teilabrechnungen nicht verpflichtet.** [5] **Einwendungen gegen die Abrechnung hat der Mieter dem Vermieter spätestens bis zum Ablauf des zwölften Monats nach Zugang der Abrechnung mitzuteilen.** [6] **Nach Ablauf dieser Frist kann der Mieter Einwendungen nicht mehr geltend machen, es sei denn, der Mieter hat die verspätete Geltendmachung nicht zu vertreten.**

(4) **Eine zum Nachteil des Mieters von Absatz 1, Absatz 2 Satz 2 oder Absatz 3 abweichende Vereinbarung ist unwirksam.**

1 **1) Allgemeines.** – Neufassg von I dch Art 11 Föderalismusreform-BegleitG vom 5. 9. 06 (BGBl I 2098), in Kraft ab 1. 1. 07, ist eine Folge des G zur Änderg des GG vom 28. 8. 06 (BGBl I 2034), dch das die soz Wohnraumförderg in die ausschließl Gesetzgebgskompetenz der Länder fällt. Desh wurde die bisher Regelg in WoFG 19 II aufgehoben u dch den Begriff der Betriebskosten in I 2, die ErmächtiggsGrdlage für den VO-Erlass in I 4 u die Anordng der Weitergeltg der BetrKV in I 3 sichergestellt, dass die Vorschr über Betriebskosten weiterh einheitl gelten. Eine sachl Änderg ist also nicht eingetreten. – **a) Zweck.** §§ 556–556 b regeln entgg der amtl Überschrift von UnterKap 1 nicht die Mietstruktur, sond enthalten nur einige Vorschr zu Betriebskosten u Zahlg der Miete. Den Part steht grdsätzl frei, welche Art u ZusSetzg der Miete sie vereinbart (§ 535 II, dort Rn 71). § 556 begrenzt die VertrFreih bei den Betriebskosten, soweit die Part über ihre Übernahme dch den
2 Mieter eine Vereinbg treffen. – **b) Anwendungsbereich:** WohnraummietVerh (Einf 88 v § 535, § 549 Rn 5),
3 auch iSv § 549 II, III (§ 549 Rn 14): MischmietVerh, wenn das Schwergewicht auf dem Wohnen liegt. – **c) Unabdingbarkeit** (IV). Sie bedeutet für I wie schon bisher nach hM (BGH NJW **93**, 1061, Karlsr NJW-RR **88**, 1036, Kblz NJW **86**, 995 mwN), dass eine Vereinbg der Umlage von Kosten, die nicht als Betriebskosten unter BetrKV 2 fallen (Rn 4), unwirks ist. Diese Kosten, zB Verwaltgskosten, können nur als Kalkulationsposten des Verm in der Miete enthalten sein. Zu unwirks ErhöhgsVorbeh s BGH NJW **93**, 1061, **04**, 1380, NJW-RR **04**, 586. Unwirks sind auch die Vereinbg unangemessen hoher Vorauszahlgen sowie die Beschränkg des Anspr auf jährl Abrechng, des FdgsAusschlusses des Verm u der Prüfgsfrist des Mieters.

4 **2) Betriebskostenvereinbarung (I 1, 2, II 1).** – **a) Betriebskosten**, deren Begriff in I 2 wie in BetrKV 1 I 1 bestimmt ist, sind ausschließl die gem BetrKV 2, 1 I 2 (Übbl Stangl ZMR **06**, 95; Einzelh: MüKo/Schmid BetrKV 2 Rn 2 ff. Sch-F/Langenberg Rn 102 ff); im Einz: lfde öff Lasten des Grdst. Kosten für Wasserversorgg, Entwässerg, Betrieb der zentralen Heizgsanlage (zu Betriebsstrom BGH NJW **08**, 1801), Betrieb der zentralen Brennstoffversorggsanlagen, eigenständ gewerbl Wärmelieferg (§ 535 Rn 100; zur Umstellg auf Wärmelieferg § 535 Rn 24, § 560 Rn 8), Reinigg u Wartg von Etagenheizgen u Gaseinzelfeuerstätten, Betrieb der zentralen Warmwasserversorggsanlage, eigenständ gewerbl Warmwasserlieferg, Reinigg u Wartg von Warmwassergeräten, verbundene Heizgs- u Warmwasserversorggsanlagen, Betrieb eines Pers- od Lastenaufzuges, Straßenreinigg u Müllbeseitigg, Gebäudereinigg u Ungezieferbekämpfg, Gartenpflege, Beleuchtg, Schornsteinreinigg, Sach- u HaftpflVers, Hauswart (nicht Pförtner, BGH NZM **05**, 452) unter Abzug bestimmter nicht umlagefäh, vom Verm darzulegder (BGH NJW **08**, 1801) Kosten, Betrieb der GemschAntennenanlage u der mit einem Breitbandkabelnetz verbundenen privaten Verteileranlage (dazu bei fehlder Vereinbg BGH NJW **07**, 3060), Betrieb der Einrichtgen für Wäschepflege sowie sonst Betriebskosten gem BetrKV 2 Nr 17 (zB Regenrinnenreinigg BGH NJW-RR **04**, 875, wiederkehrde Kosten zur Prüfg einer techn Anlage BGH NJW **07**, 1356, weitere Bsp MüKo/Schmid BetrKV 2 Rn 75). Erfdl ist, dass sie lfd entstehen (BetrKV 1 I 1). Nicht darunter fallen insbes Instandhaltgsu Instandsetzgskosten (BetrKV 1 II Nr 2, § 535 Rn 38). Nur Betriebskosten, die tats entstehen u einer ordngsgem Bewirtschaftg entsprechen, dürfen zugrunde gelegt werden. Gartenpflegekosten dürfen mit Ausn der Flächen, die nur der Verm od bestimmte Mieter allein nutzen dürfen, auf alle Mieter umgelegt werden, auch wenn diese den Garten nicht nutzen (BGH NZM **04**, 545); ebso Aufzugskosten auch auf Erdgeschossmie-

784

Figure 2. A German commentary (*Palandt*)

Many factors contribute to this extraordinary authority. Originally, it was backed by the national socialist government that introduced the *Palandt* as a means of adapting the law to its policies; later, the *Palandt* derived its authority self-referentially from the fact that it was treated as authority by the legal profession.[137] What is more, the *Palandt* has always met the expectations of practising lawyers: it is up to date (a new edition is released every year); it is well-structured; its opinions are closely related to the actual practice of the courts; and it succeeds in compressing a huge mass of easily accessible information into one single volume. Thus, the authority of the *Palandt* must primarily be attributed to its functional formal quality. Indeed, among its characteristics, the brevity is most remarkable: the *Palandt* even introduced an elaborate system of abbreviations for most technical and many everyday words (see Figure 2, §556 [1]). These abbreviations significantly reduce the printing space.

Notably, however, the *Palandt* includes—in bold letters, like most modern commentaries—the wording of the legislation to which the commentary relates (see Figure 2). This inclusion of the BGB's text contributes to the text's overall length by about 10 per cent. It deserves special attention, because there is probably no practical need for this space-consuming reprint. German civil lawyers usually have a separate version of the BGB at hand when they use the *Palandt*; many lawyers even prefer looking at this text, because it is only there that they can see a provision in its systematic context. Indeed, reprinting the reference text has not always been a common practice of legal commentaries, as it is today. The *ius commune* commentators to the *Digest* did not reprint their Roman legislative sources;[138] neither did the German and Swiss authors commenting on the legislative codifications during much of the 19th century,[139] nor the early commentators on the French *Code*

[137] Slapnicar, 'Der Wilke, der später Palandt hieß'; cf. also Wrobel: 'Otto Palandt zum Gedächtnis', 8 ff., 14 f.; Barnert, 'Von Station zu Station', 59 f., 63 f., also on the person of Otto Palandt.

[138] This can already be seen in the early commentaries by Bartolus and Baldus; cf. later Brunnemann, *Commentarius in Pandectas*; Wesenbeck, *Paratitla*; Stryk, *Usus Modernus*; Voet, *Commentarius ad Pandectas*. However, some commentaries reprinted the text of the *Institutes*, yet they did not typologically emphasize the legislation's authority; cf. Vinnius, *Commentarius*: Roman text reprinted in small, italic types.

[139] Cf. for Prussia Ludwig, *Commentar zum allgemeinen Landrecht*; Merckel, *Commentar zum allgemeinen Landrecht*; Bielitz, *Praktischer Kommentar*. For other parts of

civil.[140] And when the modern practice began to prevail at the end of the 19th century, it was, for a long time, unusual to underline the codification's text with bold print.[141] Indeed, such a typological format was not adopted by the German commentaries during the first decades of the 20th century, either.[142]

What is more, the *Palandt* does not abbreviate the legislative text of the BGB. In contrast to the commentary's explanatory remarks, the legislator's words are thus presented as sacrosanct against mundane, practical needs. As a result, the *Palandt's* doctrinal comments—i.e. the texts that are really read by the lawyer—are presented as less important than the legislation from which they claim to derive their authority, and they are written in the form of explanatory descriptions of the law. Typically, the comments are related to individual legal requirements and to the terms of the BGB's provisions; hence, they present themselves as interpretations or clarifications of the BGB's wording. Again, the commentary presents itself as an exegetical explanation of an eminent text; this reveals a striking similarity with the standard glosses.

Thereby, the commentary constructs again, by typological means, a sharp institutional separation between the law and its scholarly

Germany Spangenberg, *Commentar über den Code Napoleon*; for Switzerland Schnell, *Commentar über das Civilrecht des Kantons Bern.*

[140] See Duranton, *Cour de Droit Français*; Toullier, *Droit Civil Français*; cf. also Troplong, *Droit Civil.* Troplong's commentary reprinted the code's text, yet the comments did not relate specifically to individual provisions but usually referred to a group of three to five provisions.

[141] In one of the first commentaries to a city's local legislation, still in the times of the *ius commune,* David Mevius had reprinted the legislation in Germanic typeface, whereas the Latin translation was printed—in the same size as the commentary—in normal typeface: *Commentarii in Jus Lubecense*. During the 19th century, the codification's text was usually printed in slightly larger or slightly spaced letters. Only the paragraph or article numbers were sometimes printed in large, bold letters, in order to structure the text visually; cf. for France, Marcade, *Code Napoléon*; Saint-Prix, *Notes théoriques*; for Germany, E. Siebenhaar, *Commentar zu dem bürgerlichen Gesetzbuche für das Königreich Sachsen*; Puchelt (ed.), *Handelsgesetzbuch*; Uebel, *Civil-Prozeßordnung*. For Switzerland, Ullmer, *Gesetzbuche des Kantons Zürich*. A bold printing underlining the legislative text's status can be found rather early in Austria; cf. von Kirchstetter, *Commentar zum Oesterreichischen Allgemeinen bürgerlichen Gesetzbuche*; von Stubenrauch, *Commentar zum österreichischen Allgemeinen bürgerlichen Gesetzbuche*. Here, already Franz von Zeiller had reprinted the code's wording in very large (though not bold) letters that added visual authority to the legislation; see von Zeiller, *Commentar über das allgemeine bürgerliche Gesetzbuch*.

[142] See Planck (ed.), *Bürgerliches Gesetzbuch; J. v. Staudingers Kommentar*; Oertmann, *Schuldverhältnisse*; Warneyer, *Kommentar zum Bürgerlichen Gesetzbuch*. All these commentaries maintained the typological format of the 19th century (above n. 141).

description. Of course, most German lawyers are today aware of the fact that their private law is much more than comes only from a codification and interpretative method. During the 20th century, large parts of the law have been fundamentally changed as a result of legal developments initiated by the practical lawyers, courts, and legal scholars. Indeed, large parts of the law cannot be found at all in the BGB or other legislation; rather, there are thick layers of praetorian law specifying, fleshing out, and even correcting the codes' provisions.[143] Of course, these judgments must be included within the academic commentaries; otherwise a commentary would be without much practical value. But typographically, the commentaries nevertheless maintain and thus institutionalize the traditional separation of legal scholarship and judicial decisions on the one hand and the law on the other hand.[144] Accordingly, judgments are presented not as sources of new law, but rather as authoritative interpretations of legislation. Again, formal means are used, successfully, for creating and maintaining legal authority. Indeed, the normative legal statements, which are collected in the comments, would be without practical value or legal authority if they could not be treated as interpretations of the law. Thus, their typographical presentation as interpretative explanations helps in establishing their legitimacy and authority. True, the formal presentation may no longer be the most decisive factor in the case of a well-established commentary, such as the *Palandt*, which recommends itself with its functional quality, and whose authority is simply taken for granted by most German lawyers. Nevertheless, the significance of this factor should not be underestimated: the formal presentation of this commentary cannot be explained with functional aspects alone.

Modern lawyers might perhaps be inclined to disqualify such use of form to create authority or legitimacy as being manipulative and illegitimate. Legal authority should be the result of democratic, open, and transparent procedures, on the one hand, and of convincing legal argument on the other. It should not be created by means which are beyond

[143] See *HKK/Zimmermann*, vor § 1. 'Das Bürgerliche Gesetzbuch ...' [17]; Zimmermann and Jansen, 'Quieta Movere', 287 ff., 296 ff.; Jansen, 'Codifications, Commentators, and Courts', all with further references.

[144] For the jurisprudential discussion in Germany, see Zimmermann and Jansen, 'Quieta Movere', 302 ff., with further references.

democratic or judicial control. It is doubtful, though, whether such a critique fully appreciates and fairly assesses the function of such mechanisms in the law.[145] Indeed, all these mechanisms can also be understood as means of protecting the integrity of the legal process. Thus, even if the declaratory theory of legal argument and judicial decision making, as expressed in the standard glosses and likewise in modern commentaries, like the *Palandt*, may be denounced as a fiction, this fiction has an important institutional function. It works as a device for controlling the legal profession: it prevents lawyers from taking full control of the legal system and arbitrarily and illegitimately developing the law. Indeed, the form of the standard glosses and the *Palandt* clearly confines the interpretative 'freedom' of scholars by forcing them to present their propositions about the law in the form of interpretations of legislation, specifically related to the exact wording of the authoritative provisions. In such a presentation, gross deviations from the legislative text are normally implausible; they are difficult to justify and will usually remain exceptional. Thus, the institutional form of the standard glosses and the *Palandt* protects the integrity of the authoritative texts: while adding to the authority of scholarly writing, it limits its influence. In modern terms, the authority of the *Palandt* depends on the commentary's remaining responsive to the political process.

(c) Restatements of the law

All these observations help to understand the authority of non-legislative codifications as well. Indeed, the Restatements have been interpreted as part of the codification movement because of their formal similarities with European codifications.[146] More precisely, a restatement (Figure 3) very much resembles a codification as it is reprinted together with a scholarly comment; and the same is true for the PICC (Appendix, Figure 7): those texts present boldly printed authoritative rules, which are accompanied by explanatory Comments and Illustrations. In their formal presentation, the restatements thus replicate the civilian distinction of the legal rule and its academic comment: the rules are presented as authoritative in being the object of doctrinal explanation.

[145] Cf. also, for the analysis of procedures, Stollberg-Rilinger, 'Einleitung'.
[146] Crystal, 'Restatement Movement' 267 f.

§§ 101–102 CONTRACTS Ch. 4

§ 101. SEALED PROMISE DELIVERED UNCONDITIONALLY OR IN ESCROW.

A promise under seal may be delivered by the promisor unconditionally, in which case there is a present contract under seal; or may be delivered in escrow, in which case there is no present contract under seal. Delivery may be made either unconditionally or in escrow to the promisee or to any other person.

Comment:

a. The Section by its terms is applicable to the power of a promisor to subject himself to a duty. It does not enable a promisor by inserting in a document not only his own promise, but what purports to be a promise by the promisee, to subject the latter to a duty by delivering the document to a third person. If, however, a promisor attempts this, his own promise is likewise ineffective until the promisee by accepting the document assents to assume the stated duty (see §§ 105–107).

Illustration:

1. A delivers to B a sealed promise naming C as promisee. Though C is ignorant of the existence of the promise there is a present contract if the delivery was unconditional, a delivery in escrow if the delivery was conditional.

§ 102. WHAT AMOUNTS TO UNCONDITIONAL DELIVERY.

A promise under seal is delivered unconditionally when the promisor puts it out of his possession with the apparent intent to create immediately a contract under seal, unless the promisee then knows that the promisor has not such actual intent.

120

Figure 3. American *Restatements of the Law of Contracts* (First series)

Yet, although the authors of the first Restatements consciously chose this legislative form,[147] they apparently did not borrow it directly from the European codifications or commentaries. Rather, the immediate models were certain English textbooks,[148] and especially Albert Venn Dicey's work on the conflicts of law (Figure 4).[149] This was a book which must be seen as a genuinely scholarly contribution to the English codification debate.[150] Dicey wanted to show that the common law could be reconstructed as a systematic body of rules, and for this purpose he presented the law of conflicts in the 'form of systematically arranged Rules and Exceptions, and each of these Rules and Exceptions is, when necessary, elucidated by comment and illustrations.'[151] Dicey, who was probably inspired by some earlier textbooks also using rules to present the law in an orderly form,[152] had developed his own, rather specific format in his treatise on the *Selection of Parties* (1870); he had further refined it in his subsequent treatises on the *Law of Domicil* (1879) and on the *Conflict of Laws* (1896). Although Dicey found some followers, who again slightly modified his approach, though,[153] his form of presenting doctrinal knowledge remained exceptional.

[147] Above at 105 f.

[148] Powell, *Evidence*; Hawkins, *Wills* (rules of construction of wills, rather than rules of the law: pp. iv f.); Underhill, *Law of Torts*. All those rather short books presented the law in the form of rules. None of them, however, used the terminology of Comments and Illustrations and structured the text as clearly as Dicey. Later authors using a similar format were Stephen, *Evidence* (Stephen used 'Illustrations', but no 'Comments' to explain his rules); id., *Criminal Law* (only few illustrations); Bower, *Defamation*; id., *Misrepresentation*.

[149] The model character of Dicey's work has escaped the notice of most later observers; and it has only rarely been explicitly acknowledged by the fathers of the Restatements, too, most likely because the American Law Institute had been so critical of a textbook-like treatment of the law (above at 105). However, an exception is Cardozo, *Growth of the Law*, 7, who also pointed to the work of James Fitzjames Stephen on *Evidence*.

[150] A. Braun, 'English codification debate', at 3: '"Codification" through academic enterprise'. Stephen's *Digest of the Law of Evidence* even grew out of the Indian Evidence Act of which Stephen was an author. What is more, this book was originally written as a proposal for a similar English Act; it was published as a monograph, when it turned out that the proposal would not be submitted to Parliament: *loc. cit.*, iii. f.

[151] Dicey, *Conflict of Laws*, vii.

[152] See the works of Powell and Hawkins, above n. 148.

[153] See especially the treatises by Bower, Stephen and Underhill above n. 148.

BRITISH NATIONALITY. 181

Comment.

This Rule embodies a complete change in the law of England. By the common law marriage does not affect a woman's nationality. Now, in virtue of the Naturalization Act, 1870, s. 10, her nationality varies under English law with that of her husband.

Illustrations.

1. *S* is a Frenchwoman born in France. She marries a British subject. She becomes a British subject.

2. *S* is an Englishwoman born in England. She marries a French citizen domiciled in London. She thereupon is deemed to be a French citizen, and becomes a statutory alien.[1]

RULE 32.[2]—A widow continues to be the subject of the state of which her late husband was at his death a subject, until she changes her nationality.

Comment and Illustration.

This Rule is not, in so many words, laid down in the Naturalization Act, 1870; it may, however, be reasonably deduced from the Naturalization Act, 1870, s. 10, sub-ss. (1) and (2).

S is a natural-born British subject. She marries a French citizen living and domiciled in England. She never leaves England till his death. On the death of her husband she remains a French citizen.

RULE 33.[3]—A divorced woman continues to be the subject of the state of which her husband was a subject immediately before or at the moment of divorce, until she changes her nationality (?).

[1] Under French law, a foreign woman who marries a Frenchman follows the status of her husband. *S.*, therefore, in fact becomes on her marriage a French citizen *Semble*, however, she would under the Naturalization Act, 1870, be "deemed to be" a French citizen in England even if she were not so in fact under French law.

[2] Compare Naturalization Act, 1870, s. 10, sub-ss. (1) and (2). See *Bloxam* v. *Farre* (1883), 8 P. D. 101; (1884), 9 P. D. (C. A.) 130.

[3] Compare Rules 31, 32, *ante*.

Figure 4. Dicey, *Conflict of Laws*

Remarkably, the Restatements (First) were not drafted as a formal copy of Dicey's work; they modified Dicey's presentation in important respects. It is worth looking at these modifications more closely, because they help in better understanding the ideas underlying the restatements' form. Dicey's motive for representing the law in the form of commented rules was not to add authority to his work. Rather, he had chosen his method primarily for the practical consideration of making the law more easily accessible:

> The practical advantage of the arrangement pursued in this treatise is, that it enables the reader to see at a glance what the rule of law is, whilst it frees him from the necessity of collecting the principle for which he is in search from the decisions or statutes in which it is embodied; and that it further puts it in his power to refer with great readiness to the subject on which he may desire to be informed.[154]

Moreover, Dicey wanted to show that the seemingly complex and untidy common law could be reduced to a system of relatively few principles:

> An advantage of a more speculative nature is that this arrangement ... makes, it is hoped, apparent the fact that this somewhat complicated and intricate branch of the law, [sic] depends on and is the expression of a few simple principles.[155]

This, Dicey assumed, was necessary for showing that a codification of the common law was feasible and useful:

> The law ... is ... reduced into a series of definite rules, which being based on statutory enactments, decided cases, or inferences drawn from authoritative dicta or admitted principles, constitute, insofar as my work has been successfully performed, a code of what may be termed the English law ...[156]

Thus, Dicey's primary intention was to present the overly complex common law as an orderly and easily accessible system; his choice of form was based on this intention.

[154] Dicey, *Selection of parties*, iv.
[155] Dicey, *Selection of parties*, iv.
[156] Dicey, *Domicil*, iv f. See similarly Stephen, *Evidence*, vii: 'I have attempted ... to make a digest of the law, which ... might be used in the preparation of a code ...', cf. also xvi f. and see above n. 150.

Now, in accordance with this rather scholarly purpose, most of his treatise consists of an analysis of common law authorities that Dicey showed to support the rules in question. There is a great deal of text in relation to the rules and the text is full of references to authorities. What is more, although the rules were separated from the comments, they were not set in bold letters: Dicey was exclusively concerned about clarity; his rules were not meant to bear particular legislation-like dignity. And, perhaps most significantly, Dicey even added question marks where he felt that the rule in question was not supported with sufficient authority.[157] Thus, although Dicey used the form of normative, prescriptive rules, his treatises were clearly meant to be genuinely descriptive in approach. In effect, his rules were prescriptive in a descriptive sense. There was no doubt that Dicey's work was methodically based on the assumption of an institutional distinction between the law and its scholarly description. His rules were based on external authority and supported by legal argument.

Compared with this approach, the Restatements' (First) formal presentation is much more ambiguous. On the one hand, the Restatements (First) were clearly meant to represent the law, as it stood and was applied by the courts. Therefore, their claim to authority was of non-political, derivative nature, as well. On the other hand, however, the formal meaning of these Restatements has never been purely descriptive, either. Indeed, whereas the original Report of the Committee of 35 had considered, in accordance with Dicey's descriptive method, a 'complete citation of authorities, decisions, treatises and articles',[158] nothing like this can be found in the actual Restatements (First), because '(i)t seemed that the Restatement would be more likely to achieve an authority of its own . . . if exact rules were clearly stated without argument'.[159] *Lex iubeat, non disputet.*

Remarkably, similar observations can be made in the case of the PICC. Like the American Restatements, these principles do not

[157] Dicey, *Domicil*, v: 'I have . . . when a rule seemed doubtful, indicated the uncertainty by a printed query'.

[158] ALI, 'Report of the Committee Proposing the Establishment of an American Law Institute', 22. Otherwise, it was feared, the legal profession would not have confidence in the result. Hence, there should be a 'tangible proof of care'.

[159] Williston, 'The Restatement of Contracts', 777.

normally offer reasons for the position taken, but merely provide Comments that are meant to explain the provisions' meaning. Indeed, the official Comments 'systematically refrain from referring to national laws in order to explain the origin and rationale of the solution retained'.[160] Here the purpose is that the Rules shall not be presented as a—probably wrong—description of a common core of the world's different legal systems. Rather, the PICC shall constructively contribute to the creation of a transnational body of private law; the Principles' formal presentation was specifically designed with regard to this purpose.[161] Academic commentators have criticized this approach for its lack of information and scholarly qualities.[162] But the purpose of such restatements consists in establishing legal authority rather than in providing lawyers with comparative information or legal argument.

In accordance with the intention of making legal authority, the American Restatements contained (of course) no question marks where the law was disputed, and the Rules were printed in bold letters. What is more, the Restatements were not published like an ordinary book, but rather 'promulgated' by the American Law Institute[163] as if they were an act of legislation. Hence, the formal meaning of the Rule-Comment separation appears much more as a replication of the civilian separation of the legal rule and its academic explanation than had been the case in the work of Dicey. Similar observations hold again for the PICC, which are printed in (very) bold letters, as well. Clearly, these Rules are of greater weight, or dignity, than the Comments and Illustrations which are written

[160] Governing Council of UNIDROIT, 'Introduction to the 1994 Edition', xv; see above at 106.

[161] Cf. Governing Council of UNIDROIT, 'Introduction to the 1994 Edition', xv: 'This goal (namely, to establish a balanced set of rules designed for use throughout the world ...) is reflected in their formal presentation'. Similarly Bonell, *International Restatement*, 68, stressing the international character of the principles, which does purportedly not allow for a citation of national authorities. In contrast, uniform law instruments, especially the CISG, are cited, if they are the more or less literal source for a rule in the PICC.

[162] *PICC-Commentary*/Vogenauer, Introduction [21]; *PICC-Commentary*/Michaels, Preamble I [4]; Basedow, 'Uniform Law Conventions and the UNIDROIT Principles', 130 f.; Metzger, *Extra legem, intra ius*, 249 f.

[163] See the title of the first Restatement: *Restatements of the Law of Contracts as Adopted and Promulgated by the American Law Institute.*

as explanations, rather than as justifications, of the black-letter Rules.[164] Even if the PICC were not 'promulgated' by UNIDROIT, the Institute officially 'authorised their publication', although it could not formally approve them.[165] Thereby, the meaning of the Restatements' and PICC's formal presentation was strongly influenced by the fact that they were published not as the work of a single author, but rather as the result of complex decision procedures within an authoritative organization that represented the legal profession as a whole or, in the case of UNIDROIT, the transnational legal community. Indeed, it makes a huge difference whether a scholar, like Dicey, presented a rule as his individual academic view of how the law should be reconstructed or whether a rule is presented as the collective conviction of the legal community or as an official statement of an international organization.

All in all, by using a normative, prescriptive language for their Rules and by presenting them in the form of legislation, the American Law Institute and UNIDROIT implicitly staged their Rules as authoritative statements of the law. Yet, these Institutes did not make an obviously illegitimate claim of making the law: the Rules were published under the well-chosen title of a 'Restatement' of the common or transnational law, rather than as the result of quasi-legislative decision making. In this way the formal and conceptual presentation of the Restatements (First) and the PICC blurred the difference between a descriptive representation ('restatement') of rules actually in force and a prescriptive statement of legislation.[166] Thus, they consciously ignored, or rather transgressed,

[164] A somewhat different impression is given by UNIDROIT. Here, authors often emphasize that '(t)he Comments are an integral part of the UNIDROIT Principles' and that their function consists not only in explaining, but also in supplementing the rules: Bonell, *International Restatement*, 62; cf. also Furmston, 'UNIDROIT Principles and International Commercial Arbitration', 203. Yet, this does not really distinguish the PICC from the American Restatements. The black-letter rules remain the starting point of legal argument; they are clearly of greater importance than the Comments. Indeed, a 'supplement' is normally of lower significance than the primary rule; and the Working Group used to put disputed qualifications of the black-letter rule into the Comment (Furmston, *loc. cit.*). Thus, they were seen as of secondary significance, and they are apparently understood in this sense by the actual legal practice.

[165] See above at 69.

[166] See above at 58 f., 70 f.; Kelley, 'Reform by Descriptive Theory', especially 122 ff.

the traditional European institutional distinction between the law and its description. The Rules were presented neither as a description of the courts' practice, nor as a legislative command, but rather as an authoritative expression of the legal profession's considered view of the law. This resulting ambiguity in formal meaning made it possible for the legal profession to accept the Restatements and the PICC as authoritative statements of the law without, however, inappropriately treating them as legislation. If the authority of the Restatements' second and especially third series is indeed in decline these days, this is probably not least due to the fact that—in order to justify more innovative rules—the Restatements have increasingly complemented the statement and explanation of the Rules with legal argument and references to legal authorities.[167] Thus, these more recent Restatements present themselves increasingly as a proposal of a new rule to be accepted by the legal profession, rather than as a statement of the law. Yet, such argument will always be contested.

Interestingly, these observations are confirmed by a view on the PECL. The Lando Commission has always understood and presented its Rules as an outcome of scholarly, comparative research and as a proposal for future legislation, rather than as a system of authoritative rules that would be applicable as such.[168] Hence, the Rules are not printed in bold letters, but, more modestly, in italics. And, most importantly, the Comments and Illustrations are always followed by Notes providing a comparative overview and justification of the Rule (see Appendix, Figure 6). Thus, the PECL clearly acknowledge the institutional difference between the description and the authoritative statement of the law (indeed, the Notes often

[167] See on this development Hesselink, 'Choices Made by the Lando Commission', 77 ff.; Michaels, 'Restatements', at 2.

[168] This is so despite the strong wording of its first Art. 1:101(1) PECL: 'These Principles are intended to be applied as general rules of contract law in the European Union'. Indeed, parties are merely 'invited' to incorporate the PECL into their contract, and the official comment emphasizes that those Principles 'do not have the authority ... of law' (Art. 1:101 PECL, Comment A, C). In contrast, no such wording can be found in the Official Comment to the PICC's Preamble. There is only a brief acknowledgment of this fact by the Governing Council of UNIDROIT in the 'Introduction to the 1994 Edition', xv, which is immediately qualified, though, by a claim for the Principles' being of 'persuasive authority'.

prove the PECL's claim of adequately restating European private law to be unfounded or questionable).[169] The relatively weak authority of the PECL (as compared with the PICC and the American Restatements) may find further explanation in this observation, and the concern of some observers that the PICC might not be fully accepted because of their lack of argument and reference[170] has proved unjustified.

Of course, it may be doubted whether blurring the difference between the representation of rules actually in force and a prescriptive statement of legislation is an acceptable and legitimate means of establishing legal authority. However, the American Law Institute's Restatements would never have been understood—nor even accepted—as authoritative statements of the law, had the Institute not been regarded by the legal profession as an institution which was legitimized to make authoritative statements on American law. In this sense, the Institute was apparently seen as legitimately representing the elite of the American legal profession. It was therefore accepted as an institution which was vested with some kind of (weak) legislative authority.[171] Thus, the formal blurring of the difference between the representation and description of legal rules must be seen as an expression of a *claim* to a specific type of authority which had to be justified on the basis of reputation, representation, and procedure. This was, of course, not even close to democratic legitimacy. But the creation of legitimacy and authority by the American Law Institute was not based on illegitimate manipulation, either.

The same is apparently true for the PICC. As an institution, the UNIDROIT-Institute was certainly legitimized to take steps to unify private law and to create a transnational legal system. Of course, it may be doubted whether it was legitimate to do so by

[169] Cf. only the Notes to Art. 1:201 PECL (on Good Faith and Fair Dealing); Notes 3 and 4 to Art. 2:101 PECL (Conditions for the Conclusion of a Contract), on the basic question of consideration and *cause*; the Notes to Art. 6:110 PECL (Stipulation in Favour of a Third Party) (these rules were, however, already outdated, with respect to English law, when the PECL were published in 2000); or the Notes to Art. 9:503 (Foreseeability [of loss]).

[170] See Basedow, 'Uniform Law Conventions and the UNIDROIT Principles', 130 f.

[171] See above at 54 f. and 132 f.

procedural and formal means, which had not been provided for in the Institute's Statute.[172] But again, the formal presentation should be seen as an expression of the *claim* to formulate authoritative legal standards, which has to be justified on the basis of the Institute's reputation[173] and the perceived legitimacy (rather than substantial quality) of its Rules. And it is remarkable that the institutional distinction between the law and its description has quickly been re-established by (mostly European) legal scholars, when they treated the PICC as a reference text for an academic commentary.[174]

III. Some Results

Form proves to be much more than a pragmatic, functional device of making the law easily accessible. The formal presentation of a text has an important graphical aspect that may transport meaning. Thus, the formal presentation of a non-legislative reference text may symbolize some kind of institutional authority; it can thus be used as a means of creating or adding to its authority. This is not only true for scholarly work, such as the medieval standard glosses and a modern commentary to a civil code, but also for non-legislative codifications. The authority of the American Restatements of the Law (First) and also of the PICC was established not only by authorship and procedure, but to a significant degree also by an intelligent choice of form. The formal fiction of legitimate legislation and the transgression of the traditional separation of the law and its scholarly description helped in establishing legal authority.

At the same time, a comparative view makes apparent that there is not a standard set of formal means creating legal authority. The adequate form depends always on its authors and addressees and on the relevant legal, social, cultural, and political context. Thus, while the medieval standard glosses and the modern commentaries typographically constructed and maintained the institutional distinction between the law and its description, on which the authority of

[172] See above 69 f. Further references on this discussion at 93, n. 55.
[173] On this claim, cf. Kronke, 'A Bridge out of the Fortress'.
[174] Vogenauer and Kleinheisterkamp (eds), *PICC-Commentary*.

scholarly commentaries depends, this very distinction had to be blurred by the Restatements (First) and by the PICC. The American Law Institute's and UNIDROIT's claim to re-state the law authoritatively was based on an ambiguity of describing and prescribing the law; and this ambiguity was again created by means of formal presentation. However, this strategy would not have worked if these Institutes had not been regarded as organizations which legitimately represented the American legal profession or, respectively, the international community of global contract lawyers. Furthermore, the Restatements would not have been accepted by a legal profession which did not in its majority highly esteem the formal values of clarity and precision,[175] and which did not believe in the existence of one common national common law.[176] Similarly, the PICC would have been less successful in arbitrational practice if there had not been an evident lack of systematic reference texts for a growing body of transnational commercial contract law.

It would therefore be a misunderstanding to assume that the different forms of non-legislative, professional authority, as described in Chapter 3, were functionally equivalent in that they could be used alternatively. The form of a legal instrument must always be designed for its purposes taking the existing legal and cultural background into account. Thus, whereas a legal commentary presupposes the existence of a rather comprehensive reference text, restatements provide a legal system with a new comprehensive textual authority. Such an instrument will be helpful only if the legal system indeed needs a new textual, statutory basis. Conversely, if a legal system is already based on well-established, though inconsistent, legislative authorities, as was the case in early Canon law and may be argued to be the case in Europe today, a compilation like the *Decretum Gratiani* might be a more appropriate form for reordering the law.

[175] Cf. Gilmore, *Ages of American Law*, 73 f.

[176] Above at 97 f.

Conclusion

A comparative and historical perspective shows that non-legislative codifications, such as the American Restatements, the *Principles of European Contract Law*, and the UNIDROIT *Principles of International Commercial Contracts*, are no modern peculiarity. On the contrary: European private law has long been developed on the basis of texts that were largely independent of any political domination. This becomes apparent from the transjurisdictional character of most non-legislative codifications. Thus, private law has mostly been, and still is to a large degree, autonomous from the states' political system. Of course, the law has always been responsive to the states' or governments' political policy-making, on which it indeed depends, and the sources of private law may relate exclusively to a state's domination. But from a historical and comparative perspective, such a finding would be rather exceptional. It thus amounts to an oversimplification to base private law essentially or conceptually on the state or on a legislator's political will. Often, private law and its textual authorities are—in different degrees—beyond the state.[1]

As a result, it has been seen that legal authority, i.e. the abstract status and formal weight of a text in legal argument,[2] results from and is determined by complex processes of recognition in legal discourse. Not only the authority of non-legislative reference texts and learned commentaries, but also the authority of judicial decisions[3] and of the state's legislation ultimately depends on their reception by the legal profession. Hence, non-legislative reference texts may gain similar or even greater authority than legislative codifications. Of course, lawyers usually prefer to rely on the political authority of the state and the legislator; they have therefore

[1] See also Michaels, 'The true lex mercatoria'.

[2] See above at 43 f.: the abstract authority of a legal text consists in the legal profession accepting it as an ultimate source of the law, without requiring further legal reasons to do so.

[3] Cf. Postema, 'Philosophy of the Common Law', 596 f., 601.

long included the idea of domination in concepts of legislation and law.[4] But the legal system will independently establish its basic reference texts if the political sector proves unable, for whatever reason, to formulate the necessary authorities.

As a result of these findings, jurisprudential theories reconstructing (private) law on the basis of a single, state-oriented *Grundnorm* or rule of recognition offer an inappropriately simple reconstruction of legal systems. Such theories proceed from the seemingly evident, though nevertheless misleading, question of whether a norm is 'valid' within a legal system. In contrast, it is notable that professional private lawyers have only rarely openly addressed the question of a non-legislative reference text's validity.[5] Rather they have discussed, much more specifically, the relation of legislative and non-legislative texts, and the applicability of specific non-legislative rules. Examples are the relation of the Roman *Corpus iuris* and statutory law, or of the American Restatements and the precedents of American courts, or the discussion of the applicability of the PICC in the context of national and uniform law.[6] What matters in practical legal discourse is less the 'validity' of a norm but rather its applicability and authority, i.e. the formal weight of a normative text in legal discourse as an ultimate source of the law.

The authority of legislative and non-legislative codifications is a result of individual historical processes and cannot, therefore, be explained on the basis of abstract theory alone. Nevertheless, comparative analysis reveals rather general factors of legal authority: factors determining whether the legal profession will normally accept or reject such a text as authority in legal discourse. Notably, these factors are to a large degree, even if never fully, time-, system-, and culture-independent. Some of these factors relate to the situation of the legal profession itself. Here, the most important are the codification's

[4] Above at 85 f.

[5] Cf. also Metzger, *Extra legem, intra ius*, 251 ff., 282 ff., 385 ff., 437 ff. with comparative observations. Metzger himself nonetheless discusses the 'validity' of general principles of the law, such as the American Restatements, the PICC, or the PECL. Yet, as traditional concepts of validity are not helpful for such a discussion, he emphasizes the non-positivist meaning of 'validity' in this context.

[6] Compare Stryk, 'Discursus Praeliminaris de Usu et Auctoritate Juris Romani', and *PICC-Commentary*/Michaels, Preamble I.

fitting in with the social identity of the legal profession and the perception of a crisis in the law's administration; such a crisis has often prepared lawyers to accept new textual authorities. Other factors are text-related. Among those, representation, authorship, and procedure concern the legitimacy of law-making. Professional excellence and reputation have always contributed to a codification's authority; and in more recent times, the procedural ideals of fair representation and discursively open, transparent decision making have become important authority factors also for non-legislative codifications.

Finally, the form of a text has proved to be a key, though underestimated, text-related factor of legal authority. On the one hand, the authority of reference texts depends on whether they offer a consistent, orderly, and easily applicable expression of the actual law. On the other hand, the formal presentation of a reference text may as such symbolize its institutional character and thus contribute to its authority. Well-known texts of legal authority, such as the medieval standard glosses, a modern commentary to a civil code, or the American Restatements, show clearly that the authority both of reference texts and their commentaries depends to a significant degree on their success in presenting themselves as authoritative legal institutions.

It is noteworthy that there is no uniform set of formal devices which could be 'used' for creating legal authority. Rather, the effect of formal instruments always depends on the specific historical, cultural, institutional, and legal context. Thus, the success of a formal device will unavoidably depend on its appropriate and intelligent design. What is more, even if most of these factors are time-, system-, and culture-independent,[7] this does not mean that all of these factors have to be present at the same time. The *Corpus iuris civilis* neither had the formal qualities of other textual authorities, nor did it realize the ideals of fair representation or transparent decision making. It is the interplay and combination of such factors which contribute to the authority of a legal text. Indeed, the legal profession may accept shortcomings in some respects, if there are no

[7] One group of factors, which is clearly not independent in this sense, is the procedural ideals of fair representation and transparent decision making. These factors are an expression of modern conceptions of procedural justice; see above at 102 f.

textual alternatives. Nevertheless, it could be seen, quite clearly, that all these factors do significantly contribute to the authority of legal reference texts.

All in all, the law is much more complex than is commonly assumed. Legal authority is made—like all authority—on the basis of a combination of legally rational and—from a lawyer's perspective—perhaps more irrational, aesthetic factors, such as the typographical presentation of a text and other formal devices. Nonetheless, such factors are of the utmost importance and they are not necessarily manipulative. Indeed, they are indispensable, as legal institutions must be symbolically staged to become a part of social reality. Nevertheless, legal scholars have mostly focused on factors of purely legal rationality. Yet, to include those other aspects in legal analysis is also necessary for a full and adequate understanding of the legal process. This is of particular importance in times when the law is undergoing fundamental changes as a result, for instance, of the Europeanization and globalization of the economy, society, and its legal systems. Lawyers should be conscious of themselves establishing authoritative legal institutions by treating reference texts as legal authorities. And they should have an understanding of the mechanisms influencing their professional behaviour. Only such a full comprehension of the legal process would enable them to develop the law responsibly.

Appendix

¶ Apocalipsis. C XIII.

...dei: et habent testimonium iesu christi. Et stetit super arenam maris. C. XIII. Et vidi de mari bestiam ascendentem habentem capita septem et cornua decem et super cornua eius decem diademata: et super capita eius nomina blasfemie. Et bestia quam vidi similis erat pardo, et pedes eius sicut pedes ursi, et os eius sicut os leonis. Et dedit illi draco virtutem suam et potestatem magnam. Et vidi unum de capitibus suis quasi occisum in mortem, et plaga mortis eius curata est. Et admirata est universa terra post bestiam. Et adoraverunt draconem qui dedit potestatem bestie: et adoraverunt bestiam dicentes: Quis similis bestie, et quis poterit pugnare cum ea? Et datum est ei os loquens magna et blasfemias: et data est illi potestas facere menses xlii. Et aperuit os suum in blasfemias ad deum blasfemare nomen eius et tabernaculum eius et eos qui in celo habitant. Et datum est illi bellum facere cum sanctis: et vincere illos. Et data est ei potestas in omnem tribum et populum et linguam et gentem. et adoraverunt eam omnes qui inhabitabant terram: quorum non sunt scripta nomina in libro vite agni qui occisus est ab origine mundi. Si quis habet aures audiendi audiat. Qui in captivitatem duxerit: in captivitatem vadet. qui in gladio occiderit: oportet eum gladio occidi. Hic est patientia et fides sanctorum. Et vidi aliam bestiam ascendentem de terra, et habebat cornua duo similia agni. Et loquebatur sicut draco. Et potestatem prioris bestie omnem faciebat in conspectu eius. et fecit terram et habitantes in ea adorare bestiam primam: cuius curata est plaga mortis. Et fecit signa magna, ut etiam ignem faceret de celo descendere in terram in conspectu hominum. Et seduxit habitantes in terra propter signa que data sunt illi facere in conspectu bestie: dicens habitantibus in terra ut faciant imaginem bestie que habet plagam gladii et vixit. Et datum est illi ut daret spiritum imagini bestie. et ut loquatur imago bestie: et faciat ut quicumque non adoraverit imaginem bestie occidatur. Et faciet omnes pusillos et magnos et divites et pauperes et liberos et servos habere characterem in dextera manu aut in frontibus suis. et nequis possit emere aut vendere nisi habeat characterem aut nomen bestie aut numerum nominis eius. Hic sapientia est. Qui habet intellectum...

42

Figure 5. *Biblia Latina cum Glossa Ordinaria*

296 *Chapter 5*

Article 5:105: Reference to Contract as a Whole

Terms are to be interpreted in the light of the whole contract in which they appear.

COMMENT

It is reasonable to assume that the parties meant to express themselves coherently. It is thus necessary to interpret the contract as a whole and not to isolate clauses from each other and read them out of context. It must be presumed that the terminology will be coherent; in principle, the same term should not be understood to have different meanings in different parts of the same contract. The contract must be interpreted in a way that gives it basic coherence, so that the clauses do not contradict each other.

There is normally no particular hierarchy between the elements of a contract, save under special circumstances: for example, particular emphasis should be given to any definition of terms or to a preamble which could have been introduced into the contract.

Article 5:105 may also be applied to groups of contracts. For example one can treat a frame-work (master) contract and the various contracts made under it as a whole. By the "whole contract" must be understood the "whole group of contracts".

Illustration: Miss A, an inexperienced singer, is taken on for six months by B, the manager of a cabaret on the Champs-Elysées. The contract contains a clause authorising the manager to end the contract in the first three days of the singer starting work. Another clause allows either party to determine the contract on payment of a significant sum of money as a penalty. Miss A is fired after one day and claims payment of the sum. Her claim should fail because the penalty clause is to be read in the light of the clause allowing determination within three days, which is a trial period.

NOTES

This rule is stated in a number of texts: ITALIAN CC art. 1363; FRENCH, BELGIAN and LUXEMBOURG CCs art. 1161; SPANISH CC art. 1285; UNIDROIT art. 4.4. In PORTUGAL it is found in Law 446/1985 of 15 October 1985 and has been extended to all contracts. It is also found in NORDIC law: Swedish Supreme Court, NJA 1990, 24; for Denmark, see *Lynge Andersen* 357 ff. The rule is also found in English law, see *Chitty* §§12-053 - 2-059 and refs. there, SCOTTISH, GERMAN, AUSTRIAN and GREEK law.

The illustration is inspired by French Cass. soc. 7 March 1973, B 73 V no.145.

Figure 6. *Principles of European Contract Law* (PECL)

Art. 2.1.9 **UNIDROIT Principles**

ARTICLE 2.1.9

(Late acceptance. Delay in transmission)

(1) A late acceptance is nevertheless effective as an acceptance if without undue delay the offeror so informs the offeree or gives notice to that effect.

(2) If a communication containing a late acceptance shows that it has been sent in such circumstances that if its transmission had been normal it would have reached the offeror in due time, the late acceptance is effective as an acceptance unless, without undue delay, the offeror informs the offeree that it considers the offer as having lapsed.

COMMENT

1. Late acceptance normally ineffective

According to the principle laid down in Art. 2.1.7 for an acceptance to be effective it must reach the offeror within the time fixed by the latter or, if no time is fixed, within a reasonable time. This means that as a rule an acceptance which reaches the offeror thereafter is without effect and may be disregarded by the offeror.

2. Offeror may nevertheless "accept" late acceptance

Para. (1) of this article, which corresponds to Art. 21 CISG, states that the offeror may nevertheless consider a late acceptance as having arrived in time and thus render it effective, provided that the offeror "without undue delay [...] so informs the offeree or gives notice to that effect". If the offeror takes advantage of this possibility, the contract is to be considered as having been concluded as soon as the late acceptance reaches the offeror and not when the offeror informs the offeree of its intention to consider the late acceptance effective.

Illustration

1. A indicates 31 March as the deadline for acceptance of its offer. B's acceptance reaches A on 3 April. A, who is still interested in the contract, intends to "accept" B's late acceptance, and immediately informs B of its intention. Notwithstanding the fact that this notice only reaches B on 5 April the contract is concluded on 3 April.

48

Figure 7. UNIDROIT-*Principles of International Commercial Contracts* (PICC)

Bibliography

Adams, K.D., 'Blaming the Mirror: The Restatements and the Common law', (2007) 40 *Indiana LR* 205–270

Ajani, G. and H. Schulte-Nölke, 'The Principles of the Existing EC Contract Law: a preliminary output of the Acquis Group', in: The Research Group on the Existing EC Private Law (ed.), *Acquis Principles. Contract I*, ix–xiii

Alexander, L., and E. Sherwin, 'Judges as Rule Makers', in: Edlin (ed.), *Common Law Theory*, 27–50

Alexy, R., *Theorie der juristischen Argumentation*, 3rd ed., 1996

—— *Theorie der Grundrechte*, 3rd ed., 1996

—— *Begriff und Geltung des Rechts*, 2nd ed., 1994 (translated by S. Paulson: Alexy, *The Argument from Injustice: A Reply to Legal Positivism*, 2000)

Althoff, G., *Die Macht der Rituale. Symbolik und Herrschaft im Mittelalter*, 2003

American Bar Association, 'Report of the Special Committee Appointed to Consider and Report Whether the Present Delay and Uncertainty in Judicial Administration Can be Lessened, and If So, By What Means', (1885) 8 *Annual Report of the American Bar Association* 323–448

American Law Institute, 'Report of the Committee on the Establishment of a Permanent Organization for the Improvement of the Law Proposing the Establishment of an American Law Institute ...', (1923) 1 *Proceedings of the American Law Institute* 1–109

—— *Restatements of the Law of Contracts as Adopted and Promulgated by the American Law Institute* (first series), 1932

—— *The Restatement in the Courts. A compilation showing the use by the courts of the Restatement of the Law Prepared for the American Law Institute by Benjamin H. Oehlert, of the Philadelphia Bar, and Herbert F. Goodrich, Adviser on Professional Relations to the American Law Institute*, 1934

—— *Restatement of the Law of Contracts. Colorado Annotations*, 1936

Angehrn, E., *Interpretation und Dekonstruktion: Untersuchungen zur Hermeneutik*, 2003

Anschütz, G., *Die Verfassung des Deutschen Reiches vom 11. August 1919*, 14th ed., 1933, repr. 1966

Antoniolli, L. and A. Veneziano (eds), *Principles of European Contract Law and Italian Law. A Commentary*, 2005

Auxerre, Gottfried von, 'Epistola ad Albinum cardinalem et episcopum Albanensem. De condemnatione errorum Gilberti Porretani', *PL* 185, *pars prior*, 1859, 587–594

Azo, *Summa in ius civile*, Lyon 1574

Bachmann, G., *Private Ordnung. Grundlagen ziviler Regelsetzung*, 2006

Baldwin, J.W., *The Scholastic Culture of the Middle Ages, 1000–1300*, 1971

Bar, C. von, 'Die Study Group on a European Civil Code', in: *Festschrift für Dieter Henrich*, 2000, 1–11

Bar, C. von, E. Clive and H. Schulte-Nölke (eds), *Principles, Definitions and Model Rules of European Private Law: Draft Common Frame of Reference (DCFR): Outline Edition*, 2009

Bar, C. von and H. Schulte-Nölke, 'Gemeinsamer Referenzrahmen für ein europäisches Schuld- und Sachenrecht', (2005) *ZRP* 165–168

Barker, W.T., 'Lobbying and the American Law Institute: The Example of Insurance Defence', (1998) 26 *Hofstra LR* 573–593

Barnert, E., 'Von Station zu Station. Anm zu Otto Palandt (umstr) uam aAnl seines 130. Gebtags (mwN)', (2007) 1 *Myops* 56–67

Basedow, J., 'Die UNIDROIT-Prinzipien der internationalen Handelsverträge und das deutsche Recht', in: *Gedächtnisschrift für Alexander Lüderitz*, 2000, 1–24

—— 'Uniform Law Conventions and the UNIDROIT Principles of International Commercial Contracts', (2000) *ULR* 129–139

—— 'Transjurisdictional Codification', (2009) 83 *Tulane LR* 973–998

Basedow, J., K.J. Hopt and R. Zimmermann (eds), *Max Planck Handbook of European Private Law*, forthcoming 2010

Basile, M.E. *et al.*, 'Introduction', in: iid. (eds), *Lex Mercatoria and Legal Pluralism*, 1998, 13–214

Beale, J., *A Treatise on the Conflict of Laws*, vol. I, 1935

—— 'Dicey's "Conflict of Laws."', (1896/97) 10 *Harvard LR* 168–174

—— 'The Necessity for a Study of Legal System', (1914) 14 *Proceedings of the Association of American Law Schools* 31–45

Becker, H.-J., 'Der Friede von Venedig im Jahre 1177 und die Entstehung der Papstkirche', in: Dilcher and Quaglioni, *Inizi / Anfänge*, 261–282

Behrends, O., 'Das Bündnis zwischen Gesetz und Dogmatik und die Frage der dogmatischen Rangstufen', in: id. / Henckel (eds), *Gesetzgebung und Dogmatik*, 9–36

Behrends, O. and W. Henckel (eds), *Gesetzgebung und Dogmatik. Abhandlungen der Akademie der Wissenschaften in Göttingen. Philologisch-historische Klasse*, 3. Folge 178, 1989

Bellomo, M., *L'Europa de diritto comune*, 7th ed., 1994 (Engl. trans. [from the 2nd ed.] by L.G. Cochrane: *The Common Legal Past of Europe. 1000–1800*, 1995)

Berger, P., 'The relationship between the UNIDROIT Principles of International Commercial Contracts and the new *lex mercatoria*', (2000) *ULR* 153–170

Berman, H.J., *Law and Revolution. The Formation of the Western Legal Tradition*, 1983

Bernstein, A., 'Restatement Redux', (1995) 48 *Vanderbilt LR* 1663–1695

Bertelsmeier-Kirst, C., *Kommunikation und Herrschaft. Zum volkssprachlichen Verschriftlichungsprozeß des Rechts im 13. Jahrhundert*, 2008

Biblia Latina cum Glossa Ordinaria, Straßburg 1480 f.; repr., with an Introduction by K. Froehlich and M.T. Gibson, 1992

Bielitz, G.A., *Praktischer Kommentar zum allgemeinen Landrechte für die preußischen Staaten*, Erfurt 1823

Blackstone, W., *Commentaries on the Laws of England*, 4th ed., Dublin 1771

Bodenheimer, E., *Jurisprudence*, 1940

Bonell, M.J., *An International Restatement of Contract Law*, 3rd ed., 2005

—— *The UNIDROIT Principles in Practice. Caselaw and Bibliography on the UNIDROIT Principles of International Commercial Contracts*, 2nd ed., 2006

Boockmann, H. *et al.* (eds), *Recht und Verfassung im Übergang vom Mittelalter zur Neuzeit. I. Teil. Bericht über Kolloquien der Kommission zur Erforschung der Kultur des Spätmittelalters 1994–1995. Abhandlungen der Akademie der Wissenschaften in Göttingen. Philologisch-historische Klasse*, 3. Folge 228, 1998

Bortolotti, F., 'The UNIDROIT Principles and the arbitral tribunals', (2000) *ULR* 141–152

Bourdieu, P. and L.J.D. Wacquant, *An Invitation to Reflexive Sociology*, 1992 (repr. 2004)

Bower, G.S., *A Code of the Law of Actionable Defamation with a Continuous Commentary* ..., 1908

—— *The Law of Actionable Misrepresentation Stated in the Form of a Code, Followed by a Commentary* ..., 1911

Braun, A., 'The English codification debate and the role of jurists in the development of legal doctrines', forthcoming in: Lobban and Moses (eds), *Social and Legal Philosophy*

Braun, J., *Einführung in die Rechtswissenschaft*, 2nd ed., 2001

Brauneder, W., 'Privatrechtsfortbildung durch Juristenrecht in Exegetik und Pandektistik in Österreich', (1983) 5 *ZNR* 22–43

Brie, S., 'Die Stellung der deutschen Rechtsgelehrten der Rezeptionszeit zum Gewohnheitsrecht', in: *Festgabe für Felix Dahn*, 1905, 129–164

Brockmöller, A., *Die Entstehung der Rechtstheorie im 19. Jahrhundert in Deutschland*, 1997

Brödermann, E., 'The Growing Importance of the UNIDROIT Principles in Europe—Review in Light of Market Needs, the Role of Law and the 2005 Rome I Proposal', (2000) *ULR* 749–770

Brunnemann, J., *Commentarius in Quinquaginta Libros Pandectarum*, Frankfurt/Oder 1677

—— *Commentarius in Codicem Justiniani*, Leipzig 1599

Brynteson, W.E., 'Roman Law and Legislation in the Middle Ages', (1966) 41 *Speculum* 420–437

Bürge, A., *Das französische Privatrecht im 19. Jahrhundert*, 2nd ed., 1995

Burkart, F., *Interpretatives Zusammenwirken von CISG und UNIDROIT Principles*, 2000

Busch, D., 'The Principles of European Contract Law before the Supreme Court of the Netherlands. On the influence of the PECL in Dutch legal practice', (2008) 16 *ZEuP* 549–562

Busch, D. and H.N. Schelhaas (eds), *The Principles of European Contract Law and Dutch Law. A Commentary*, 2 vols, 2002/2006

Bussani, M. and V.V. Palmer, *Pure Economic Loss in Europe*, 2003

Caemmerer, E. von, 'Wandlungen des Deliktsrechts', in: *Festschrift zum hundertjährigen Bestehen des deutschen Juristentages*, 1960, 49–136

Cairns, J.W., 'The de la Vergne Volume and the *Digest* of 1808', forthcoming in the *Tulane European and Civil Law Forum*

Calasso, F., 'Il concetto di diritto comune', in: id., *Introduzione al diritto comune*, 1951, 33–76

Canaris, C.-W., *Die Feststellung von Lücken im Gesetz*, 2nd ed., 1983

—— *Systemdenken und Systembegriff in der Jurisprudenz*, 2nd ed., 1983

—— 'Die Stellung der "UNIDROIT Principles" und der "Principles of European Contract Law" im System der Rechtsquellen', in: J. Basedow (ed.), *Europäische Vertragsrechtsvereinheitlichung und deutsches Recht*, 2000, 5–31

Cancik, H., 'Der Text als Bild. Über optische Zeichen zur Konstitution von Satzgruppen in antiken Texten', in: H. Brunner *et al.* (eds), *Wort und Bild*, 1979, 81–100

Cardozo, B., *The Growth of the Law*, 1924

Caroni, P., 'Kodifikation', in: A. Erler and E. Kaufmann (eds), *Handwörterbuch zur deutschen Rechtsgeschichte*, vol. II, 1978, cols. 907–922

—— *Gesetz und Gesetzbuch. Beiträge zu einer Kodifikationsgeschichte*, 2003

Cashin Ritaine, E. and E. Lein (eds), *The UNIDROIT Principles 2004. Their Impact on Contractual Practice, Jurisprudence and Codification*, 2007

Chartier, R., *Lesewelten. Buch und Lektüre in der frühen Neuzeit*, 1990

Christensen, K., 'Introduction', in: Gratian, *Treatises on Laws (Decretum DD. 1–20)*, 1993, ix–xxvii

Classen, C.D., 'Die Drittwirkung der Grundrechte in der Rechtsprechung des Bundesverfassungsgerichts', (1997) 122 *AöR* 65–107

Cohen, F.S., 'Transcendental Nonsense and the Functional Approach', (1935) 35 *Columbia LR* 809–847

Coing, H., *Europäisches Privatrecht*, vol. I: *Älteres Gemeines Recht, 1500–1800*, 1985

—— 'Zur Romanistischen Auslegung von Rezeptionsgesetzen: Fichards Noten zur Frankfurter Reformation von 1509', (1936) 56 *ZRG (rom.)* 264–277

—— 'Die europäische Privatrechtsgeschichte der neueren Zeit als einheitliches Forschungsgebiet', (1967) 1 *Ius Commune* 1–11

—— 'Zur Vorgeschichte der Kodifikation: Die Diskussion um die Kodifikation im 17. und 18. Jahrhundert', in: B. Paradisi (ed.), *La formazione storica del diritto moderno in Europa*, 1977, 797–817

—— 'Die Juristische Fakultät und ihr Lehrprogramm', in: id. (ed.), *Handbuch der Quellen und Literatur der neueren europäischen Privatrechtsgeschichte*, vol. II/1, 1977, 1–69

Colli, V. (ed.), *Juristische Buchproduktion im Mittelalter*, 2002

Conring, *De origine iuris germanici*, Helmstedt 1643

Cook, C.M., *The American Codification Movement. A Study of Antebellum Legal Reform*, 1981

Crystal, N.M., 'Codification and the Rise of the Restatement Movement', (1979) 54 *Washington LR* 239–273

Dannemann, G., 'Introduction', in: The Research Group on the Existing EC Private Law (ed.), *Acquis Principles. Contract I*, xxiii–xxxii

Dasser, F., 'Mouse or Monster? Some Facts and Figures on the *lex mercatoria*', in: Zimmermann *et al.* (eds), *Nichtstaatliches Privatrecht—Geltung und Genese*, 129–158

Dawson, J.P., *The Oracles of the Law*, 1968

DeMott, D., 'The First Restatement of Agency: What Was the Agenda', (2007/08) 32 *Southern Illinois University LJ* 17–38

Dezalay, Y. and B.G. Garth, *Dealing in Virtue, International Commercial Arbitration and the Creation of a Transnational Legal Order*, 1996

Dicey, A.V., *A Treatise on the Rules for the Selection of the Parties to an Action*, London 1870

—— *The Law of Domicil as a Branch of the Law of England in the Form of Rules*, London 1879
—— *A Digest of the Law of England with References to the Conflict of Laws*, 2nd ed., 1908
Dilcher, G., 'Oralität, Verschriftlichung und Wandlungen der Normstruktur in den Stadtrechten des 12. und 13. Jahrhunderts', in: Keller *et al.* (eds), *Pragmatische Schriftlichkeit im Mittelalter*, 9–19
—— 'Die stadtbürgerliche Gesellschaft und die Verrechtlichung der Lebensbeziehungen im Wandlungsprozeß zwischen Mittelalter und Neuzeit', in: Boockmann *et al.* (eds), *Recht und Verfassung im Übergang vom Mittelalter zur Neuzeit I*, 93–114
Dilcher, G. and D. Quaglioni (eds), *Gli inizi del diritto pubblico. L'età di Federico Barbarossa: legislazione e scienza del diritto / Die Anfänge des öffentlichen Rechts. Gesetzgebung im Zeitalter Friedrich Barbarossas und das Gelehrte Recht*, 2007
Dölemeier, B., 'Kodifikationsbewegung', in: H. Coing (ed.), *Handbuch der Quellen und Literatur der neueren europäischen Privatrechtsgeschichte*, vol. III/2, 1982, 1421–1439
Dolezalek, G., '*Libri magistrorum* and the Transmission of Glosses in Legal Textbooks (12th and Early 13th Century)', in: Colli (ed.), *Juristische Buchproduktion im Mittelalter*, 315–349
Donahue, C., 'Equity in the Courts of Merchants', (2004) 72 *TR* 1–35
—— 'Benvenuto Stracca's De Mercatura: Was there a Lex mercatoria in Sixteenth-Century Italy?', in: V. Piergiovanni (ed.), *From lex mercatoria to commercial law*, 2005, 69–120
—— 'Private Law Without the State and During Its Formation', in: Jansen and Michaels (eds), *Beyond the State*, 121–143
Dreier, H., 'Kanonistik und Konfessionalisierung—Marksteine auf dem Weg zum Staat', (2002) *JZ* 1–13
Drosdeck, T., *Die herrschende Meinung—Autorität als Rechtsquelle*, 1989
Dulckeit, G., 'Zur Lehre vom Rechtsgeschäft im klassischen römischen Recht', in: *Festschrift Fritz Schulz*, vol. 1, 1951, 148–190
Duranton, M., *Cour de Droit Français Suivant le Code Civil*, 2nd ed., Paris 1828
Dürig, G., 'Grundrechte und Zivilrechtsprechung', in: *Vom Bonner Grundgesetz zur gesamtdeutschen Verfassung. Festschrift zum 75. Geburtstag von Hans Nawiasky*, 1956, 157–190
Duve, T., 'Mit der Autorität gegen die Autoritäten? Überlegungen zur heuristischen Kraft des Autoritätsbegriffs für die Neuere Privatrechtsgeschichte', in: Oesterreicher *et al.* (eds), *Autorität der Form*, 239–256

Dworkin, R., *Taking Rights Seriously*, 1977
—— 'No Right Answer?', in: P.M.S. Hacker and J. Raz (eds), *Law, Morality, and Society. Essays in Honour of H.L.A. Hart*, 1977, 58–84; = (1978) 53 *New York University LR* 1–32
Eckert, J., 'Gesetzesbegriff und Normanwendung im späten Naturrecht. Die Spruchpraxis preußischer Gerichte unter dem Allgemeinen Landrecht', (1998) 37 *Der Staat* 571–590
Eckhardt, K.A., *Sachsenspiegel IV: Eike von Repchow und Hoyer von Falkenstein*, 1966
Edlin, D.E. (ed.), *Common Law Theory*, 2007
Ehrlich, E., 'Internationales Privatrecht', (1906) 126 *Deutsche Rundschau* 419–432
Eidenmüller, H., F. Faust, C. Grigoleit, N. Jansen, G. Wagner and R. Zimmermann, 'The Common Frame of Reference for European Private Law—Policy Choices and Codification Problems', (2008) 28 *OJLSt.* 659–708
Eisenberg, M.A., 'The Concept of National Law and the Rule of Recognition', (2002) 29 *Florida State U. LR* 1229–1263
—— 'The Principles of Legal Reasoning in Common Law', in: Edlin (ed.), *Common Law Theory*, 81–101
Encinas de Munagorri, R., 'Qu'est-ce que la technique juridique? Observations sur l'apport des juristes au lien social', (2004) *Dalloz Chroniques* 711–715
Engel, C. and W. Schön (eds), *Das Proprium der Rechtswissenschaft*, 2007
Engelmann, W., *Die Wiedergeburt der Rechtskultur in Italien durch die wissenschaftliche Lehre*, 1938
Enneccerus, L. and H.C. Nipperdey, *Allgemeiner Teil des Bürgerlichen Rechts*, 15th ed., 1959
Ernst, W., 'Gelehrtes Recht—Die Jurisprudenz aus der Sicht des Zivilrechtslehrers', in: Engel and Schön (eds), *Proprium der Rechtswissenschaft*, 3–49
European Group on Tort Law, *Principles of European Tort Law*, 2005
Falck, N., *Juristische Encyclopädie*, ed., by R. von Jhering, 5th ed., Leipzig 1851
Falk, U. and H. Mohnhaupt (eds), *Das Bürgerliche Gesetzbuch und seine Richter. Fallstudien zur Reaktion der Rechtspraxis auf die Kodifikation des deutschen Privatrechts*, 2000
Fauvarque-Cosson, B., 'Faut-il un Code civil européen?', (2002) *Rtd civ.* 463–480
Fernandez, M.F., *From Chaos to Continuity. The Evolution of Louisiana's Judicial System 1712–1862*, 2001

Ferrari, F. *et al.* (eds), *The Draft UNCITRAL Digest and Beyond: Cases, Analysis, and Unresolved Issues in the U.N. Sales Convention*, 2005
Finnis, J., *Natural Law and Natural Rights*, 1980
Fleischer, H., 'Gesellschafts- und Kapitalmarktrecht als wissenschaftliche Disziplin—Das Proprium der Rechtswissenschaft', in: Engel and Schön (eds), *Proprium der Rechtswissenschaft*, 50–76
Flume, 'Vom Beruf unserer Zeit für Gesetzgebung', (1990) *ZIP* 1427–1430
Fögen, M.T., *Römische Rechtsgeschichten. Über Ursprung und Evolution eines sozialen Systems*, 2002
—— 'Römisches Recht und Rombilder im östlichen und westlichen Mittelalter', in: B. Schneidmüller and S. Weinfurter (eds), *Heilig. Römisch. Deutsch. Das Reich im mittelalterlichen Europa*, 2006, 57–83
—— *Das Lied vom Gesetz*, 2007
Frank, J.P., 'Law Institute 1923–1998', (1998) 26 *Hofstra LR* 615–639
Freising, Otto von, *Ottonis Gesta Friderici I. imperatoris*, ed. by G. Waiz and B. von Simson, in: *MG* 46, 3rd ed., 1978, 1–161
Fried, J., *Die Entstehung des Juristenstandes im 12. Jahrhundert*, 1974
Friedberg, E., *Die künftige Gestaltung des deutschen Rechtsstudiums nach den Beschlüssen der Eisenacher Konferenz*, Leipzig 1896
Friedman, L.M., *A History of American Law*, 3rd ed., repr. 2007
Froehlich, K., 'The Printed Gloss', in: *Biblia Latina cum Glossa Ordinaria*, vol. I, xii–xxvi
Funke, A., *Allgemeine Rechtslehre als juristische Strukturtheorie*, 2004
Furmston, M.P., 'The UNIDROIT Principles and International Commercial Arbitration', in: Institute of International Business Law and Practice (ed.), *A New Lex Mercatoria?*, 199–209
Gail, A. von, *Practicarum Observationum tam ad processum iudiciarium, praesertim Imperialis Camerae ... libri duo*, Cologne 1668
Garré, R., *Consuetudo: Das Gewohnheitsrecht in der Rechtsquellen- und Methodenlehre des späteren ius commune in Italien (16.-18. Jahrhundert)*, 2005
Gebhardt, J., 'Verfassung und Symbolizität', in: Melville (ed.), *Institutionalität und Symbolisierung*, 585–601
Gibson, M.T., 'The Glossed Bible', in: *Biblia Latina cum Glossa Ordinaria*, vol. I, vii–xi
Gilmore, G., *The Ages of American Law*, 1977
Glenn, H.P., *On Common Laws*, 2005
Golding, M.P., 'Kelsen and the Concept of a "Legal System"', (1961) 47 *ARSP*, 355–386

Gordley, J., 'Myths of the French Civil Code', (1994) 42 *AmJCompL* 459–506

—— *The Enforceability of Promises in European Contract Law*, 2001

Görich, K., 'Fragen zum Kontext der roncalischen Gesetze Friedrich Barbarossas', in: Dilcher and Quaglioni (eds), *Inizi / Anfänge*, 305–325

Governing Council of UNIDROIT, 'Introduction to the 1994 Edition', in: UNIDROIT (ed.), *Principles of International Commercial Contracts*, 2nd ed., 2004, xiv–xvi

—— 'Introduction to the 2004 Edition', in: UNIDROIT (ed.), *Principles of International Commercial Contracts*, vii–viii

Gratian, *The Treatises on Laws (Decretum DD. 1–20)*, trans. by A. Thompson, *with The Ordinary Gloss*, trans. by J. Gordley, 1993

Graziadei, M., 'Comparative Law as the Study of Transplants and Receptions', in: Reimann and Zimmermann (eds), *Oxford Handbook of Comparative Law*, 441–475

Graziadei, M. *et al.*, *Commercial Trusts in European Private Law*, 2005

Grimm, D., 'Rechtsentstehung', in: id. (ed.), *Einführung in das Recht*, 2nd ed., 1991, 40–94

Grossi, P., *L'ordine giuridico medievale*, 1996

Habermas, J., 'Wahrheitstheorien', in: id., *Vorstudien und Ergänzungen zur Theorie des kommunikativen Handelns*, 1995, 127–183

—— *Faktizität und Geltung*, 1992

Haferkamp, H.-P., 'The Science of Private Law and the State in Nineteenth Century Germany', in: Jansen and Michaels (eds), *Beyond the State*, 245–267

—— 'Karl Adolph von Vangerow (1808–1870). Pandektenrecht und "Mumiencultus"', (2009) 17 *ZEuP* 813–844

Hähnchen, S., 'Die Rechtsform des CFR und die Frage nach der Kompetenz', in: Schmidt-Kessel (ed.), *Der gemeinsame Referenzrahmen*, 147–171

Haltern, U., *Europarecht. Dogmatik im Kontext*, 2nd ed., 2007

Harding, A., *Medieval Law and the Foundations of the State*, 2002

Hart, H.L.A., *Definition and Theory in Jurisprudence*, 1953

—— *The Concept of Law*, 2nd ed., 1994

—— 'Kelsen Visited', in: id., *Essays in Jurisprudence and Philosophy*, 1983, 286–308

Hawkins, F.V., *A Concise Treatise on the Construction of Wills*, London 1863

Heidemann, M., *Methodology of Uniform Contract Law. The UNIDROIT Principles in International Legal Doctrine and Practice*, 2007

Helmholz, R.H., *The Spirit of Classical Canon Law*, 1996

Herberger, M., *Dogmatik: Zur Geschichte von Begriff und Methode in Medizin und Jurisprudenz*, 1981

—— 'Rangstufen der Rechtsdogmatik im Hinblick auf deren Bedeutung für die Gesetzgebung', in: Behrends and Henckel (eds), *Gesetzgebung und Dogmatik*, 66–79

Hesselink, M., 'Principles of European Contract Law: Some Choices Made by the Lando Commission', in: id., *The New European Private Law*, 2002, 75–147

—— 'The Common Frame of Reference as a Source of European Private Law', (2009) 83 *Tulane LR* 919–971

Hohfeld, W.N., 'A Vital School of Jurisprudence and Law: Have American Universities Awakened to the Enlarged Opportunities and Responsibilities of the Present Day?', (1914) 14 *Proceedings of the Association of American Law Schools*, 76–139

Holmes, O.W., *Holmes-Laski Letters*, vol. I. *The Correspondence of Mr. Justice Holmes and Harold J. Laski, 1916–1935*, ed. by M. de Wolfe Howe, 1953

Homeyer, G., 'Johannes Kledonk wider den Sachsenspiegel', (1855) *Abhandlungen der Königl. Akademie der Wissenschaften zu Berlin* 376–432

Hondius, E., 'Das neue Niederländische Gesetzbuch. Allgemeiner Teil', (1991) 191 *AcP* 378–395

Howell, M. and W. Prevenier, *Werkstatt des Historikers*, 2004

Huber, U., *Heedendaegse Rechtsgeleertheyt*, 5th ed., transl. and ed. by P. Gane, *The Jurisprudence of My Time*, 1939

Huber, U., 'Das geplante Recht der Leistungsstörungen', in: W. Ernst and R. Zimmermann (eds), *Zivilrechtswissenschaft und Schuldrechtsreform*, 2001, 31–183

Hull, N.E.H., 'Restatement and Reform: A New Perspective on the Origins of the American Law Institute', (1990) 8 *Law and History Rev.* 55–96

Ibbetson, D., 'Case-Law and Doctrine: a Historical Perspective on the English Common Law', in: R. Schulze and U. Seif (eds), *Richterrecht und Rechtsfortbildung in der Europäischen Rechtsgemeinschaft*, 2003, 27–40

Immel, G., 'Typologie der Gesetzgebung des Privatrechts und Prozeßrechts', in: H. Coing (ed.), *Handbuch der Quellen und Literatur der neueren europäischen Privatrechtsgeschichte*, vol. II/2, 1976, 3–96

Institute of International Business Law and Practice (ed.), *UNIDROIT Principles for International Commercial Contracts: A New Lex Mercatoria?*, 1995

Jakobs, H.H., *Magna Glossa. Textstufen der legistischen glossa ordinaria*, 2006

Jansen, N., *Binnenmarkt, Privatrecht und europäische Identität*, 2004

—— 'Dogmatik, Erkenntnis und Theorie im europäischen Privatrecht', (2005) 13 *ZEuP* 750–783

—— 'Traditionsbegründung im europäischen Privatrecht', (2006) *JZ* 536–546

—— 'Principles of European Tort Law? Grundwertungen und Systembildung im europäischen Haftungsrecht', (2006) 70 *RabelsZ* 732–770

—— 'Comparative Law and Comparative Knowledge', in: Reimann and Zimmermann (eds), *Oxford Handbook of Comparative Law*, 305–338

—— 'The State of Art of European Tort Law. Present Problems and Proposed Principles', in: M. Bussani (ed.), *European Tort Law. Eastern and Western Perspectives*, 2007, 15–45

—— '*Negotiorum Gestio* und *Benevolent Intervention in Another's Affairs*: Principles of European Law?', (2007) 15 *ZEuP* 958–991

—— 'Das gelehrte Recht und der Staat', in: Zimmermann *et al.* (eds), *Nichtstaatliches Privatrecht—Geltung und Genese*, 159–186

—— '*Ius Commune*', forthcoming in: Basedow, Hopt and Zimmermann (eds), *Handbook of European Private Law*

—— 'Codifications, Commentators, and Courts in Tort Law: The Perception and Application of the Civil Code and the Constitution by the German Legal Profession', forthcoming in: Lobban and Moses (eds), *Social and Legal Philosophy*

Jansen, N. and R. Michaels, 'Private Law and the State. Comparative Perceptions and Historical Observations', (2007) 71 *RabelsZ* 345–397

—— (eds), *Beyond the State. Rethinking Private Law*, 2008

Jansen, N. and R. Zimmermann, 'Restating the Acquis communautaire? A Critical Examination of the "Principles of the Existing EC Contract Law"', (2008) 71 *MLR* 505–534

Jellinek, G., *Allgemeine Staatslehre*, 3rd ed., 1914

Kannowski, B., *Die Umgestaltung des Sachenspiegelrechts durch die Buch'sche Glosse*, 2007

—— 'Der Sachsenspiegel und die Buch'sche Glosse—Begegnung deutschrechtlichen und romanistischen Denkens?', in: G. Dilcher and E.-M. Distler (eds), *Leges—Gentes—Regna. Zur Rolle von germanischen Rechtsgewohnheiten und lateinischer Schrifttradition bei der Ausbildung der frühmittelalterlichen Rechtskultur*, 2006, 503–521

—— 'Europäisches Rechtsdenken bei Johann von Buch', in: H. Lück (ed.), *Tangermünde, die Altmark und das Reichsrecht*, 2008, 77–92

Kantorowicz, E.H., 'Kingship under the Impact of Scientific Jurisprudence', in: M. Clagett *et al.* (eds), *Twelfth-Century Europe and the Foundations of Modern Society*, 1961, 89–111

Keller, H., 'Die Veränderung gesellschaftlichen Handelns und die Verschriftlichung der Administration in den italienischen Stadtkommunen', in: id. *et al.* (eds), *Pragmatische Schriftlichkeit*, 21–36

Keller, H., K. Grubmüller, and N. Staubach (eds), *Pragmatische Schriftlichkeit im Mittelalter. Erscheinungsformen und Entwicklungsstufen*, 1992

Kelley, P.J., 'The First Restatement of Torts: Reform by Descriptive Theory', (2007/08) 32 *Southern Illinois University LJ* 93–134

Kelly, D.R., 'Ancient Verses on New Ideas: Legal Tradition and the French Historical School', (1987) 26 *History and Theory* 319–338

Kelsen, H., *Reine Rechtslehre*, 2nd ed., 1960 (Engl. trans. by M. Knight: *Pure Theory of Law*, 1967)

Kessedjian, C., 'La codification privée', in: *E Pluribus Unum. Liber Amicorum Georges A.L. Droz*, ed., by A. Borrás *et al.*, 1996, 135–149

—— 'Un exercice de rénovation des sources du droit des contrats du commerce international: Les Principes proposés par l'UNIDROIT', (1995) *Revue critique de droit international privé* 641–670

Kiefer, T., *Die Aquilische Haftung im "Allgemeinen Landrecht für die Preussischen Staaten" von 1784*, 1989

Kieninger, E.-M. *et al.*, *Security Rights in Movable Property in European Private Law*, 2004

Kilbourne, Jr., R.H., *A History of the Louisiana Civil Code. The Formative Years, 1803–1839*, 1987

Kirchstetter, L. von, *Commentar zum Oesterreichischen Allgemeinen bürgerlichen Gesetzbuche mit vorzüglicher Berücksichtigung des gemeinen deutschen Privatrechts*, Leipzig *et al.* 1868

Kisch, G., *Sachsenspiegel and Bible*, 1941

Koch, P., *Die Statutengesetzgebung der Kommune Vercelli im 13. und 14. Jahrhundert*, 1995

Kohl, H., *Erinnerungen, 1990–1994*, 2007

Koschaker, P., *Europa und das römische Recht*, 4th ed., 1966

Kötz, H., *Europäisches Vertragsrecht*, vol. 1, 1996

Krause, H., 'Kaiserrecht und Rezeption', (1952) *Abhandlungen der Heidelberger Akademie der Wissenschaften, Philosophisch-Historische Klasse*, 1–147

Kroeschell, K., 'Rechtsaufzeichnung und Rechtswirklichkeit. Das Beispiel des Sachsenspiegels', in: P. Classen (ed.), *Recht und Schrift im Mittelalter*, 1977, 349–380

—— 'Von der Gewohnheit zum Recht. Der Sachsenspiegel im späten Mittelalter', in: Boockmann *et al.* (eds), *Recht und Verfassung im Übergang vom Mittelalter zur Neuzeit I*, 68–92

Kronke, H., 'A Bridge out of the Fortress: UNIDROIT's Work on Global Modernisation of Commercial Law and its Relevance for Europe', (2008) 16 *ZEuP* 1–5

Kroppenberg, I., 'Der gescheiterte Codex. Überlegungen zur Kodifikationsgeschichte des Codex Theodosianus', (2007) *RG* 112–126

—— 'Mythos Kodifikation—Ein rechtshistorischer Streifzug', (2008) *JZ* 905–912

Kull, A., 'Restitution and Reform', (2007/08) 32 *Southern Illinois University LJ* 83–92

Kuttner, S., 'The Father of the Science of Canon Law', (1941) 1 *Jurist* 1–19

—— 'Quelques observations sur l'autorité des collections canoniques dans le droit classique de l'Église', in: *Actes du Congrès de droit canonique (Paris 22–26 avril 1947)*, 1950, 305–312

Kysar, D.A., 'The Expectation of Consumers', (2003) 103 *Columbia LR* 1700–1790

Landau, P., 'Quellen und Bedeutung des Gratianischen Dekrets', (1986) 52 *SDHI* 218–235

—— 'Der Einfluß des kanonischen Rechts auf die europäische Rechtskultur', in: R. Schulze (ed.), *Europäische Rechts- und Verfassungsgeschichte*, 1991, 39–57

—— 'Der Entstehungsort des Sachsenspiegels. Eike von Repgow, Altzelle und die anglo-normannische Kanonistik', (2005) 61 *Deutsches Archiv* 73–101

Lando, O., 'Preface', in: id. and H. Beale (eds), *Principles of European Contract Law I/II*, xi–xvi

Lando, O. and H. Beale (eds), *Principles of European Contract Law, Parts I and II*, 2000

Lando, O., E. Clive, A. Prüm and R. Zimmermann (eds), *Principles of European Contract Law, Part III*, 2003

Lange, H. and M. Kriechbaum, *Römisches Recht im Mittelalter*, vol. II: *Die Kommentatoren*, 2007

Langenbucher, K., *Die Entwicklung und Auslegung von Richterrecht*, 1996

LaPiana, W.P., '"A Task of No Common Magnitude": The Founding of the American Law Institute', (1987) 11 *Nova LR* 1085–1126

Lauterbach, W.A., *Collegium Theoretico-Practicum*, Tübingen 1726

Leible, S., 'Auswirkungen des CFR auf eine gemeinschaftsrechtskonforme Auslegung', in: Schmidt-Kessel (ed.), *Der gemeinsame Referenzrahmen*, 217–233

Lepsius, S., 'Taking the Institutional Context Seriously. A Comment on James Gordley', in: Jansen and Michaels (eds), *Beyond the State*, 233–243

Lerch, K.D. (ed.), *Die Sprache des Rechts. Strukturen, Formen und Medien der Kommunikation im Recht*, 2005

'Lex mercatoria', in: Basile *et al.* (eds), *Lex Mercatoria and Legal Pluralism*, 1–40

Lobban, M. and J. Moses (eds), *The Making of Modern Tort Law: Social and Legal Philosophy*, forthcoming

Lötscher, A., 'Gesetze als Texte: Wie wird Recht in Textstrukturen gebracht?', in: Lerch (ed.), *Sprache des Rechts*, 183–207

Lübbe-Wolf, G., 'Expropriation der Jurisprudenz?', in: Engel and Schön (eds), *Proprium der Rechtswissenschaft*, 282–292

Lück, H., *Über den Sachsenspiegel. Entstehung, Inhalt, und Wirkung des Rechtsbuchs*, 1999

—— 'Johann von Buch (ca. 1290–ca. 1356)—Stationen einer juristisch-politischen Karriere', (2007) 124 *ZRG (germ.)* 120–143

Ludwig, C.W., *Commentar zum allgemeinen Landrecht für die preußischen Staaten*, Breslau 1804

Luhmann, N., *Das Recht der Gesellschaft*, 1995 (Engl. transl.: *Law as a Social System*, 2004)

—— 'Die Geltung des Rechts', (1991) 22 *Rechtstheorie* 273–286

Luig, K., 'Institutionenlehrbücher des nationalen Rechts im 17. und 18. Jahrhundert', (1970) 3 *Ius Commune* 64–97

—— 'Der Geltungsgrund des römischen Rechts im 18. Jahrhundert in Italien, Frankreich und Deutschland', in: *La formazione storica del diritto moderno in Europa* (Atti del terzo congresso internazionale della Società Italiana di Storia del Diritto), vol. II, 1977, 819–845

—— 'Conring, das deutsche Recht und die Rechtsgeschichte', in: M. Stolleis (ed.), *H. Conring (1606–1681). Beiträge zu Leben und Werk*, 1983, 355–395

Lurga, B., *Grundfragen der Vereinheitlichung des Vertragsrechts in der EU*, 2002

Lütke Westhues, P., *Die Kommunalstatuten von Verona im 13. Jahrhundert*, 1995

MacCormick, N., 'The Maastricht-Urteil: Sovereignty Now', (1995) 1 *ELJ* 259–266

—— *Institutions of Law. An Essay in Legal Theory*, 2007

MacQueen, H.L. and R. Zimmermann (eds), *European Contract Law: Scots and South African Perspectives*, 2006

Maggs, G.E., 'Ipse Dixit: The Restatements (Second) of Contracts and the Modern Development of Contract Law', (1998) 66 *George Washington LR* 508–555

Mangoldt, H. von, 'Schriftlicher Bericht des Abgeordneten Dr. von Mangoldt über den Abschnitt I. Die Grundrechte', in: Parlamentarischer Rat Bonn 1948/49, *Schriftlicher Bericht zum Entwurf des Grundgesetzes für die Bundesrepublik Deutschland* (= Anlage zum stenographischen Bericht der Sitzung des Parlamentarischen Rates am 6. Mai 1949), 1949

—— *Das Bonner Grundgesetz*, 1953

Mangoldt, H. von and F. von Klein, *Das Bonner Grundgesetz*, 2nd ed., 1957

Marcade, V., *Explication du Code Napoléon* . . ., 6th ed., Paris 1869

Marella, F., 'Choice of Law in Third-Millennium Arbitrations: The Relevance of UNIDROIT Principles of International Commercial Contracts', (2003) 36 *Vanderbilt J. Transnational L.* 1137–1188

Mazal, O., *Geschichte der Buchkultur*, vol. 3/1, *Frühmittelalter*, 2003

Meder, S., 'Die Krise des Nationalstaates und ihre Folgen für das Kodifikationsprinzip', (2006) *JZ* 477–487

Mehren, A.T. von, *Law in the United States. A General and Comparative View*, 1988

—— 'Some Reflections on Codification and Case Law in the Twenty-First Century', (1998) 31 *University of California, Davis LR* 659–670

Melville, G., (ed.), *Institutionalität und Symbolisierung. Verstetigungen kultureller Ordnungsmuster in Vergangenheit und Gegenwart*, 2001

Merckel, J.C., *Commentar zum allgemeinen Landrecht für die Preußischen Staaten*, 2nd ed., Breslau and Leipzig 1812

Mertens, B., *Gesetzgebungskunst im Zeitalter der Kodifikation*, 2004

Metzger, A., *Extra legem, intra ius: Allgemeine Rechtsgrundsätze im Europäischen Privatrecht*, 2009

Mevius, D., *Commentarii in Jus Lubecense Libri Quinque* . . ., 4th ed., Frankfurt and Leipzig 1700

Michaels, R., 'Privatautonomie und Privatkodifikation. Zu Anwendbarkeit und Geltung allgemeiner Vertragsrechtsprinzipien', (1998) 62 *RabelsZ* 580–626

—— 'The Re-State-Ment of Non-State Law. The State, Choice of Law, and the Challenge from Global Legal Pluralism', (2005) 51 *Wayne LR* 1209–1259

—— 'The true lex mercatoria: Law Beyond the State', (2008) 14 *Indiana Journal of Global Legal Studies* 447–468

—— 'Umdenken für die UNIDROIT-Prinzipien: Vom Rechtswahlstatut zum Allgemeinen Teil des transnationalen Vertragsrechts', (2009) 73 *RabelsZ* 866–888

—— 'Restatements', forthcoming in: Basedow, Hopt and Zimmermann (eds), *Handbook of European Private Law*

Michaels, R. and N. Jansen, 'Private Law Beyond the State? Europeanization, Globalization, Privatization', (2006) 54 *AmJCompL* 843–890

Mihm, A., 'Vom Dingprotokoll zum Zwölftafelgesetz. Verschriftlichungsstufen städtischer Rechtstraditionen', in: H. Keller, C. Meier and T. Scharff (eds), *Schriftlichkeit und Lebenspraxis im Mittelalter. Erfassen, Bewahren, Verändern*, 1999, 43–67

Moeller, E. von, *Hermann Conring: der Vorkämpfer des deutschen Rechts: 1606–1681*, 1915

Mohnhaupt, H., 'Gesetzgebung des Reichs und Recht im Reich vom 16. bis 18. Jahrhundert', in: B. Dölemeyer and D. Klippel (eds), *Gesetz und Gesetzgebung im Europa der Frühen Neuzeit*, 1998, 83–108

Möllers, C., *Staat als Argument*, 2000

Möllers, T. and A. Heinemann, *The Enforcement of Competition Law in Europe*, 2007

Moreau Lislet, L., *A Digest of the Civil Laws now in force in the Territory of Orleans (1808). Containing Manuscript References to its Sources and Other Civil Laws on the Same Subjects*, repr. 1971

Morin, R., *La révolte du droit contre le code. La révision nécessaire des concepts juridiques (Contrat, responsabilité, propriété)*, 1945

Movsesian, M.L., 'Williston as Conservative-Pragmatist', (2007/08) 32 *Southern Illinois University LJ* 135–143

Nicolini, U., 'Autonomia e diritto proprio nelle città italiane del Medio Evo', in: *Festschrift für Helmut Coing*, vol. I, 1982, 249–267

Nipperdey, H.C., 'Gleicher Lohn der Frau für gleiche Leistung', (1950) *Recht der Arbeit*, 121–128

—— *Grundrechte und Privatrecht*, 1961

Noll, P., *Gesetzgebungslehre*, 1973

Oberreuter, H., 'Institution und Inszenierung. Parlamente im Symbolgebrauch der Mediengesellschaft', in: Melville (ed.), *Institutionalität und Symbolisierung*, 659–670

Oertmann, P., *Recht der Schuldverhältnisse*, 3rd/4th ed., 1910

Oesterreicher, W., 'Autorität der Form', in: id. *et al.* (eds), *Autorität der Form*, 13–16

Oesterreicher, W. *et al.* (eds), *Autorität der Form—Autorisierung—Institutionelle Autorität*, 2003

Oestmann, P., *Rechtsvielfalt vor Gericht*, 2002

—— (ed.), *Zwischen Formstrenge und Billigkeit*, 2009
—— 'Lotharische Legende', in: *Enzyklopädie der Neuzeit*, vol. 7, 2008, cols. 1009–1011
—— 'Die Zwillingsschwester der Freiheit. Die Form im Recht als Problem der Rechtsgeschichte', in: id. (ed.), *Formstrenge und Billigkeit*, 1–54
Oser, D., *The Unidroit Principles of International Commercial Contracts. A Governing Law?*, 2008
Pahlmann, B. and J. Schröder (1996), 'Eike von Repgow', in: G. Kleinheyer and J. Schröder (eds), *Deutsche und Europäische Juristen aus neun Jahrhunderten*, 4th ed., 1996, 123–126
Palandt, *Bürgerliches Gesetzbuch*, 68th ed., 2009
Palmer, V.V., 'Two Worlds in One: The Genesis of Louisiana's Mixed Legal System, 1803–1812', in: id. (ed.), *Louisiana: Microcosmos of a Mixed Jurisdiction*, 1999, 23–39
Papier, H.-J., 'Drittwirkung der Grundrechte', in: D. Mertens and H.-J. Papier (eds), *Handbuch der Grundrechte in Deutschland und Europa*, vol. II, 2006, 1331–1361
Patzelt, W., 'Symbolizität und Stabilität. Vier Repräsentationsinstitutionen im Vergleich', in: Melville (ed.), *Institutionalität und Symbolisierung*, 603–637
Pfeiffer, T., 'Von den Principles of European Contract Law zum Draft Common Frame of Reference', (2008) 16 *ZEuP* 679–707
Planck, G. (ed.), *Bürgerliches Gesetzbuch nebst Einführungsgesetz*, Berlin 1899
Postema, G., 'Law's Autonomy and Public Practical Reason', in: R.P. George, *The Autonomy of Law. Essays on Legal Positivism*, 1996, 79–118
—— 'Philosophy of the Common Law', in: J. Coleman and S. Shapiro (eds), *The Oxford Handbook of Jurisprudence and Philosophy of Law*, 2002, 588–622
—— '*A Similibus ad Similia*. Analogical Thinking in Law', in: Edlin (ed.), *Common Law Theory*, 102–133
Pound, R., *Interpretations of Legal History*, 1923
—— 'The Causes of the Popular Dissatisfaction with the Administration of Justice', (1906) 29 *Annual Report of the American Bar Association* 395–417
Powell, E., *The Principles and Practice of the Law of Evidence*, 2nd ed., London 1859
Pozzo, B., *Property and Environment*, 2007
Puchelt, E.S. (ed.), *Commentar zum allgemeinen deutschen Handelsgesetzbuch. Mit bes. Berücksichtigung der Praxis des Reichs-Oberhandelsgerichts*, Leipzig 1874

Puchta, G.F., *Cursus der Institutionen*, vol. I, 5th ed. by A. Rudorff, Leipzig 1856

Quaritsch, H., *Staat und Souveränität*, vol. I. *Die Grundlagen*, 1970

Raeschke-Kessler, H., 'Should an Arbitrator in an International Arbitration Procedure apply the UNIDROIT-Principles?', in: Institute of International Business Law and Practice (ed.), *A New Lex Mercatoria?*, 167–180

Raible, W., 'Die Semiotik der Textgestalt', (1991) *Abhandlungen der Heidelberger Akademie der Wissenschaften. Philosophisch-historische Klasse*, Abh. 1

Rawls, J., *A Theory of Justice*, rev. ed., 1999

Raz, J., 'Legal Principles and the Limits of Law', (1972) 81 *Yale LJ* 823–854

Rehberg, K.S., 'Institutionen als symbolische Ordnungen. Leitfragen und Grundkategorien zur Theorie und Analyse institutioneller Mechanismen', in: G. Göhler (ed.), *Die Eigenart der Institutionen. Zum Profil politischer Institutionentheorie*, 1994, 47–84

Reimann, M., 'The CISG in the United States: Why It Has Been Neglected and Why Europeans Should Care', (2007) 71 *RabelsZ* 115–129

Reimann, M. and R. Zimmermann (eds), *The Oxford Handbook of Comparative Law*, 2006

Reinhard, W., *Geschichte der Staatsgewalt. Eine vergleichende Verfassungsgeschichte Europas von den Anfängen bis zur* Gegenwart, 3rd ed., 2002

Rethorn, D., 'Verschiedene Funktionen von Präambeln', in: J. Rödig (ed.), *Studien zu einer Theorie der Gesetzgebung*, 1976, 296–327

Reventlow, Graf H., *Epochen der Bibelauslegung*, vol. II. *Von der Spätantike bis zum Ausgang des Mittelalters*, 1994

Rheinstein, M., 'Leader Groups in American Law', (1971) 38 *U. of Chicago LR* 687–696

Riesenhuber, K., 'Systembildung durch den CFR—Wirkungen auf die systematische Auslegung des Gemeinschaftsrechts', in: Schmidt-Kessel (ed.), *Der gemeinsame Referenzrahmen*, 173–215

Rödl, F., 'Law Beyond the Democratic Order? On the Legitimatory Problem of Private Law "Beyond the State"', in: Jansen and Michaels (eds), *Beyond the State*, 323–347

Röhl, K.F., *Allgemeine Rechtslehre*, 2nd ed., 2001

—— 'Bilder in gedruckten Rechtsbüchern', in: Lerch (ed.), *Sprache des Rechts*, 267–348

Röthel, A., 'Integration durch eine unverbindliche lex academica: Der Referenzrahmen als Modellgesetz?', in: Schmidt-Kessel (ed.), *Der gemeinsame Referenzrahmen*, 287–309

Rückert, J., *Autonomie des Rechts in rechtshistorischer Perspektive*, 1988

Ruffert, M., *Vorrang der Verfassung und Eigenständigkeit des Privatrechts*, 2001

Saint-Prix, F.B., *Notes théoriques sur le code civil ...*, Paris 1856

Savigny, F.C. von, *Vom Beruf unserer Zeit für Gesetzgebung und Rechtswissenschaft*, Heidelberg 1814

—— *Landrechtsvorlesung 1824*, edited by C. Wollschläger, *Landrechtsvorlesung 1824. Drei Nachschriften*, vol. I, 1994

—— *System des heutigen römischen Rechts*, Berlin 1840 ff.

Schilter, J., *Praxis Juris Romani in Foro Germanico*, Frankfurt/Main 1733

Schlosser, J.G., *Briefe über die Gesetzgebung*, Frankfurt/Main 1789

Schmidt-Kessel, M., *Reform des Schadenersatzrechts*, vol I: *Europäische Vorgaben und Vorbilder*, 2006

—— 'Auf dem Weg zum Gemeinsamen Referenzrahmen: Anmerkung zur Mitteilung der Kommission vom 11. Oktober 2004', 2005 *GPR* 2–8

—— (ed.), *Der gemeinsame Referenzrahmen. Entstehung, Inhalte, Anwendung*, 2008

Schmoeckel, M., J. Rückert and R. Zimmermann (eds), *Historisch-kritischer Kommentar zum BGB*, vol. I, 2003, vol. II, 2007

Schnell, S.L., *Theoretisch-praktischer Commentar über das positive Civilrecht des Kantons Bern*, Bern 1811

Schröder, J., *Recht als Wissenschaft*, 2001

—— '"Communis opinio" als Argument in der Rechtstheorie des 17. und 18. Jahrhunderts', in: G. Köbler (ed.), *Wege europäischer Rechtsgeschichte. Karl Kroeschell zum 60. Geburtstag*, 1987, 404–418

—— 'Das Verhältnis von Rechtsdogmatik und Gesetzgebung in der neuzeitlichen Rechtsgeschichte (am Beispiel des Privatrechts)', in: Behrends and Henckel (eds), *Gesetzgebung und Dogmatik*, 37–66

Schulte-Nölke, H., 'Contract Law or Law of Obligations?—The Draft Common Frame of Reference (DCFR) as a multifunctional tool', in: R. Schulze (ed.), *Common Frame of Reference and Existing EC Contract Law*, 2008, 47–64

Schulz, F., *History of Roman Legal Science*, 1946

—— *Geschichte der römischen Rechtswissenschaft*, 1961

Schulze, R. *et al.* (eds), *Der akademische Entwurf für einen Gemeinsamen Referenzrahmen. Kontroversen und Perspektiven*, 2008

Schwartz, V. E., K. Kelly and D. F. Partlett, *Prosser, Wade and Schwartz's Torts*, 11th ed., 2005

Schwarz, A. B., 'Zur Entstehung des modernen Pandektensystems', (1921) 42 *ZRG (rom.)* 578–610

Schwenzer, I. (ed.), *Schlechtriem/Schwenzer. Kommentar zum Einheitlichen UN-Kaufrecht*, 5th ed., 2008

Sefton-Green, R., *Mistake, Fraud and Duties to Inform in European Contract Law*, 2005

Siebenhaar, E., *Commentar zu dem bürgerlichen Gesetzbuche für das Königreich Sachsen und zu der damit in Verbindung stehenden Publicationsverordnung vom 2. Januar 1863*, Leipzig 1864

Siegel, H., *Die deutschen Rechtsbücher und die Kaiser Karl-Sage. Sitzungsberichte der Kais. Akademie der Wissenschaften in Wien. Philosophisch-historische Classe*, vol. 140, Wien 1899

Simpson, A. W. B., 'The Common Law and Legal Theory', in: id. (ed.), *Oxford Essays in Jurisprudence (Second Series)*, 1973, 77–99

Slapnicar, K. W., 'Der Wilke, der später Palandt hieß', (2000) *NJW* 1692–1699

Lord Smail, D., 'Notaries, Courts, and the Legal Culture of Late Medieval Marseille', in: K. L. Reyerson and J. Drendel (eds), *Urban and Rural Communities in Medieval France: Provence and Languedoc, 1000–1500*, 1998, 23–50

Smalley, B., 'Glossa ordinaria', in: *Theologische Realenzyklopädie*, vol. 13, 1984, 452–457

Smits, J., 'The Principles of European Contract Law and the Harmonisation of Private Law in Europe', in: A. Vaquer Aloy (ed.), *La Tercera Parte de los Principios de Derecho Contractual Europeo. The Principles of European Contract Law Part III*, 2005, 567–590

—— 'European Private Law and Democracy: A Misunderstood Relationship', in: *Essays in the Law and Economics of Regulation. In Honour of Anthony Ogus*, ed., by M. Faure and F. Stepien, 2008, 49–59

Snyder, D. V., 'Private Lawmaking', (2003) 64 *Ohio State LJ* 371–449

Soetermeer, F., 'Exemplar und Pecia. Zur Herstellung juristischer Bücher in Bologna im 13. und 14. Jahrhundert', in: Colli (ed.), *Juristische Buchproduktion im Mittelalter*, 481–516

Spangenberg, E. P. J., *Ernst Spangenbergs Commentar über den Code Napoleon*, Göttingen 1810

Stapleton, J., 'Controlling the Future of the Common Law by Restatement', in: M. S. Madden (ed.), *Exploring Tort Law*, 2005, 262–294

Staudenmayer, D., 'Weitere Schritte im Europäischen Vertragsrecht', (2005) 16 *Europäische Zeitschrift für Wirtschaftsrecht* 103–106

Stephen, J. F., *A Digest of the Law of Evidence*, London 1876

—— *A Digest of the Criminal Law (Crimes and Punishments)*, London 1877

Stern, K., *Das Staatsrecht der Bundesrepublik Deutschland*, vol. III/1, 1988

Stintzing, R. von and E. Landsberg, *Geschichte der Deutschen Rechtswissenschaft*, München & Leipzig 1880/1884

Stollberg-Rilinger, B., 'Einleitung', in: id. (ed.), *Vormoderne politische Verfahren. Zeitschrift für historische Forschung, Beiheft* 25, 2001, 9–24

—— 'Die Würde des Gerichts. Spielten symbolische Formen an den Höchsten Reichsgerichten eine Rolle?', in: Oestmann (ed.), *Formstrenge und Billigkeit*, 191–216

Stolleis, M., 'Condere leges et interpretari. Gesetzgebungsmacht und Staatsbildung in der frühen Neuzeit', in: id., *Staat und Staatsräson in der frühen Neuzeit. Studien zur Geschichte des öffentlichen Rechts*, 2002, 167–196

Stone Sweet, A., *Governing with Judges. Constitutional Politics in Europe*, 2000

—— *The Judicial Construction of Europe*, 2004

Struve, T., 'Die Rolle des römischen Rechts in der kaiserlichen Theorie von Roncaglia', in: Dilcher and Quaglioni (eds), *Inizi / Anfänge*, 71–99

Stryk, S., *Specimen Usus Moderni Pandectarum*, Halle 1708 ff.

—— 'Discursus Praeliminaris de Usu et Auctoritate Juris Romani in Foris Germaniae', in: id. *Usus Modernus*, vol. I, 1–38

Stubenrauch, M. von, *Commentar zum österreichischen Allgemeinen bürgerlichen Gesetzbuche*, 6th ed., Wien 1892

Student Note (anonymous), 'Just What You'd Expect: Professor Henderson's Redesign of Products Liability', (1998) 111 *Harvard LR* 2366–2383

Study Group on a European Civil Code/C. von Bar, *Benevolent Intervention in Another's Affairs (PEL Ben. Int.)*, 2006

Study Group on a European Civil Code/M. Barendrecht *et al., Service Contracts (PEL SC)*, 2007

Study Group on a European Civil Code/U. Drobnig, *Personal Security (PEL Pers. Sec.)*, 2007

Study Group on a European Civil Code/M. Hesselink *et al., Commercial Agency, Franchise and Distribution Contracts (PEL CAFDC)*, 2006

Study Group on a European Civil Code/E. Hondius *et al., Sales (PEL S)*, 2008

Study Group on a European Civil Code/K. Lilleholt *et al., Lease of Goods (PEL LG)*, 2008

Summers, R. S., *Form and Function in a Legal System—A General Study*, 2006

J. v. Staudingers Kommentar zum Bürgerlichen Gesetzbuch und dem Einführungsgesetze, 5th/6th ed., 1910

Symeonides, S. C., 'The First Conflicts Restatement Through the Eyes of Old: As Bad as Its Reputation?', (2007/08) 32 *Southern Illinois University LJ* 39–82

Tamanaha, B. Z., *A General Jurisprudence of Law and Society*, 2001

Teubner, G. *Recht als autopoietisches System*, 1989 (Engl. transl.: *Law as an Autopoietic System*, 1993)

The Research Group on the Existing EC Private Law (Acquis Group) (ed.), *Principles of the Existing EC Contract Law (Acquis Principles). Contract I. Pre-contractual Obligations, Conclusion of Contract, Unfair Terms*, 2007

Thibaut, A. F. J., *System des Pandekten-Rechts*, 4th ed., Jena 1814

Thieme, H., 'Statutarrecht und Rezeption', in: *Festschrift für Guido Kisch*, 1955, 69–86

Thier, A., 'Dynamische Schriftlichkeit: Zur Normbildung in den Kanonessammlungen', (2007) 124 *ZRG (kan.)* 1–33

de Tocco, C., *Leges Langobardorum cum argutissimis glosis*, Venice 1537, repr. and newly ed., by G. Astuti, 1964

Toullier, C.-B.-M., *Le Droit Civil Français suivant l'ordre du code*, 5th ed., Paris 1830

Troplong, M., *Le Droit Civil expliqué suivant l'ordre des articles du code ... De la vente ...*, Paris 1837

Trstenjak, V., 'Der Gemeinsame Referenzrahmen und der Europäische Gerichtshof', in: Schmidt-Kessel (ed.), *Der gemeinsame Referenzrahmen*, 235–253.

Trusen, W., 'Die Rechtsspiegel und das Kaiserrecht', (1985) 102 *ZRG (germ.)* 12–59

Uebel, G. F. C., *Commentar der Civil-Prozeßordnung für das deutsche Reich und des Einführungsgesetzes hiezu vom 30. Januar 1877*, Bamberg 1878

Ullmer, R. E., *Commentar zum privatrechtlichen Gesetzbuche des Kantons Zürich*, Zürich 1870

Underhill, A., *A Summary of the Law of Torts, or Wrongs Independent of Contract*, London 1873

Unger, R. M., *Knowledge and Politics*, 1975

UNIDROIT (ed.), *Principles of International Commercial Contracts*, 2nd ed., 2004 (1st ed., 1994); the black letter rules are available at <http://www.unidroit.org/english/principles/contracts/main.htm>; for the official comments, see <http://www.unilex.info/dynasite.cfm?dssid=2377&dsmid=13637&x=1>

van Crefeld, M., *The Rise and Decline of the State*, 1999

van den Berg, P. A. J., *The Politics of European Codification. A History of the Unification of Law in France, Prussia, the Austrian Monarchy and the Netherlands*, 2007

van Groenewegen, S., *Tractatus de legibus abrogatis et inusitatis in Hollandia vicinisque regionibus*, Leiden 1649

Vandall, F. J., 'Constructing a Roof Before the Foundation is Prepared: The Restatement (*Third*) of Torts: *Products Liability* Section 2(b) Design Defect', (1997) 30 *U. of Michigan Journal of Law Reform* 261–279

Vandall, J. F. and Vandall, F. J., 'A Call for an Accurate Restatement (Third) of Torts: Design Defect', (2003) 33 *U. of Memphis LR* 909–944

Varga, C., *Codification as a Socio-Historical Phenomenon*, 1991

Vendrell Cervantes, C., 'The Application of the Principles of European Contract Law by Spanish Courts', (2008) 16 *ZEuP* 534–548

Vinnius, A., *In Quattuor Libros Institutionum Imperialium Commentarius*, 4th ed., Amsterdam 1666

Voet, J., *Commentarius ad Pandectas*, Venice 1770

Vogenauer, S., 'Sources of Law and Legal Method in Comparative Law', in: Reimann and Zimmermann (eds), *Oxford Handbook of Comparative Law*, 869–898

Vogenauer, S. and J. Kleinheisterkamp (eds), *Commentary on the UNIDROIT Principles of International Commercial Contracts (PICC-Commentary)*, 2009

Wagner, G., 'The Project of Harmonizing European Tort Law', (2005) 42 *CMLR* 1269–1312

Waldhoff, C., 'Der Gesetzgeber schuldet nichts als das Gesetz. Zu alten und neuen Begründungspflichten des parlamentarischen Gesetzgebers', in: *Staat im Wort. Festschrift für Josef Isensee*, 2007, 325–343

Wallinga, T., *Tanta / ΔΕΔΩΚΕΝ. Two Introductory Constitutions to Justinian's Digest*, 1989

Warneyer, O., *Kommentar zum Bürgerlichen Gesetzbuch für das Deutsche Reich*, 1923

Weber, M., *Wirtschaft und Gesellschaft*, 5th ed., 1972 (Engl. transl. by G. Roth and C. Wittich: *Economy and Society*, 1968)

—— 'Die "Objektivität" sozialwissenschaftlicher und sozialpolitischer Erkenntnis', in: id., *Gesammelte Aufsätze zur Wissenschaftslehre*, 7th ed., 1988, 146–214

—— 'Die drei Typen der legitimen Herrschaft', *ibid.*, 475–488

Wechsler, H., 'Restatements and Legal Change: Problems of Policy in the Restatement Work of the American Law Institute', (1968) 13 *St. Louis University LJ* 185–194

Wehle, S., *Typographische Kultur. Eine zeichentheoretische und kulturgeschichtliche Studie zur Typographie und ihrer Entwicklung*, 2000

Weigand, R., 'Glossen, kanonische', in: *Theologische Realenzyklopädie*, vol. 13, 1984, 457–459

Weimar, P., 'Accursius', in: M. Stolleis (ed.), *Juristen. Ein biographisches Lexikon. Von der Antike bis zum 20. Jahrhundert*, 1995, 18–19

Wendehorst, C., 'The State as a Foundation of Private Law Reasoning', in: Jansen and Michaels (eds), *Beyond the State*, 145–182

Werro, F. and V. V. Palmer, *The Boundaries of Strict Liability in European Tort Law*, 2004

Wesenbeck, M., *Commentarii in Pandectas Juris Civilis et Codicem Justinianeum Olim Dicti Paratitla*, cum notis & observantibus Reinhardi Bachovii, Amsterdam 1665

Whittaker, S., 'The "Draft Common Frame of Reference". An Assessment commissioned by the Ministry of Justice': <http://www.justice.gov.uk/docs/eu-contract-law-common-frame-reference.pdf>

—— 'A Framework of Principle for European Contract Law?', (2009) 125 *LQR* 616–647

Wieacker, F., *Privatrechtsgeschichte der Neuzeit*, 2nd ed., 1967

—— 'Aufstieg, Blüte und Krisis der Kodifikationsidee', in: *Festschrift für Gustav Boehmer*, 1954, 34–50

—— 'Der Kampf des 19. Jahrhunderts um die Nationalgesetzbücher', in: id., *Industriegesellschaft und Privatrechtsordnung*, 1974, 79–93

Williston, S., 'The Restatement of Contracts: Statement by Samuel Williston', (1932) 18 *American Bar Association Journal* 775–777

Williston, S. and G. J. Thompson, *A Treatise on the Law of Contracts*, Revised (3rd) ed., 1936–38

Windscheid, B., *Lehrbuch des Pandektenrechts*, 7th ed., Frankfurt a.M. 1891

—— 'Das römische Recht in Deutschland', in: id., *Gesammelte Reden und Abhandlungen*, ed., by P. Oertmann, 1904, 25–49

Winroth, A., *The Making of Gratian's Decretum*, 2000

Wolfram, C. W., 'Bismarck's Sausages and the ALI's Restatements', (1998) 26 *Hofstra LR* 817–834

Wrobel, H., 'Otto Palandt zum Gedächtnis 1.5.1877–3.12.1951', (1982) *KJ* 1–17

Wurmnest, W., 'Common Core, Kodifikationsentwürfe, Acquis-Grundsätze—Ansätze von internationalen Wissenschaftlergruppen zur Privatrechtsvereinheitlichung in Europa', (2003) 11 *ZEuP* 714–744

Wüstendörfer, H., 'Die deutsche Rechtswissenschaft am Wendepunkt', (1913) 110 *AcP* 219–380

Zasius, U., *In primam partem digestorum paratitla* (*Opera omnia*, Lyon 1550, vol. I)

Zeiller, F. von, *Commentar über das allgemeine bürgerliche Gesetzbuch für die gesammten Deutschen Erbländer der Oesterreichischen Monarchie*, Wien & Triest 1811

Zekoll, J., 'Das American Law Institute—ein Vorbild für Europa?', in: Zimmermann *et al.* (eds), *Nichtstaatliches Privatrecht—Geltung und Genese*, 101–127

Zimmermann, R., *The Law of Obligations. Roman Foundations of the Civilian Tradition*, paperback ed., 1996

—— 'Römisch-holländisches Recht—ein Überblick', in: R. Feenstra and R. Zimmermann (eds), *Das römisch-holländische Recht: Fortschritte des Zivilrechts im 17. und 18. Jahrhundert*, 1992, 9–58

—— 'Das römisch-kanonische ius commune als Grundlage europäischer Rechtseinheit', (1992) *JZ* 8–20

—— 'Codification: History and Present Significance of an Idea', (1995) 3 *ERPL* 95–120

—— 'Statuta sunt stricte interpretanda?', (1997) 56 *Cambridge LJ* 315–328

—— 'Europa und das römische Recht', (2000) 299 *AcP* 243–316

—— *Roman Law, Contemporary Law, European Law. The Civilian Tradition Today*, 2001

—— *Die Principles of European Contract Law als Ausdruck und Gegenstand Europäischer Rechtswissenschaft*, 2003

—— 'Principles of European Contract Law and Principles of European Tort Law. Comparison and Points of Contact', in: H. Koziol and B. C. Steininger (eds), *European Tort Law 2003*, 2004, 2–31

—— 'Die Unidroit-Grundregeln der internationalen Handelsverträge 2004 in vergleichender Perspektive', (2005) 13 *ZEuP* 264–290

—— '*Ius Commune* and the Principles of European Contract Law: Contemporary Renewal of an Old Idea', in: MacQueen and Zimmermann (eds), *European Contract Law*, 1–42

—— 'The Principles of European Contract Law: Contemporary Manifestation of the Old, and Possible Foundations for a New, European Scholarship of Private Law', in: F. Faust and G. Thüsing (eds), *Beyond Borders: Perspectives on International and Comparative Law, Symposium in Honour of Hein Kötz*, 2006, 111–148

—— 'Comparative Law and the Europeanization of Private Law', in: Reimann and Zimmermann (eds), *Oxford Handbook of Comparative Law*, 539–578

—— *et al.* (eds), *Globalisierung und Entstaatlichung des Rechts*, vol. II: *Nichtstaatliches Privatrecht—Geltung und Genese*, 2008

Zimmermann, R. and N. Jansen, 'Quieta Movere. Interpretative Change in a Codified System', in: P. Cane and J. Stapleton (eds), *The Law of Obligations. Essays in Celebration of John Fleming*, 1998, 285–315

Zimmermann, R. and S. Whittaker, *Good Faith in European Contract Law*, 2000

Zweigert, K. and H. Kötz, *Einführung in die Rechtsvergleichung*, 3rd ed., 1996

Index